The Angry Young Men

HUMPHREY CARPENTER

The Angry Young Men

A LITERARY COMEDY OF THE 1950S

ALLEN LANE
an imprint of
PENGUIN BOOKS

ALLEN LANE
THE PENGUIN PRESS

Published by the Penguin Group
Penguin Books Ltd, 80 Strand, London WC2R ORL, England
Penguin Putnam Inc., 375 Hudson Street, New York, New York 10014, USA
Penguin Books Australia Ltd, 250 Camberwell Road, Camberwell, Victoria 3124, Australia
Penguin Books Canada Ltd, 10 Alcorn Avenue, Toronto, Ontario, Canada M4V 3B2
Penguin Books India (P) Ltd, 11, Community Centre, Panchsheel Park, New Delhi – 110 017, India
Penguin Books (NZ) Ltd, Cnr Rosedale and Airborne Roads, Albany, Auckland, New Zealand
Penguin Books (South Africa) (Pty) Ltd, 24 Sturdee Avenue, Rosebank 2196, South Africa

Penguin Books Ltd, Registered Offices: 80 Strand, London WC2R ORL, England

www.penguin.com

First published 2002
1

Set in 10.5/14 pt PostScript Adobe Linotype Sabon
Typeset by Rowland Phototypesetting Ltd, Bury St Edmunds, Suffolk
Printed in Great Britain by Clays Ltd, St Ives plc

A CIP catalogue record for this book is available from the British Library

ISBN 0-713-99532-7

Contents

List of Illustrations

Photographic acknowledgements are given in parentheses.

1. The young Kingsley Amis. *(Ida Kar/Camera Press)*
2. Philip Larkin in his role as librarian. *(Camera Press)*
3. The Amis family at Swansea in 1956. *(Evening Standard/Hulton Getty)*
4. John Osborne. *(Slim Aarons/Hulton Getty)*
5. John Wain. *(Ida Kar/Camera Press)*
6 & 7. Two characteristic images of the Fifties. *(6, Hulton Archive; 7, Hulton Getty)*
8. Colin Wilson in his sleeping-bag on Hampstead Heath. *(Courtesy of Colin Wilson)*
9. (a) Bill Hopkins and (b) Stewart Holroyd. *(Courtesy of Bill Hopkins and Colin Wilson)*
10. Colin Wilson and Joy Stewart in their London bedsitter. *(Keystone/Hulton Archive)*
11. Cartoon by Cecil Keeling on the front of *Twentieth Century* magazine.
12. Kenneth Haig, Alan Bates and Mary Ure in *Look Back in Anger*. *(Houston Rogers/Theatre Museum, V&A)*
13. Colin Wilson doing a Jimmy Porter. *(Keystone/Hulton Deutsch)*
14. The *Daily Mail*'s Flook becomes an AYM. *(By kind permission of George Melly and Wally Fawkes)*
15. Sir Laurence Olivier in *The Entertainer*. *(Hulton Getty)*
16. The young John Braine. *(Camera Press)*
17. John Braine trying to look like Joe Lampton in *Room at the Top*. *(Camera Press)*
18. Doris Lessing. *(The Observer/Hulton Archive)*

19. John Osborne and Mary Ure protesting about the Bomb. *(Keystone/Hulton Deutsch)*

20. John Braine buys a new house in stockbroker country. *(Keystone/Hulton Archive)*

21. Kingsley Amis in 1986. *(Press Association)*

Prologue:
A bottle of whisky

The taxi carries me past the sign saying 'NO VISITORS EXCEPT BY APPOINTMENT', and up to the house, which is slightly ramshackle and spills over into the garden. There are large dogs, and several elderly-looking cars. The dogs are in the charge of a man in an anorak and a pork-pie hat, and I recognize him at once, though I only know him from photographs taken half a century ago. There's still the same boyish cowlick of hair flopping down over his forehead, the same half-eager, half-myopic gaze through the glasses, and his hair has scarcely begun to turn grey, even though he's in his early seventies. This is Colin Wilson, the last survivor of the Angry Young Men.

Though we have been in touch by e-mail for some weeks, there has been a last-minute muddle over the date of my visit, and I have arrived in Cornwall just as he has to hurriedly write an article for the *Sunday Times*. It's about the Moors murderer Ian Brady, who has written a book about serial killers, encouraged by Wilson. 'I've been in correspondence with quite a lot of serial killers,' Wilson tells me. 'It's not really a good idea to befriend them – they tend to unload all their troubles on you.'

The taxi departs, I leave my suitcase just inside the front door of the house, and Wilson hustles the two enormous dogs into the back of an old Land Rover. We drive off to a nearby wood to take them for a walk, even though it's now almost dark (this is November).

As we follow the animals through the foliage, Wilson talks about Brady and his accomplice Myra Hindley, and about sexually motivated killings in general. His recent books include *The Corpse Garden* (1998), a chronicle of the slaughter carried out by Fred and Rosemary West. I can't help recalling that Kingsley Amis claimed, not altogether jokingly, to find Wilson's interest in murder somewhat alarming. 'Between ourselves,' Amis wrote in 1987 to Harry Ritchie, who was working on a book about the Angry Young Men, 'I was too afraid to drink a bottle of whisky Colin Wilson once gave me, and there it stayed on my shelf till an intrepid psychiatrist pal guzzled it with no ill effects, or none but the usual.'*

Wilson is telling me that there weren't any sex murders before the Victorian period: 'Until then, people only killed for money or some other basic need.' Sex has always interested him as a subject; his first book, *The Outsider*, opens with a voyeur peeping through a hole in the wall, and another of his early books is *Origins of the Sexual Impulse*. 'I found I was sexually wide awake at the age of about twelve or thirteen,' he tells me as we walk on in almost complete darkness. 'On my way to school, there was a huge advertisement for Ovaltine, with a girl in her underwear standing on a pair of scales, and I used to go past this thing every day with an erection.'

The Outsider appeared in the same month that John Osborne's *Look Back in Anger* opened at the Royal Court Theatre in London. By this time, John Wain and Kingsley Amis had both published their first novels, *Hurry On Down* and *Lucky Jim*. There had been claims in the press that Wain and Amis were key figures in a new literary group, 'The Movement', and now – in the summer of 1956 – the media lumped them together with Wilson and Osborne to form the Angry Young Men ('AYM' for short). John Braine's name was added a year later, with the publication and instant success of his first book, *Room at the Top*.

As we walk, Wilson claims to me that being labelled an AYM was an unpleasant experience: 'I did not enjoy becoming famous, not one little bit – it was just no fun.' He tells me that he disliked *Look Back in Anger*, and found himself unable to enjoy *Lucky Jim* or *Hurry On Down*. He would therefore presumably not disagree with Kingsley Amis's assertion (in a 1968 letter) that 'the Angry Young Man "movement" was a phantom creation of literary journalists'. John Osborne said the same in a 1957 article, at the height of the AYM craze: 'The

---

* Wilson writes: 'I only ever once gave Amis a bottle of whisky, and that was in 1957, before I had written about crime.'

"Angry Young Men" cult ... is a cheap, journalistic fiction ... Fleet Street ... created the A Y M ... It didn't matter much whether they were Angry or even Young ...'

On the other hand, at the time, Wilson gave the impression that he loved the publicity. He certainly courted the press avidly, making no attempt to deny the validity of the A Y M label. And, writing in *Encounter* in 1959, he indicated that he did think he had something in common with the other Angries:

I sometimes feel a peculiar discomfort in talking to writers of an older generation: a sense of different worlds, different languages. This disappears when I
speak with contemporaries like John Braine, Kingsley Amis, John Osborne.
They've been through the same mill-race ...

It also becomes clear, as Wilson talks to me, that for a group which did not exist, the A Y M certainly saw quite a lot of each other. He reminisces about encounters with the other Angries, and spends some time impersonating John Braine's exaggeratedly 'bluff Yorkshire' manner. Nor does he question that the A Y M are a valid subject for a book.

My own interest in them began when I was writing a biography of Dennis Potter (1998), who had briefly tried to be a kind of latter-day Angry before discovering his *métier* as a television playwright. In my next book, *That Was Satire That Was* (2000), an account of the 'satire boom' of the 1960s, the Angries began to look to me like forerunners of the Sixties satirists, trying to overturn the worn-out and conservative mores of the society in which they found themselves.

To my surprise, I discovered that no 'group biography' of the Angries had been written. Kenneth Allsop's *The Angry Decade*, published in 1958 before the A Y M craze had ended, includes important material, but was completed too hastily and too close to the events it describes to be a balanced summing-up. Harry Ritchie's *Success Stories* (1988) is a brilliantly researched account of the media's role in creating the A Y M, but does not attempt to cover all the individual Angries. I have tried to fill that gap, as entertainingly as possible.

During his heyday as an Angry, Colin Wilson became notorious for his unembarrassed claims that he was a genius. In this respect, nothing has changed. As we finish our walk and head back to his house through darkened Cornish lanes, he tells me about a conversation he once had with Roald Dahl: 'The first time I took Roald out to dinner, he said, "Let's admit it, you and I are second-raters – we won't be remembered." And I said, "I don't know whether *you* are, but I'm not. I shall be regarded as one of the major writers of the twentieth century." Roald said, "You don't mean that, do you?" And I said, "Yes, I do." And I could see he was slightly worried about that.'

I make no comment, but explain to him that my narrative will begin not with any of the AYM themselves, but with Philip Larkin, whose friendship with Kingsley Amis arguably kicked the whole thing off. Given his negative views about the writings of Osborne, Wain and Amis, I expect Wilson to be dismissive about Larkin. But I am wrong. 'I admire Larkin,' he tells me, adding that he particularly likes 'The Whitsun Weddings'. I ask if he can stomach the melancholy, pessimistic side of Larkin, which is certainly very far from Wilson's own outlook as expressed in *The Outsider* and many of his subsequent books. 'It strikes me,' he answers, 'that when you do something as well as he does, it doesn't terribly matter if you're pessimistic or optimistic, because you're doing something with the real you.' Whereupon we reach the Wilson driveway, with its warning sign to visitors, and he parks the Land Rover and takes me into the house. Waiting for us – prepared by his wife Joy, who is out at a meeting – is a splendid supper of Cornish oysters and smoked eel, with two vintage wines. And no whisky.

I

All women are stupid beings

' "They fuck you up, your mum and dad" is my best-known line,' said Philip Larkin in an interview with the *Observer*, 'and I wouldn't want it to be thought that I didn't like my parents. I did like them. But at the same time they were rather awkward people and not very good at being happy. And these things rub off.'

He once described the family home as 'dull . . . and slightly mad', with an atmosphere of 'tense boredom'; yet his father's death from cancer in 1947 left him, in his biographer Andrew Motion's word, 'desolate', and he immediately arranged for his mother to share his own house.

Philip Arthur Larkin was born on 9 August 1922, the second child of Sydney Larkin, Deputy Treasurer (and Treasurer-elect) of Coventry Corporation. 'My father was a local government official and we lived in quite respectable houses and had a succession of maids and that sort of thing, as one did before the war.' Moreover 'the house was full of books'.

Though Sydney Larkin's chief intellectual talent was at mathematics (he had trained in accountancy at the University of Birmingham), he was also a keen reader of the classics and contemporary literature, who bought – as they were published – novels by H. G. Wells and Arnold Bennett, plays by Shaw, and poetry collections by Thomas Hardy. Philip was named after the poet Philip Sidney. Larkin's mother Eva was bookish, too; before marriage she had thought of becoming a librarian, and took up teaching for a little while.

Sydney's political sympathies were right-wing, and during the Thirties he openly admired Hitler's success in bringing the German economy under control; but so did many people. It is true that he owned a clockwork Hitler which gave the Nazi salute, but this implies mockery more than approval. It would be wrong to represent him as a bully: when Philip discovered jazz in schooldays, his father bought him a subscription to the magazine *Down Beat* and even purchased for him a learner's drum kit.

Philip had a sister, Kitty, but she was ten years his elder, so he was virtually brought up as an only child, indulged and even pampered. Although, in a 1950 poem, he described his childhood as 'a forgotten boredom', he was keen to emphasize that his public image as the poet of gloom did not altogether correspond with his own view of himself:

Actually, I like to think of myself as quite funny . . . But it's unhappiness that provokes a poem. Being happy doesn't provoke a poem . . . And I think writing about unhappiness is probably the source of my popularity, if I have any – after all, most people *are* unhappy, don't you think?

In 1930 he entered King Henry VIII School, Coventry. 'I was an unsuccessful schoolboy. You must remember that I was very short-sighted and nobody realized it, and also that I stammered, so that really classes were just me sitting with bated breath dreading lest I should be called on to say something.'

This was true, academically speaking, until he reached the sixth form; but socially he was happy: 'I had friends whom I played football and cricket with and Hornby trains and so forth.' By the time he sat for a closed scholarship (reserved for King Henry VIII boys) to St John's College, Oxford, he was a prominent figure in school life, helping to edit the literary contributions to the school magazine, and himself writing prose and poetry prolifically.

He won the scholarship and arrived at Oxford, aged eighteen, in October 1940, two terms before Kingsley Amis (who writes: 'Oxford must have been an administrators' nightmare then, with so many dons away on some form of war service, and a new intake of undergraduates appearing every term instead of the normal once a year in the autumn'). The university and city in wartime were not (as Larkin puts it) 'the Oxford of . . . Charles Ryder and his plovers' eggs'. Life in college was austere:

Because of Ministry of Food regulations, the town could offer little in the way of luxurious eating and drinking, and college festivities, such as commemoration balls, had been suspended for the duration. Because of petrol rationing, nobody ran a car. Because of clothes rationing, it was difficult to dress stylishly . . . It became a routine after ordering one's books in Bodley* after breakfast to go and look for a cake or cigarette queue.

Moreover (Larkin goes on in the same essay) the usual preoccupations of undergraduates – competition with each other, and hopes and plans for the future – seemed to be almost completely in suspension:

There were none of the pressing dilemmas of teaching or the Civil Service, industry or America, publishing or journalism: in consequence, there was next to no careerism. National affairs were going so badly, and a victorious peace was clearly so far off, that effort expended on one's post-war prospects could hardly seem anything but a ludicrous waste of time.

In Larkin's third term, his tutorial partner Norman Iles, who had been looking at a list in the college lodge, 'hailed the mention of a newcomer, name of Amis'. Iles had met Amis when they were both sitting for a scholarship at Cambridge, and he described him as 'the hell of a good man', further explaining: 'He shoots guns.' Larkin writes:

I did not understand this until later in the afternoon when we were crossing the dusty first quadrangle a fair-haired young man came down staircase three and paused on the bottom step. Norman instantly pointed his right hand at him in the semblance of a pistol and uttered a short coughing bark to signify a shot – a shot not as in reality, but as it would sound from a worn soundtrack on Saturday afternoon in the ninepennies.
  The young man's reaction was immediate. Clutching his chest in a rictus of agony, he threw one arm up against the archway and began slowly crumpling downwards, fingers scoring the stonework. Just as he was about to collapse on the piled-up laundry, however . . . he righted himself and trotted over to us.

* The Bodleian Library.

3

'I've been working on this,' he said, as soon as introductions were completed. 'Listen. This is when you're firing in a ravine.'

We listened.

'And this when you're firing in a ravine and the bullet ricochets off a rock.'

We listened again. Norman's appreciative laughter skirled freely: I stood silent. For the first time I felt myself in the presence of a talent greater than my own.

* *

Kingsley William Amis was a few months older than Larkin – an only child, born on 16 April 1922 in a nursing-home in Clapham, south London. His second given name was after his father, the former after a cousin of his mother, 'one of a pair of twins,' writes Amis's biographer Eric Jacobs, 'the second of whom was called Queenie, which would probably have been Kingsley's name if he had turned out a girl'. Some close friends ignored 'Kingsley' and called him 'Bill'; to his first wife he would be 'Billy', to rhyme with her own nickname, 'Hilly'.

Martin Amis claims that a dictionary gives the meaning of the family surname as 'Of the lower classes, *esp.* slaves'. It is the French word for 'friends', but Kingsley said that if the family had originally come from France, 'there was no trace whatever' of it. He also alleged, in a 1951 letter to Larkin, that C. S. Lewis (with whom he had had a drink) 'took about three minutes to have it explained to him that my name wasn't Aimless'.

If the family had ever come from France, Amis senior was (said his son) 'the most English human being I have ever known'. William Robert Amis was employed by Colman's Mustard, in the City of London, as what we would now call a sales manager, though he gave his job as 'mustard manufacturer's clerk' on Kingsley's birth certificate. 'He got no further than a senior clerk's responsibilities and pay with the horrible mustard people, and considered himself a failure,' writes Kingsley, adding: 'He was never bitter about this, but meant to see that I had a better chance than he.'

The family lived in a small house at 16 Buckingham Gardens, Norbury, a district which Kingsley scorned in the memorable phrase: 'Norbury, SW16 is not a place'. He describes his parents' social ambience during the 1920s and 1930s as a 'semi-detached, morning coffee, 8.5 to Blackfriars, dinner-dance, carless and, by modern standards, almost drinkless world'.

His parents had met when they were both attending a Baptist chapel, where his maternal grandfather was the organist, but 'my mother and father had abandoned nearly all religious observances by the 1920s . . . they gave me no religious instruction of any kind'. He declared that he himself had 'no belief in the existence of God, not the first beginning of one, not a shred, and never have had as far back as I can remember'. He assumed that his father was an atheist, but 'I only suspect this, because he was not one for that sort of discussion'. Moreover, 'when plunged into unusually deep despair about my shortcomings, he was likely to put them down to my complete lack of religion'.

William Amis's father had run a wholesale glassware business, J. J. Amis & Co. Kingsley preferred his maternal grandfather, who had worked in a gentlemen's outfitters in Brixton:

He liked and collected books, real books, poetry books, had lined part of a room in his little Camberwell house with them . . . He would read his favourite passages aloud to . . . his wife, my Gran . . . and she would make faces and gestures at him while his head was lowered to the page, which helped to make me hate her very much.

Kingsley's father, too, was an habitual maker of faces, possessing 'a talent for physical clowning and mimicry that made him . . . one of the funniest men I have known. Every story called for the full deployment of facial, vocal and bodily resources . . . My mother used the same techniques, so that at one stage I thought they were standard in anecdote-telling.'

His fundamental affection for his father is demonstrated by the fact that, when his mother died in 1957, Kingsley brought William to stay with the family in Swansea, and even took him to America for his sabbatical year (1958–9). But Martin Amis says Kingsley was uneasy in his father's company: 'My father loved his mother without much complication . . . but I never saw him altogether easy in the company of my grandfather.'

Kingsley himself puts it more bluntly, recalling that 'we quarrelled violently at least every week or two for years'. He puts this down largely to 'my father's constant concern to prevent my getting away from him'. (He portrays this in his 1994 novel, *You Can't Do Both*.) This may have contributed to the fear of solitude which haunted Kingsley throughout his life – though he had maybe also inherited his mother's anxious nature. Martin describes him as someone 'who refused to drive and refused to fly, who couldn't easily be alone in a bus, a train or a lift (or in a house, after dark)'.

Kingsley's quarrels with his father were also largely about sex and art:

We were divided on the issue of sex to fully the expected degree, my father a card-carrying anti-self-abuser-cum-anti-fornicationist, myself opposed to neither. There was once a very big scene over the first of these, full of warnings about thinning of the blood and eventual hopeless insanity. I had the remarkable good sense not merely not to believe this, but to keep my disbelief to myself. Thereafter I went my own sexual way under a pact of silence and dissimulation.

As to art, this was

not a word or a concept my father had much truck with . . . [It] consisted for him of Gilbert and Sullivan, the Edwardian ballads . . . that he and my mother and their friends sang at the piano, West End stage successes . . . and detective stories.

Kingsley 'had my own ideas of what art consisted of '. He disparaged his father's musical taste 'and wanted to know why there was no Schubert or Wolf (Wolf ! Was I mad or just trendy?) under the lid of the piano-stool'. In return, his father complained about 'the damned wireless or gramophone blaring through the house', especially when Kingsley was listening to jazz. 'There was a piece of Duke Ellington's . . . which put my father in mind, or so he said, of a lot of savages dancing round a pot of human remains.'

Even looking at pictures and reading were contentious activities:

If I chose to waste a fine afternoon in an art gallery or to ruin my eyes over a book when I could have been out in the fresh air, then that . . . was up to me

6

. . . When I was at home, as when not at school I usually was, I kept finding that reading in public was deemed rude, while reading in private was anti-social.

On the other hand his mother prodded him gently towards literary activity, 'suggesting on rainy afternoons when I had no book or comic to read . . . that I should do a bit of writing'. He began to write poetry at school, and some of it was published in the school magazine.

His first two schools were private fee-paying establishments in Norbury. In 1934, aged twelve, he was sent to the City of London School, on the Victoria Embankment, where his father and two uncles had been educated. Again, his father paid fees at first, 'gambling successfully that I would get a scholarship in the year that followed'. He also experienced public-school life when in 1939 the City of London boys were evacuated to Marlborough, though he and his fellow evacuees were cold-shouldered socially by the Marlburians. After five terms there, he won an exhibition to St John's College, Oxford.

* *

For his part, Amis, who remembered his first meeting with Philip Larkin at St John's as 'much less dramatically satisfying' than Larkin's highly-coloured recollection, found the eighteen-year-old Larkin 'almost aggressively normal', without any sign of the 'solitary creature' that he became in later years. Larkin's preferred clothes, which included wine-coloured trousers and a bow tie (neither of them commonplace at Oxford, both slightly camp), seemed to Amis 'not very serious'.

Larkin remarks, in turn, that no one took the freshman Amis seriously because he was such a good mimic: 'It was not a BBC Variety Hour knack of "imitations" . . . rather, he used it as the quickest way of convincing you that something was horrible or boring or absurd.' However, there was a serious side to Amis, and it was political:

In those days of Help for Russia Week, when the hammer and sickle flew with the Union Jack in Carfax, he became editor of the University Labour Club *Bulletin* . . . In his contentious mood he could be (intentionally) very irritating, especially to those who thought party politics should be suspended until the war was over. I . . . shared his convictions to the extent of visiting the club's social room in the High once or twice for coffee after closing time.

Amis himself recalls that he went further left than the Labour Party:

I had also joined the 'student' branch of the Communist Party, in which at that time high positions were held by John (then 'Jack') Terraine, now a military historian, and Iris Murdoch ... Belonging was at least cheap and it involved girls, not very nice-looking ones, though, most of them, but it also meant reading, or trying to read, Marx, Lenin and Plekhanov (aargh), going to 'study groups' and meetings, *speaking* at meetings, on balance a poor return for having, in this most banal of ways, rebelled against my father (these words too probably deserve their inverted commas), and the only useful lesson I learnt, for later, was the cunning and the unquenchable assiduity with which Communists infiltrate other groups, non-political (religious, for instance) as well as political.

Though Larkin did not go as far as this politically, he recalls that they were of one mind in their love of jazz. He and a school friend had brought their joint record collection to Oxford, 'so that we need not be without our favourite sound ... Kingsley's enthusiasm flared up immediately'. John Osborne has said of the love of jazz that was shared by most of the Angry Young Men:

A lot of people in my generation ... were very influenced by jazz ... It was a special voice that we all latched on to, because it was exotic and it was powerful, and it was completely different from the kind of voice that we knew at the time.

Although he was versed in the big band swing of the day, Amis had not previously paid close attention to other types of jazz. Now it became as much a preoccupation and passion for him as it already was for Larkin. Besides collecting records (sometimes by shoplifting), the two of them occasionally performed – at least to each other; Amis recalls Larkin playing blues piano 'with some proficiency' on a battered instrument in a dingy Oxford pub, while he himself 'would sometimes sing, or rather bawl'.

They were also of one mind about Oxford's English Language and Literature syllabus. Most undergraduates hated having to study Anglo-Saxon and Early Middle English, but from Chaucer onwards they could usually find texts that they liked. Not so Larkin. 'I have no recollection,' Amis writes, 'of ever hearing Philip admit to having enjoyed . . . any author or book he studied, with the possible exception of Shakespeare.' This might seem to consort oddly with the fact that Larkin wrote poetry. 'But so did I,' remarks Amis, who published two of Larkin's poems in the Labour Club *Bulletin*; 'so did half the people one talked to.'

The best of Larkin's poems at this time were heavily influenced by W. H. Auden (far too modern to be on the Oxford English syllabus). Writing in 1943, Larkin described Auden as having risen 'like a sun' over his generation of would-be poets – to read Auden's *The Orators* was 'like being allowed half an hour's phone conversation with God'.

* *

Amis's first taste of Oxford was soon over. 'The army claimed me in the summer of 1942.' Larkin was exempted because of poor eyesight.

After basic training, Amis became a signals officer, and though he eventually got to Europe in the wake of the D-Day landings (his first journey abroad), he claimed afterwards that he had come through the war 'without having had to walk a step [in action] or fire a shot'. But if he encountered little military action, his war was full of sexual experience. His first surviving letter to Larkin, written in the autumn of 1943, when he was twenty-one, refers to two affairs he had been having, one with an ATS (female soldier) called May, the other with a married woman: 'Betty . . . came to see me off at Darlington. I liked this because I wanted to take her trousers down, but I didn't like it because I couldn't then . . . We certainly want to make the beast with two backs, eh? . . . Her married name is Simpson, Mrs E. A. Simpson.'*

A year later, he was copying out, for Larkin's amusement, passages from a letter that he alleged had been written to him by a clergyman's daughter whom he had managed to ensnare, and who described her sexual longings in some detail. 'It's true all right,' Amis assured Larkin. 'What do you think of all this?'

---

* Zachary Leader, editor of Amis's letters, says the Betty affair lasted two years, and is 'thinly fictionalized' in the unpublished novel Amis co-wrote during the war with E. Frank Coles, a fellow officer. Martin Amis emphasizes that it was 'no casual dalliance'. Several of the poems in *Bright November*, Amis's first collection, are about Betty Simpson or addressed to her.

What Larkin thought was that 'all women are stupid beings . . . Marriage seems a revolting institution,' he wrote to Amis. 'A lonely bacherlorhood interspersed with buggery and strictly-monetary forni- cation seems to me preferable.'

He added that he was writing a story about sexual loneliness. 'It concerns a young man who invents a younger sister, and falls in love with her.' In a letter to another friend he gave a more detailed description:

It concerns a very poor young man who goes to Oxford who is exceptionally nervous and rather feminine, who is forced to share a room with his exact antithesis. As a result of adverse conditions, and also of telling his room-mate that he had a sister a year younger than himself (or two or three years) – which is untrue – he begins to construct a complicated sexless daydream about an imaginary sister, who serves as a nucleus for a dream-life. Then he meets a girl who is exactly like this imaginary sister (the sister-aspect having by now changed into rather a more emotional relationship) and the rest of the story, in action and in a long dream, serves to disillusion him completely . . . It could lengthen into a novel, if ever I could do it.

He could, though he reported to Amis that *Jill*, as he called it, was soon 'getting more infantile', incorporating material about the imaginary Jill's schooldays which had originated in an elaborate sexual joke shared with Amis.

While Amis was still at Oxford, the two had collaborated in writing what Amis described as 'soft porn fairy stories', which have long since vanished. What does survive, however, is the next stage of the joke, in which Larkin discovered a taste for inventing tales about schoolgirl lesbianism. These were written under the pseudonym 'Brunette Cole- man', and mostly set in an imaginary hothouse of a boarding-school called Willow Gables.

Larkin had himself been homosexually inclined at school; his letters to Amis are peppered with references (albeit joking) to boys with whom he had been in love, and in his second year at Oxford he seems to have fallen for a fellow undergraduate, Philip Brown, who later admitted that there had been 'a few messy encounters between us'.

(Only Amis was the recipient of such sexual confessions; there is nothing like them in Larkin's letters to any of his other friends.)

While doing a vacation job in the Borough Treasurer's department in Warwick, Larkin mentioned to Amis that he would sleep with the office boy, Derek, 'without overmuch repulsion', and remarked to Amis that 'the greatest artists and philosophers did not enjoy the benefits of heterosexuality'. At the beginning of the 1942 Michaelmas term he was eyeing 'a whole tableful of freshmen' and reporting disappointedly: 'I have fallen for only one of them.'

The invention of Brunette, a lesbian *alter ego*, seems (as Andrew Motion suggests) to have been both an attempt to mock his own chiefly latent homosexuality, and to express the sexual arousal he certainly also experienced with women. All this found an echo in Amis, who was curious about homosexuality. 'Did you know *Golding* at school?' he asked Larkin of a fellow undergraduate. 'Was he *homo*? *Never mind why I'm asking.*' When threatened with a military posting to India, he reported to Larkin: 'I am told that all the boys (and women) there have syphilis.' And he was avid to play his own part, in his letters to Larkin, in the schoolgirl lesbian fantasies:

'I am beginning to wonder if all this is worth while,' said Marsha, turning towards the window with her head drooping slightly, so that the evening sun gave her flaxen hair a rosy sheen. Jennifer made as if to move towards her, then spoke instead: 'You sound very disillusioned, darling,' she said softly. The younger girl reacted instantly. She whirled round, ran to the back of Jennifer's chair, and flung her arms round her neck, so that the prefect's head rested on her breast. 'No, no, no,' came her voice muffled by Jennifer's thick hair; 'I didn't mean that, dearest; I was only thinking how we never seem to be able to get far enough away from other people; all I want is to be close to you, but somehow we never seem to be close enough to one another.' For answer, Jennifer pulled her on to her lap and held her mouth in a long, shuddering kiss. Marsha flexed her slim body and pressed herself to her. And then there was nothing but their closeness as the shadows lengthened and the sunlight paled and dusk swam into the still, silent room, and Barbara, passing by in the chilly garden, stooped and picked a furled rose from the flower-bed beneath their window.

Occasionally Amis wrote to Larkin in the persona of the lesbian lover of Larkin's *alter ego*, beginning one letter 'Darling Brunette', and signing off: 'All my love, dearest'. Martin Amis believes his father's feelings for Larkin were in fact far more than friendship: 'It was love, unquestionable love, on my father's part. He wanted to be with Larkin *all the time*; that this was impossible, continued to irk and puzzle him. Larkin, I think, felt the same way, or rather he felt the Larkinesque equivalent. But he had less talent for love.'

Meanwhile Larkin's occasional attempts at heterosexual relationships seemed doomed to failure; his clumsy passes at female undergraduates only resulted in a string of rejections, and he soon began to retreat into miserly, masturbatory misogyny: 'Cunt and bugger Oxford women . . . I *don't* want to take a girl out and spend *circa* £5 when I can toss off in five minutes, free, and have the rest of the evening to myself.' (He mentioned in several letters that he had been masturbating.)

Amis continued to be highly successful with women, yet his reports of sexual conquests were often reported equally misogynistically. 'Hilary was stupider and more boring than ever,' he told Larkin when, back at Oxford in 1946 to resume his degree, he had begun to pursue a seventeen-year-old Ruskin College art student, Hilary ('Hilly') Bardwell.

We have been arguing for the past week about sleeping in the same bed as each other. First she said no, and I said she would have to say yes, then she said yes, and I said I had forced her into it and what she meant was no, then she said no, and I feel hurt and angry and disappointed and am trying to make her say yes, and there for the moment the matter rests. It has absorbed more of my attention and energy . . . than I think is right and this increases my bitterness. If only one could be ruthless about these things! . . . Women appear to me as basically dull, but as basically pathetic too . . .

Hilary soon yielded. 'Her breasts are concave on top,' Amis told Larkin.

On Amis's side, his friendship with Larkin was uniquely close – no other male was playing a similar part in his life. Larkin, however, had quite a few close men friends. Among them was a rather camp, flashy former St John's College undergraduate named Bruce Montgomery. Larkin writes of him:

He had a grand piano; he had written a book called *Romanticism and the World Crisis*, painted a picture that was hanging on the wall of his sitting-room, and was a skilled pianist, organist and even composer. During the vacation . . . he had spent ten days writing, with his J nib and silver pen-holder, a detective story called *The Case of the Gilded Fly*. This was published the following year under the name of Edmund Crispin.

Amis emphasizes the camp element in Montgomery:

This man, along with an indefinable and daunting air of maturity, had a sweep of wavy auburn hair, a silk dressing-gown in some non-primary shade and a walk that looked eccentric and mincing . . . When more fully attired, he inclined to a fancy-waistcoated, suede-shoed style with cigarette-holders and rings.

Amis's letters to Larkin reveal a distinct envy, not merely of Montgomery's precocious literary success but of his capacity to arouse Larkin's affection. 'Whatever made you think I didn't like Bruce?' he asked Larkin tetchily after he and Montgomery had first met. 'I'm only jealous of his sodding – and apparently undeserved – good luck abt books and money . . .' And in another letter, after Montgomery had been to stay with Larkin: 'Wheres Bruce gone then expect youll miss him wont you.' Some letters even give the impression that Amis's relationship with Hilary was less intense than his feelings for Larkin. On one occasion he hinted at the possibility of a *ménage à trois*: 'Don't breathe a word of this old boy, but Hilly told me that the only man she likes the thought of being pocked by APART FROM ME is you.'

2

A marvellous welter of derisive hatred

By the time Amis got back to Oxford, in the autumn of 1945, Larkin had gone. Despite his hatred of the syllabus, he had achieved a First in English at Oxford. During the two years since then, he had been in charge of a small public library, at Wellington in Shropshire. 'The library is a very small one, I am entirely unassisted in my labours, and spend most of my time handing out tripey novels to morons.' However, Bruce Montgomery was teaching at Shrewsbury public school, only a few miles away, so they could meet for 'spasmodic drinking bouts'; and the undemanding nature of the job meant that Larkin could 'find time for "my writing"'. He had soon 'finished one complete version of *Jill*, as my novel is called . . .'

It was not – as it might appear at first – a novel about a working-class boy experiencing Oxford, but a painful exposé of Larkin's own sexual dilemma. Its hero John Kemp is caught between an unconscious but growing homosexual attraction to his muscular college room-mate Christopher Warner, 'lustfully and playfully savage', and his pathetic fantasies about pubescent schoolgirls – the nearest he can get to hetero-sexual feeling.

The book's chief weakness is the improbability that someone from Kemp's background (a north of England grammar school) would be sufficiently familiar with the world of 'Brunette Coleman' to write fantasy narratives about public-schoolgirls' crushes for each other. Larkin admitted this in a letter to Amis: 'A little twerp like John Kemp couldn't possibly think of anything so subtly perverse.' Amis agreed: 'Kemp the Warner-fearer and Kemp the Jill-imaginer are not . . . the same person.'

But after the reader has endured this re-hash of Willow Gables, *Jill*

14

moves powerfully into nightmare mode, as John Kemp finds a 'real' Jill – an Oxford schoolgirl – and begins to pursue her relentlessly, with disastrous consequences for himself.

The book might seem to be Larkin's warning to himself against attempting such relationships; yet by the summer of 1945 he was involved romantically with a real-life Jill, a Wellington schoolgirl called Ruth Bowman, who was only sixteen when they first met. In his letters to Amis, Larkin referred to her as 'the school captain', and explained: 'The heart of my relationship with her is not perversion [i.e. sex] at all (I wish it were) but boredom and flattery. As long as she keeps talking about me I am flattered. When she criticizes me, or speaks of herself, I am bored.' He said he could hardly be bothered to try to seduce her: 'I have formed a very low opinion of women and the idea of having one perpetually following me abait is wearisome.' But Amis kept egging him on: 'Do something about it, man . . . An efficient Elephant can undress in fifteen seconds.' He reassured Larkin about contraceptives: 'As regards Durex products . . . I've used them upwards of 100 times and never been landed yet.'

After about two years, Larkin got Ruth into bed, earning congratulations from Amis: 'I was very glad to hear that you had slipped a length on misruth.' This was the first occasion on which Larkin had slept with a woman.

Almost by accident, *Jill* quickly found a publisher, albeit an incompetent one who did almost nothing to further Larkin's career. Larkin had been asked to contribute to a volume called *Poetry from Oxford in Wartime*, which was published during 1945 by the Fortune Press. This turned out to be a one-man operation run by an eccentric called Reginald Ashley Caton, who lived off the income from rented houses in Brighton, issued a regular stream of pornography (Larkin came across his *Boy Sailors* on a Leicester Square bookstall and was 'enthralled'), and occasionally lured a poet or novelist on to his list.*

While *Poetry from Oxford in Wartime* was still at the printer, Caton wrote to Larkin, inviting him to 'submit a volume of poems for

---

* According to his biographer Timothy d'Arch Smith, 'He died owning 91 houses there, "not a bathroom among them" he used to boast.'

consideration', and Larkin eventually sent a collection called *The North Ship*, soon followed by *Jill*. Caton accepted both books without giving evidence that he had read either; and after seemingly endless delays, during which Caton persistently failed to reply to letters or answer the telephone, the poems were published in the summer of 1945 and the novel in the autumn of 1946.

This was publication only in the most primitive sense; Caton paid no royalties – indeed, he liked his authors to pay *him* – and he made virtually no attempts at publicity or marketing. *The North Ship* earned just one review, in Larkin's home town – the *Coventry Evening Telegraph* – and he later ruefully recalled that the publication of *Jill* had 'aroused no public comment'. Amis wrote to Larkin that he hadn't 'seen any Jills in Blackwells' (the Oxford bookshop), though he later claimed to have found a copy in a London shop 'displayed between "Naked and unashamed" and "High-heeled Yvonne"'.*

Nevertheless he was envious of Larkin for getting into print: 'Your ability to write and get it published is a constant source of irritation and gloom in me, who can't put pen to fucking paper.' Moreover, Larkin had soon completed his second novel, *A Girl in Winter*, which was accepted by no less than Faber & Faber. 'You are a lucky boy,' wrote Amis. 'It's not the thought that I'm unsuccessful that worries me, [because] I'm not; but the only difference is that I'm only not unsuccessful *yet*, which does not go far to console me.'

A Girl in Winter had been recommended to Faber by Bruce Montgomery's literary agent. Montgomery was now turning out an 'Edmund Crispin' whodunit every year, and Amis admitted to being still jealous of Larkin's relationship with Montgomery. 'Won't Bruce not like me being around when he's around when you're around?' he asked Larkin, when the three of them were likely to coincide in Oxford for a weekend.

The historian of the detective story, Julian Symons, has described Montgomery as 'the last and most charming' of that school of detective writers he calls 'the *farceurs*', who combined comedy and wit with

---

* Amis's use of Caton's name for the character of a dishonest (but always offstage) publisher in *Lucky Jim* and later novels is well known. He actually makes his first fictional appearance in Amis's unpublished first novel, 'The Legacy'.

detection. Amis would not have agreed. 'I don't like all those silly literary allusions,' he told Larkin after reading the 1946 Crispin, *Holy Disorders*, 'and some of the funny bits are funny but not many, and the blend of fantasy and detective novel isn't done skilfully enough, and there is a lot of pointless facetiousness and sheer bad writing.' Despite Symons's judgement, Amis was not being unfair; the Crispin novels now seem strained and dated (but then so does most British detective fiction from the so-called 'golden age' of the whodunit).

Taking pity on Amis – or perhaps as a joke – Larkin encouraged him to send a collection of his poems to the impossible Caton. Characteristically, Caton accepted them, then fell silent. Amis (who had decided to call the book *Bright November*, 'which is CORNY and reminds me of Jaybee Priestley') was soon raging to Larkin about 'THAT SOD CATON' who *still* hasn't replied to my letter'. Like *The North Ship*, *Bright November* eventually emerged from the Fortune Press during 1947. 'The print is pretty fucking awful but we mustn't look a gift horse up the arse, must we?' Amis asked Larkin, adding: 'WHY MUSTN'T WE?'

To be fair to Caton, Larkin's and Amis's first poetry collections would not easily have found acceptance by a 'real' publisher. Larkin was nowhere near finding his own poetic identity; twenty years later he described *The North Ship* as having been written in several voices:

the ex-schoolboy, for whom Auden was the only alternative to 'old-fashioned' poetry; the undergraduate, whose work a friend affably characterized as 'Dylan Thomas, but you've a sentimentality that's all your own'; and the immediately post-Oxford self, isolated in Shropshire with a complete Yeats stolen from the local girls' school . . . It might be pleaded that the war years were a bad time to start writing poetry, but in fact the principal poets of the day – Eliot, Auden, Dylan Thomas, Betjeman – were all speaking out loud and clear . . .

The surprise name on this list is John Betjeman; Larkin and Amis liked to giggle at his schoolgirl-fantasy poems like 'Myfanwy', which were much like the outpourings of 'Brunette Coleman'; but both also acquired from him what Larkin described (in a 1960 review) as the ability to 'shimmer . . . continually between laughter and rage'.

Larkin apparently wrote a review of Amis's *Bright November* (which has not been traced), since Amis responded:

Thank you . . . for your review: it was in truth a little deep wreck o'Tory, but there's not much too bad to be said abt. the bad poems in that book . . . You don't seem however to like the good poems as much as you did: or rather, you would admit fewer as good poems, no? . . . But never mind that: the truth never harmed anyone yet ('Now, that's a *lie*, isn't it?') I feel stimulated to try again . . .

The North Ship and *Bright November* each contained one good poem. Amis's was an elegant grumble, partly written in pastiche Anglo-Saxon verse, about having to study *Beowulf* at Oxford: 'Someone has told us this man was a hero. / But what have we to learn in following / His tedious journey to his ancestors . . . ?' In Larkin's case it was the book's title-poem, a ballad about three ships which set sail respectively to the east, west and north; the first finds riches, the second encounters a storm, and both of them return home; but the northbound ship 'went wide and far / Into an unforgiving sea . . . / And it was rigged for a long journey'. Larkin knew very well that he was writing about his own life, which was turning out to be an increasingly ice-bound emotional journey.

His second novel, *A Girl in Winter*, whose heroine, like Larkin, is employed in a provincial public library, had turned out to be set in an even bleaker region of the heart than *Jill*. 'It is a deathly book,' Larkin wrote to a friend, 'and has for theme the relinquishing of live response to life. The central character, Katherine, picks up where John [Kemp] left off and carries the story on into the frozen wastes.' Katherine, an émigrée from an unspecified country, working in England during wartime, receives a surprise visit from Robin, a young man with whom she had had a brief romantic friendship during an earlier visit to Britain; but though they spend the night together, the experience is disappointing for both of them, and will clearly lead to nothing.

Amis emphasized the emotional bleakness of *A Girl in Winter* when he reviewed it for the Oxford literary periodical *Mandrake* – and clearly he saw the book as reflecting this aspect of its author:

The book is a study in hopelessness; this was made clearer by its original title, 'The Kingdom of Winter'.* In its main part Katherine is surrounded by those gripped by unacknowledged despair: the accurately observed Anstey, her boss, has the ugliness but also the qualifications for pity of the man unable to escape; the woman he wants to marry is tied to a feeble-minded mother who carries the atmosphere to a moment of horror; horror also emerges intermittently during a visit to a dentist too spiritually stunted to know of kindliness . . .

Of the two major characters besides Katherine, Jane, Robin's sister, who appears only in the flashback, has gained perception of her position as one who no longer desires to do anything . . . Robin, once the possessor of a self-assurance impregnable even before the foreign vitality of the schoolgirl Katherine, shows himself at the end to have lost purpose. Katherine has become lonely, has lost her ardour and her curiosity, and her final surrender to Robin's impromptu advances is a more important surrender by being loveless and regarded by her as unimportant . . .

For fuller understanding . . . the reader is referred to Mr Larkin's poems in *The North Ship* . . .

Reading this review, Larkin might have felt that Amis was suggesting that his fiction had got itself into the same emotional impasse as his life. But, writing to another friend, he seemed to think he could extricate himself:

Now I am thinking of a third book in which the central character will pick up where Katherine left off and develop *logically* back to life again. In other words, the north ship will come back instead of being bogged up there in a glacier. Then I shall have finished this particular branch of soul-history (my own, of course), and what will happen then I don't know.

But soon he was telling Amis that his next novel had ground to a halt. 'I'm very sorry you've stopped,' Amis responded; 'it is a definite halt, I suppose?' It was; and a permanent one for Larkin as far as novel-writing was concerned.

* *

* Changed by Larkin at Faber's request.

By the time that *A Girl in Winter* was published, Amis was writing to Larkin every few days. Larkin kept all the letters carefully, eventually filing them in a series of ring-binders, whereas only a few of Larkin's replies survive among Amis's papers. Yet at the time Amis had depended heavily on receiving them, complaining like a lover should Larkin not respond rapidly to his latest monologue.

Whenever he wrote to Larkin, it was an elaborate performance, compounded of private jokes and virtually an invented language. He mostly used a typewriter, and never crossed out his frequent mistakes, but incorporated them into what he was writing, creating a crazy language of typographical errors. Individual words like 'thinking' or 'themselves' are reborn as 'thiknign' and 'methsleevs', and such accidental coinages often thereafter become standard Amis-lingo. Whole sentences roll out in this fashion: 'Well it was great seng your ulgy mug again.' 'Ulgy mug' it remains in later letters, while 'seriously though' invariably appears as 'serously htuogh'.

He manufactures superb obscenities out of innocent material – 'self cunt-roll' (for 'self-control') is a particularly fine example – and innocent-seeming terms are born out of naughty ones, such as 'R-slicker'. Names are similarly doctored: 'Petrol Damn' is Amis's weird version of his friend Peter Oldham; and Monica Jones, who began to become a significant figure in Larkin's life when he moved to a librarian's job at Leicester University in 1946, becomes 'Money-cur' (a dig maybe at Larkin's parsimony where women were concerned).

Many Amis spellings mimic accents: 'shagged out' becomes 'shegged 8', people 'groan 8 laid', and Americans speak ponderously of 'creadive wriding'. Each letter to Larkin (and Larkin did the same in turn) incorporates the word 'bum' into its closing words, at first quite straightforwardly – 'shiftless bum . . . smelly bum . . . senex bum' – but later as part of a more elaborately allusive valediction; for example, when Amis was having to read Chaucer's *Troilus and Criseyde*: 'The double sorwe of Troilus for to tellen bum'.

Whereas Amis's letters abound with praise for his most recently acquired jazz records (and again there are puns galore, so that Red Nichols's band the Five Pennies becomes '5 Penis'), the Oxford English Literature syllabus is the target of constant abuse. Chaucer's masterpiece becomes 'the Cuntherbelly Tails', and when Amis's tutor J. B.

Leishman praises Chaucer's humour 'I could hardly keep myself from BREAKING WIND IN HIS FACE'. Dryden is dismissed as 'A SECOND-RATE FUCKING JOURNALIST', and Amis – his spelling starting to go wild – plans a very specific revenge on Wordsworth and his circle:

I started on Lerlyrical Berballads this week . . . I am beginning to cherish a warm personal disregard for all the peolpe who surrounded W[ordsworth]'s life – Dorothy, Godwin . . . They ought all to be put together in a big house, so that they could not get out and be scalded to death with urine-steam.

Amis's term for this habitually obscene rubbishing of literary giants is 'horsepissing', and throughout the mid and late 1940s he horsepissed contemporary culture as well. At this period it was dominated by the BBC Third Programme (founded in 1946), and Amis caricatures its pretensions in several letters to Larkin:

A man called Mister C. Day Lewis is reading a poem by W[alter] de la M[are], VERY BADLY: 'Deepp in my heartttse . . . once in despair (wunntttce inn de-spaiire)'. Hay I HATT the way he reads, and the SILLY WOMAN speaking nay, as though they were reading words they have been told are full of religious content, but find they seem somehow *obscene*. And WHY, WHY do they make every sound GO ON so long? Christ, there are ij of them at it, each trying to outdo the other in reverence and shocked morality. BORL-ZICH. And I didn't think much of the Betjeman one. Now they are talking AB8 *VALUES*.

In another 1946 letter, he fumes about a 'Turd Pro-gram' dramatization of Evelyn Waugh, whose *Brideshead Revisited*, published the previous year, had bewitched most of Amis's undergraduate contemporaries – and indeed most of the British reading public – with its lush portrayal of Oxford in the 1920s, and of its narrator-hero Charles Ryder's love-affairs with Sebastian Flyte and his sister Julia. Amis, however, refused to be captivated by it.

'I was unable to decide whether the man speaking the story was meant to be mad, or nasty, or wrong, or unwise,' he wrote of *Brideshead*, in the faux-naïf style he often adopted when addressing Larkin, but a lot of it, especially the Oxford bit, is in a sort of neo-Beverley Nichols vein . . . full of things you hope are good, but know are bad, but put in. 'He was entrancing, with that epicene beauty that in extreme youth cries aloud for love and withers at the first cold wind.' *Burp.* 'The languor of youth (sorry, Youth) – how unique and quintessential it is!' *Burps.* 'I was made free of her narrow loins.' *Burppss.* I may have missed the irony, but I cannot believe that a man could write as badly as that for fun. *Nay,* if it had been made QUITE CLEAR that the man was BUGGERING THE BOY'S ARSE and *shagged the boy's sister* when he couldn't BUGGER THE BOY'S ARSE any more, I shouldn't mind so much.

Another target of Amis abuse was a 1947 issue of one of the leading forums for contemporary British literature, *Penguin New Writing*, edited by John Lehmann. Amis told Larkin:

I must say that I thought everything I read in it was as poor as PISS. There [were] two shy tor fool poems by Mister Looey Muckneass, they made me want to spew. And another thing I can't BARE is all this TAKL about Mister Ellyut's Fork wart ets, CAN'T THEY SEA that it doesn't matter a twopenny damn, old boy, whether Eliot is quoting Sane tore gust teen or Tom erse suck wine ass or Mare e. stew wart, or not, that IT MAKES NO DIFFERENCE TO ANYTHING THAT MAKES ANY DIFFERENCE TO THE POEM if he quotes from The good ship venus or The great farting contest at shitham on tees?

He was becoming a master of invective; but it had become so richly obscene, so wildly contemptuous of contemporary culture – indeed, of the entire human race apart from Larkin – that there seemed to be no possibility of making anything publishable out of it; and he wanted to be published. Bruce Montgomery (of whom he was no longer jealous) suggested that he try his hand at a detective story. 'Do you think he is right?' Amis asked Larkin. He tried reading examples of the genre, by 'Carter Dickson' (John Dickson Carr) and Margery Allingham, but gave up in disgust. By September 1946 he had begun to write a novel called 'The Legacy'.

The hero is a nineteen-year-old poet called Kingsley Amis – though he is not an authorial self-portrait; Amis seems to be mocking the tendency of first novels to be autobiographical. The fictional Kingsley will inherit £30,000 from his father, Lionel, on his twenty-first birthday, providing he joins the family firm (a wholesale grocery) and marries Stephanie Roche, a girl chosen by his parents. Kingsley initially wants to marry a girl called Jane Taylor (who resembles the real Kingsley's wartime girlfriend Betty Simpson) and hopes to spend his time writing poetry. However, in the end he surrenders to his family's plans for him.

'The Legacy' gives a first try-out to characters who will appear in *Lucky Jim*. Sidney, Kingsley's boorish brother, anticipates Bertrand Welch, while Stephanie is an early version of Margaret. But it is very much an apprentice work, clumsy and jejune compared with Larkin's accomplished *Jill* and *A Girl in Winter*.

* *

1947 was Amis's final year as an Oxford undergraduate, and despite the continual horsepissing of literature in his letters to Larkin, he got a First,* and immediately signed up to do a B.Litt. The subject of his dissertation was to be the decline of the audience for poetry from the Pre-Raphaelite period to the present day, which should have suited his cynical approach; but he found himself with a very uncongenial supervisor, Lord David Cecil of New College. Cecil was regarded by the literary and academic establishments as one of his generation's most accomplished biographers and critics; but to Amis he represented everything that was wrong with academia.†

'Tell Monica,' Amis wrote to Larkin, 'that Cecil in the flesh strikes me as a *silly, unhelpful, posturing oaf*.' Another letter to Larkin curses his supervisor as 'that POSTURING QUACK Cess-hole', and in later years one of Amis's party pieces was a deft impersonation of Cecil's

---

* Martin Amis emphasizes that, for all his father's candid contempt for much (if not most) of English literature ('I knew him to be incapable of equivocation or euphemism on any literary question'), he had a superb memory for verse, which must have served him well in the Oxford final examinations. 'I would sometimes think,' writes Martin, ' "My God, he knows *all English poetry*." Ten lines here, twenty lines there, of Shakespeare, Milton, Marvell, Rochester, Pope, Gray, Keats, Wordsworth, Byron, Tennyson, Christina Rossetti, Housman, Owen, Kipling, Auden, Graves . . .'

† The thesis was eventually turned down by the Oxford examiners, who included Cecil. 'They thought I hadn't borne out my main contention,' Amis explained to Larkin. By this time he had an academic job, and the rejection had no effect on his career.

lecturing manner, with a precise phonetic rendering of the drawling, lisping aristocratic diction:

Laze – laze and gentlemen, when we say a man looks like a poet – dough mean – looks like Chauthah – dough mean – looks like Dvyden – dough mean – looks like *Theck-thpyum* [or something else barely recognizable as 'Shakespeare'] – Mean looks like Shelley [pronounced 'Thel-lem' or thereabouts]. Matthew Arnold [then *prestissimo*] called Shelley beautiful ineffectual angel Matthew Arnold had face [*rallentando*] like a *horth*. But my subject this morning is not the poet Shelley. Jane – Austen.

Including this in his *Memoirs* towards the end of his life, Amis admits that it was 'appropriated by me without acknowledgement' from its originator, John Wain.

The first reference to Wain in Amis's letters to Larkin is in October 1946. Wain had come up to St John's College from a Staffordshire grammar school in 1943, at the age of eighteen. Having (like Larkin) failed his army medical because of poor eyesight, he was able to complete his degree without interruption, getting a First in English. Luckily, he had been 'farmed out' for tutorials to the Magdalen College tutor in English, no less than C. S. Lewis, whose 'Inklings' (Lewis himself, J. R. R. Tolkien, Charles Williams and various lesser figures) were then a prominent though eccentric Oxford cabal.* Wain was invited to join them as a representative of the younger generation.

As soon as his degree was completed, Wain was given a junior fellowship at St John's – somewhat to Amis's disgust, since Wain was three years younger than him, a mere twenty-one. 'Did you know JBWain is nay a FELLO of John's?' Amis asked Larkin, adding in a footnote that 'fello' was a variant of fellatio.

The news fills me with the liveliest horror . . . I talked to Arthur Boyarse about it: 'I see Wain is now a fellow.' 'Yes a remarkable achievement isn't it.' 'Do

---

* See the present writer's *The Inklings* (1978). Their *raison d'être* was the revival of Christian-influenced literature. The group, at evening gatherings in Lewis's college rooms and lunchtime beer-drinking sessions in Oxford pubs, chiefly the 'Bird and Baby' (Eagle and Child) opposite St John's, listened as its chief members read aloud from work in progress, most of all Tolkien's *The Lord of the Rings*.

you think so.' 'Yes you've got to remember hes only 21 years of age.' 'You mean hes not old enough to know better.'

Arthur Boyars was co-editor with Wain of *Mandrake*, the Oxford literary periodical in which Amis reviewed *A Girl in Winter*.

Amis's resentment of Wain's precocious success – not just his fellow-ship but his co-editorship of *Mandrake* and consequent power in the local literary scene – surfaces now and then in the letters to Larkin: 'John Wain was in a minor car smash recently and was cut rather badly about the forehead. I am glad. (Here wait a sec old boy haven't you a scrap of ordinary human feeling NO).' But after Amis had begun his B.Litt., Wain offered to fix him up with some teaching of undergraduates, to add to his income; and in his *Memoirs*, Amis affectionately recalls the Wain of the mid and late 1940s: 'I found him most attractive, lightly caustic with a voice and manner to match, knowledgeable, worldly-wise, a budding academic without the crap.' Moreover, Wain 'was a lover of jazz and knew about it' – an almost essential qualification for Amis's approval in those days. (Wain's son Will recalls that his father 'wasn't a musician as such', but – like Amis – could easily be persuaded to bawl out a blues.)

Amis was soon giving Wain a taste of his novel-in-progress: 'The legacy is swimming ahead . . . I read bits to John Wain when he called the other day; he delighted me by being as far as I could see genuinely horrified by the characters of Sidney, Whetstone etc.' Wain later said that it was from this that he himself 'caught the virus' of writing novels:

When, a few years later, I sat down . . . to 'see if ' I could write a novel, Amis's example was certainly one of my motives. He had made it seem . . . simple and natural to be trying to shape one's day-to-day reactions to life into fiction. I'm quite certain that I would never have written *Hurry On Down* without the example of that first, undergraduate novel of Amis's.

Amis himself wasn't sure he'd caught the virus. At one point he put 'The Legacy' on one side to attempt a children's book with an Arthurian plot. 'To-morrow I am going to start on book for young human beings,' he told Larkin in May 1947. And two weeks later: 'I am working quite hard on the Arthur thing now. The only trouble I'm finding is that I am much too clever for most grown-ups to understand, and so even cleverer than almost any child's understanding. But I still feel fairly interested in it.' The following month he submitted it to a publisher, without success:

I have already had Arthur back. They said *exactly* what I said they'd say – 'Thank you for letting us see – we were interested to read – not *quite* in line with the *kind of* material we are using *in our list at the present time*.' . . . Oh dear: I don't like thinking abt. all the TIME I've WASTED doing that: still, it's not *the end of the world*.

The following February he thought about writing a historical novel, 'a comic eighteenth-century story,' he told Larkin,

about a ship of the Royal Navy on a secret mission and carrying a detachment of Welsh soldiers on the same voyage. The skipper is very interested in textual criticism, and points out corruption in the text of his sealed orders. An officer out for promotion risks his life to bring him a re-pirated edition of the bad quarto of *Hamlet*. There are rescues and storms and cutting-out expeditions. There is a ship's doctor interested in medicine. The hero is a deserter from the army who has changed clothes with a deserter from the navy. If I can think of a funny style to write it in, I shall try and do it; one day when we're looking at each other's faces we will try and develop the idea.

Another letter to Larkin about this project refers to the soldiers as 'Welch' rather than 'Welsh'.

Two other projects distracted him from 'The Legacy': libretto-writing for Bruce Montgomery (the two of them planned and worked on various projects which came to little), and a short monograph on Graham Greene, commissioned for an ill-fated series and never published. Meanwhile, despite Amis's faith in Durex, his girlfriend Hilary Bardwell had become pregnant.

'Hilly and I are making a man at the moment which is worrying me rather,' Amis wrote to Larkin in December 1947, just after taking his Oxford finals. They decided on an abortion – then highly illegal – and only called it off reluctantly at the last moment, because of the medical risk Hilly would run at the hands of the seedy back-street doctors who were the only people prepared to perform the operation. The sole alternative, according to the middle-class moral code of those days, was a hasty wedding.

'As regards the impending marriage,' Amis told Larkin, writing for once in uncharacteristically un-comic language,

it's hard not to look on it as a *faute de mieux* . . . I don't want a filthy baby, but Hilly is so overjoyed by the prospect that it seems unkind not to allow it . . . Since I enjoy living with Hilly better than I enjoy living anywhere else, it's difficult to believe that I shan't enjoy living with her all the time, especially since it'll mean in addition that I shall be able to do as I like, eat the food I like, and stop worrying about not being able to ejaculate when I want to.

Despite the fact that Amis was 'doing the decent thing' by Hilly, his own father and Hilly's parents threatened to boycott the wedding, until dissuaded by Amis's mother. The marriage took place in the Oxford registry office in January 1948, and the couple moved into rented accommodation in the city – though Amis's in-laws lived only a few miles from Oxford, so that he had to pay frequent visits to them.

He had already taken against the Bardwells *en masse*, condemning one of his brothers-in-law for his taste in clothes and the other for having been a conscientious objector during the war. Worst of all was 'the father', Leonard Bardwell, a civil servant who (Amis told Larkin) 'does folk dancing (polk dancing? pock dancing? fock dancing?)'. Over the next few years his contempt for 'Daddy B', as his father-in-law was known within the family, became obsessive, a constantly recurring theme in his letters to Larkin. He was bored with the man's rambling monologues about morris dancing and Welsh philology – it was like listening to the 'Welch Home Service' of the BBC. During 1948, as the completed typescript of 'The Legacy' received rejection after rejection from London publishers,* he began – in the intervals of revising and trying to improve it – to contemplate quite a different kind of novel.

It was partly inspired by what he had seen when visiting Larkin at

---

* Bruce Montgomery tried it on his own publishers, Gollancz, and Kenneth Tynan, with whom Amis made friends at Oxford in 1948, seems to have offered it to Longmans.

University College, Leicester. Larkin was comparatively happy there, but Amis only felt amused contempt for the building – a hastily converted Victorian lunatic asylum – and the provincial academics. 'I looked round a couple of times,' Amis writes in his memoirs, 'and said to myself, "Christ, somebody ought to do something with this." Not that it was awful – well, only a bit . . .' He was soon mentioning the idea to Larkin, who had broken off an engagement to his Wellington girlfriend Ruth Bowman because he could not bear the thought of marriage, and was now sending Amis reports on the beginnings of an equally on–off relationship with Monica Jones at Leicester. 'I laffed like bogray over the Monicker business,' was Amis's response to one such bulletin from Larkin. 'The relationship wd dateless go well into my leicester novel.' And in another letter, in the summer of 1948: 'You know, when I've finished the legacy I'm going to start a comic novel, featuring Monica . . . it would be a marvellous welter of derisive hatred.'

He still loved Larkin dearly. Hilly had become jealous of this – Amis reported her saying to him: 'The way you hang on Philip's lips makes me laugh; if you do or say something and he doesn't think it's funny, you're upset, and if he does, you're delighted.' Yet when her baby was born, she agreed that it should be christened Philip, and that Larkin should be its godfather. Nevertheless Amis was well aware that the romantic and sexual misadventures of a Larkinesque anti-hero would have immense comic possibilities. So would a caricature of a self-obsessed academic like Lord David Cecil; and then there were the 'Welch' obsessions of Daddy Bardwell. By January 1949, these too were added to the scheme. 'I have jotted down a few notes for my next book about Daddy B,' he told Larkin. 'I don't see how I can avoid doing him in fiction if I am to refrain from stabbing him under the fifth rib in fact. I have been thinking of a kind of me-and-the-Bardwells theme for it all, ending with me poking one of Hilly's brothers' wife as a revenge on them all.'

Professor Welch, the character to which Daddy Bardwell contributed so heavily in *Lucky Jim*, is such a magnificent comic creation that few have stopped to consider the cruelty behind it. Yet Martin Amis remembers his Bardwell grandfather with an affection and admiration that is totally at odds with Kingsley's caricature of him:

He was . . . an amateur musician and a morris dancer . . . I loved him, and was always amazed by the amount of energy he devoted to entertaining me . . . He had gone to the trouble of mastering three languages of limited utility: Swedish, Welsh and Romansh . . . Kingsley cultivated an ornate resentment towards his father-in-law, but the truth is that he was irritated by Daddy B's innocence. My father, as we shall see, was generally irritated by innocence.*

* Or maybe his rage with his father-in-law was really rage with his own father in disguise. He writes: 'Boredom, I am sorry to say, came to be my chief reaction to my father's company, though I did not want to feel this and grew better at hiding it – I hope.' He scarcely needed to hide it with Hilly's father.

3

Nine times in the morning

On Sunday, 18 January 1948, three days before Kingsley Amis's hastily arranged wedding, a lanky eighteen-year-old south Londoner joined a bunch of jobbing actors on a train from Paddington to South Wales. It was tantamount to running away to join a circus. He had given up a boring but steady job writing articles for a trade journal called *Gas World* for the risk-ridden world of touring theatre.

The production was *No Room at the Inn*, which he describes as 'a melodrama about wartime evacuees being farmed out to unscrupulous foster-parents ... The tour was to last for six months ... My duties were to be Assistant Stage Manager, understudying the five men and teaching the children ... It was difficult to understand how anyone could have thought me capable of understudying five actors aged between twenty-one and seventy.'

John James Osborne's only acting experience had been in an amateur dramatic society in Leatherhead, plus a few brief appearances on stage while attending a minor public school in Devon. He was not, however, from the middle-class stratum of society which such a schooling might suggest. His school fees were paid by the National Advertising Benevolent Society, which had supported him and his mother following the death from tuberculosis in 1940 of his father, an advertising copy-writer.

At school he had shown some prowess in English literature, and wanted to go to Oxford; but this aspiration was mocked by his head-master, with whom he literally came to blows – Osborne hit back when struck, and was expelled. Joining the theatre company was a similar act of rebellion, motivated not merely by Osborne's desire to extract himself from a boring job, but also to escape from his mother,

Nellie Beatrice Osborne, née Grove, with whom he had been living as an only child since the death of his sister (from tuberculosis and meningitis) when he was two.

The two volumes of Osborne's autobiography are called *A Better Class of Person* and *Almost a Gentleman*, titles which allude to his having been born into one of the lower levels of the English class system. A dominant theme in both volumes is the rich social tragi-comedy that was acted out daily by his mother's family, the Groves, who occupied a place in the pecking order that could be loosely defined as lower-lower-middle-class, or (less flatteringly) upper-working-class. Osborne describes them in old age – using words from his own play *The Hotel in Amsterdam* – as 'Retired rotten, grafting publicans, shop assistants, ex-waitresses. They live on and on. Having hernias and arthritic hips and strokes. But they go on: writing poisonous letters to one another. Complaining and wheedling and paying off the same old scores . . .' Those complaining letters – quoted lengthily throughout both volumes of Osborne's memoirs – amused him, but they also provided him with his first taste of rhetoric and rant, two fundamental ingredients of his individuality as a playwright.

Moreover, if the Groves were nothing to be proud of socially, they provided the young John with – in the words of Alan Bennett, reviewing *A Better Class of Person* – 'a childhood of Dickensian richness and oddness'. Bennett also remarks that 'dates are quite hard to come by in this book: nowhere, for instance, is Osborne's date of birth plainly stated'. (It was 12 December 1929.) Osborne himself admits that there is a shortage of solid history, at least about his relatives. 'I spent years of unforced, curious listening in my boyhood, trying to establish hard details about what any of them actually *did* or were, but information was difficult to come by. It was rather like saying to a singer of ancient ballads, "Yes, but what were the real *facts*?"'

He does at least inform us that his mother was the daughter of a publican, and that she was working as a barmaid near Fleet Street when she met his father, then a young man newly up from South Wales. Osborne describes his parents' marriage as a 'blundering mis-alliance', and at the time of his birth they were living apart, though this seems to have been partly the consequence of Thomas Osborne's tubercular condition:

My father, when he was not in Brompton Hospital or in Colindale Sanatorium ... (by this time he had only one lung) ... seemed to stay in digs a long way from us in Harrow or Hounslow on his own, and my mother would occasionally deliver a clean shirt and socks to his landlady. He would come over to see us when he was able and I have a vague remembrance of them hitting each other.

Young John and his mother were then lodging in a series of dingy rooms near her own parents in the Fulham area of London, living on next to nothing. 'Fulham in the 1930s,' he writes, 'was a dismal district ... gloomy and uninteresting ... full of pubs, convents, second-hand clothes shops, bagwash laundries and pawnbrokers. Everything seemed very broken down.' There was little entertainment for John other than the histrionic harangues and complaints of his Grove relatives; he says he proved 'an eager and attentive listener' to these performances by members of what he ironically dubs 'the Grove Repertory Company'.*

Grandpa Grove, a grumbling old man who ate eel pie and faggots as he leafed through the *News of the World*, had come to the end of a not inglorious career as a pub landlord, at the height of which (according to family legend) he would consume a breakfast of 'half a bottle of 3-star brandy, a pound of porterhouse steak, oysters in season and a couple of chorus girls all the year round'. Indeed he had reputedly once risen to the peak of spending a naughty weekend at Brighton with that greatest of music-hall divas, Marie Lloyd – 'the only recorded link I have with anything to do with the theatrical profession,' writes Osborne sardonically. Rather oddly, this grandfather seems to have been the first person to put the idea of becoming a playwright into his head: 'He told me that he would live to see the day when one of two things would happen: one, I would be the next Prime Minister of England; or, two, I would be the next George Bernard Shaw.'†

He grew up in an environment that may have been Dickensian but

---

* In a 1957 article, Osborne points out that his father's family were very different from the Groves: 'Not only were their voices soft, but they actually *listened* to what you were saying. They came from South Wales and cared for the language they spoke.'
† Osborne says that in his teens he read Shaw's polemical play-prefaces, which were then 'frowned upon, unread, by most adults'.

was far from illiterate. His father occasionally wrote short stories and poems ('I was probably the only person who ever read them,' said Osborne), and other members of the family devoured such popular novels as the works of Warwick Deeping, borrowed from the lending library. Yet it was a home where literature had nothing to do with life: 'I grew up believing that there was a language one read in books and another one spoke, and that the divide between the two was impassable.'

His father's health remained precarious throughout his childhood, but by the time that he was seven it had rallied enough for Thomas Osborne to go back to work. Moreover his parents now became sufficiently reconciled to live under the same roof. They left Fulham and went out of London to a nondescript suburb of Epsom called Stoneleigh. This had no more identity than Kingsley Amis's Norbury – it was merely a station surrounded by shopping parades, housing estates, and a mock-Tudor pub where Osborne's mother later got a job behind the bar. It was not even Stockbroker's Tudor but 'Bankclerk's Tudor', Osborne writes contemptuously, sneering at Stoneleigh as a 'Byzantium of pre-war mediocrity'.

After little more than a year at Stoneleigh, while he commuted to his copywriter's job, Thomas Osborne's tuberculosis flared up again, and the National Advertising Benevolent Society paid for him to go off to a foreign sanatorium. He had scarcely returned when war broke out in September 1939, whereupon the Society generously evacuated him, his wife and ten-year-old son to Ventnor in the Isle of Wight, 'where we would be safer and the climate would be more suitable for his health'. It was to little effect: John soon learnt that his father had only a few weeks left to live, and then came a nightmare day:

I was sitting in the kitchen reading about two weeks after Christmas, when I heard my mother scream . . . I ran to see what was happening and stared up to the landing where my father was standing. He was completely naked with his silver hair and grey, black and red beard. He looked like a naked Christ. 'Look at him!' she screamed. 'Oh, my God, he's gone blind.' He stood quite still for a moment and then fell headlong down the stairs on top of us . . . She was quite right. He had gone blind.

Thomas Osborne died a few days later. John went back to Stoneleigh with his mother, and soon contracted rheumatic fever. 'For ten months, I read all day and listened to the wireless. The lady from next door lent me her entire set of a 1919 edition of a children's encyclopaedia.' The radio greatly expanded his cultural horizons, and he developed a taste for classical music: 'I listened all day to . . . the BBC . . . discovering how to pronounce Dvořák and Dohnányi and what the mysterious Köchel might be.' He also subscribed to a correspondence course in how to write fiction. He has said of his ambitions in those days: 'I thought I'd be a newspaper editor, opera singer, or priest. But . . . I thought whatever I did do, I'd do it better than anyone else could do it.'

To complete his recovery, he was sent by the Benevolent Society to a convalescent home in Dorset – 'more like a Borstal for sick or dying boys'. Next, the Society parcelled him off to 'the lower depths of boarding schools', Belmont College in Devon (which he calls 'St Michael's' in his autobiography). This was an establishment that offered 'the merest, timid trappings of a fake public school for the minimum expense'. Nevertheless at least one of the teaching staff made a strong impression on him, 'and I looked forward to and enjoyed his growling passion for Dickens, Thackeray, Richardson, Fielding, Tennyson, Matthew Arnold'. In his first year he won 'a prize for my Literature and Living Papers', and he began to act in sketches at school entertainments.

Much of the early part of his autobiography is devoted to an irritable caricature of his mother. (She was still alive when this first volume was published in 1981; when accused of having portrayed her cruelly, Osborne responded: 'I don't think it's really a bitter attack. It's simply a record of my feelings at the time . . . She wouldn't read it, anyway.') Yet for all his grumbles about Nellie Beatrice's lack of emotional warmth – the 'Black Looks' he says she would invariably throw in his direction, and the 'loveless clinch' which was the best she could manage for a hug – he has to admit that she spent much of her hard-earned wages and tips as a barmaid on giving him his first experience of the professional theatre. On her days off, she would take him up to the West End, for 'cream cakes at the Regent Palace, gin and It for my mother, and then on to The Show! Ivor Novello, *Dancing Years, Perchance to Dream, Lisbon Story*, all of the George Black shows at the Hippodrome.' Moreover Nellie Beatrice herself was an accomplished performer – behind the bar. 'I have seen none better,' comments Osborne. 'No one could draw a pint with a more perfect head on it or pour out four glasses of beer at the same time, throwing bottles up in the air and catching them as she did so.'

After his fracas with the headmaster had prematurely concluded his school career, he was sent by the Benevolent Society to a school of shorthand and typing, and they then found him the job on *Gas World*. The war was now over, but National Service lurked – though with his background of poor health he was not surprised to be rejected on medical grounds. In the event, his early experiences in professional theatre were to prove just as physically and emotionally taxing as two years in the army might have been.

* *

No Room at the Inn, the production he had joined, was in its way a well-made play: 'With its short scenes of melodramatic information, sentiment and broad humour, it was a skilful example of music-hall drama.' Meanwhile, though he had become engaged to an eighteen-year-old girl back home, 'Renee Shippard of the Halifax Building Society', who was writing adoring letters to him daily, Osborne began to pursue the company's juvenile lead, 'Sheila, a twenty-two-year-old . . . with elfin Elstree winsomeness'.

After a week in Cardiff, the production moved on to Southport, second in the list of 'the forty-eight different towns we were to visit'. Next came Grimsby. 'We seldom progressed logically . . . but would go from Torquay to Hanley to Eastbourne to Sheffield, making for long wearisome Sunday train calls.' The scenery and props would follow in a goods train, and at 7.30 each Monday morning Osborne would go down to the railway yard to see it unloaded and transported to the theatre. As for his understudying, 'I had to rely on scripts then known as "Sides" to learn my lines. These . . . contained only the last few words of your cue followed by the speech.'

He was soon judged insufficiently experienced to be teaching the children in the cast. During the extra time which this gave him, 'I began . . . in the dressing-room at the Empire, Sunderland . . . writing my first play, a melodrama about a poetic Welsh loon called *Resting Deep* . . . It had nothing to do with my own experience.'

Sheila the juvenile lead soon proved to be 'neurotically frigid'. When the tour was extended for a further six months and the cast acquired some new recruits, these included an actress called Stella Linden, married (in name only) to a not very successful theatrical entrepreneur called Patrick Desmond. 'Stella was about thirty, very dark with a large, handsome head and a very fine striking nose. To me, she had the appearance and authority of what was thought to be a Leading Lady.' Osborne describes his own appearance at the age of eighteen as 'unprepossessing', but he was actually very handsome; a tall face and a strong nose combined to give him what were then called 'matinée idol' looks. Despite the fact that he was earning very little, and that – during this period of severe postwar austerity – fashionable clothes were hard to find, he splashed out some of his first theatrical earnings on a pair of yellow silk pyjamas.

He showed Stella his play, *Resting Deep*. Her verdict was harsh: 'Speeches were too long; wordy scenes; slack; audiences left hanging in the air; ending unresolved.' Yet she told him that, if he was prepared to sit down with her and rework the script from scratch, she and her husband might be able to put on the play as part of a season they were planning at a run-down music-hall, the Granville at Walham Green.

Of course he agreed, and they began the rewrites together – renaming the play *The Devil Inside* – with Stella telling Osborne that his ideas were too highbrow and poetic, and injecting broad jokes. Then, during a week while *No Room at the Inn* was playing at Llandudno, it became apparent that she had proposed the collaboration largely as a means of luring the handsome eighteen-year-old into her bed. One evening she 'began making love to me at alarming speed'. He was glad of the chance to show off his silk pyjamas.

Recalling his sexual prowess in those days, he quotes from his play *A Sense of Detachment*: 'Christ, I was only nineteen! I could do it *nine times* in the morning.' Yet by the time the tour of *No Room at the Inn* had finished in December 1948, and he went to live with Stella in her Brighton basement flat, the pleasures of this sexual athleticism had begun to pall. Also there was little work to be found. He took a brief Christmas job as a pirate in a Brighton production of *Treasure Island*, did menial jobs in several restaurants and hotels, but often had to sign on for the dole. Each weekend he visited his mother simply to eat as much as he could, returning to Brighton laden with tinned food, on which he and Stella (who was also out of work) lived during the week.

He and Stella tried writing another play together. Called *Happy Birthday*, 'it was to take place in a middle-class house and concerned the events during the birthday celebrations of a middle-aged woman'. But Stella was offered a job in rep at Kendal, and once there she quickly began an affair with another very young actor. Osborne consequently found himself ejected from the Brighton flat.

He got a job as an ASM at Leicester, and now began to be assigned small acting roles of his own, walk-on parts which 'seemed to have been written with stage managers specifically in mind . . . It [was] like being the hind legs of a pantomime horse.' The season's programme at Leicester 'consisted of the staple repertory diet of the time: Home Counties comedies and murder mysteries; plays with maids and middle-class girls compromised in their cami-knickers; and the occasional northern comedy . . . Whoever wrote them knew their audience.'

Suddenly, to his astonishment, Stella's husband Pat Desmond, who was producing a season in Huddersfield, wrote to Osborne that he would put on the Osborne–Stella collaboration *The Devil Inside* for a week. Stella would be there too. So one spring Monday in 1950, at the age of twenty, Osborne found himself sitting in the stalls of the Theatre Royal,

watching the world opening performance of my play, holding hands with my co-author . . . After less than eighteen months in the theatre, I was watching my own play – or a version of it . . . (it seemed to have only dismembered resemblance to what I dimly remembered having written) . . . being performed in a professional theatre. I was getting paid and I had an ex-mistress saying affectionate encouraging things to me. Stella's coarse jokes worked, as she said they would, but my remaining wastergrounds of poetry palled even for me.

Moreover at the end of the week, 'my share of the royalty was just over nine pounds', no more than a paltry week's salary. His Leicester job had finished, and there seemed no alternative but to return, from this glimpse of a playwright's life, to his mother's Black Looks and the bypass-Tudor life of Stoneleigh.

4

Star pupil

There could scarcely be more contrast between the melodramatic upbringing and early theatrical career of John Osborne and the placid, safe, even pampered childhood, adolescence and young manhood of the member of St John's College who had aroused the envy of Kingsley Amis for his academic achievements, John Barrington Wain. Yet Wain himself never regarded the early part of his life as trouble-free; to him, at least until he reached Oxford, it was a story of perpetual anxiety, even fear.

Three years younger than Amis and Larkin, he was the son of a dentist in Stoke-on-Trent who had raised himself to prosperity from very humble beginnings. Wain writes that his father's family were 'too poor to have ancestors'. His paternal grandfather was a labourer in the Potteries, who died before he was fifty of silicosis contracted from clay-dust. His mother's father had been a printer's compositor. Until his parents' generation, his ancestors had been 'simply part of the swarming, anonymous life of the working class'. Yet Wain himself had been born, if not with a silver spoon in his mouth, then with plenty of them on display in his parents' substantial home.

'I can't make the fashionable claim to a "working-class background",' he wrote in the 1960s.

The circumstances of my childhood were exceedingly comfortable; there was never any shortage, either of food and clothing or of space, recreation, equipment. Our house was large and cheerful; I always had a room to myself; the garden was ample, with space for secret hiding-places as well as a lawn big enough to use for games; I was taken to the seaside for at least a fortnight a year.

38

When he was three, his parents had moved out of Stoke to a big house on the summit of a hill, overlooking the green Staffordshire countryside. At least, it overlooked it if the young Wain was careful not to lower his eyes; for the valley directly beneath it had been filled up with 'the Sutton dwelling', a slum clearance housing estate that was 'bursting' with working-class children. Though he was only one generation removed from that class himself, he was brought up to fear and even hate it.

His father was openly contemptuous of the inability of his working-class patients to look after their health, while his mother, who 'had had her own childhood darkened and most of the confidence crushed out of her by an over-harsh father', was timorous by nature, and seems to have encouraged John to keep away from the 'rough' boys in the valley below. John was not an only child: he had an elder sister and a younger brother, but neither of these seems to have offered him much companionship. 'Mine,' he writes, 'was a lonely childhood,' and his solitary hours were often darkened by a fear of the Sutton houses below the hill, which gave him 'the perpetual sense of living in a beleaguered garrison'.

In his early years, he was taken out for walks by one of the servant-girls the Wains could afford to employ (they also retained a teenage 'house-boy' to clean the shoes and the car, and sweep the paths). The servant would take the child past a huddle of derelict cottages with tumbledown privies in the garden, and she seems to have sadistically encouraged him to fear these: ' "Now we're coming to the dirty lava-tories," the girl would say. "Run!" ' And he ran.

It was just as bad when he began formal education. At five, he was enrolled into the most genteel of dame-schools; yet even here there was a 'rough' boy to be avoided ('rough' was the parental term of disapproval of children who were 'dangerous, uncouth, coarsely dressed'). He might have learnt to fight back, but his parents were both pacifists, passionate supporters of the Peace Pledge Union and the Anglican Pacifist Fellowship; and also (as he puts it) 'simple-lifers [who] distrusted drugs and were strong on herbal remedies, wholewheat biscuits, and natural living'. Hitting back was not an option for their son.

By the time he went on to a Froebel preparatory school, he was (as he puts it) 'underweight, pale and "peaky"', accustomed to a parental background chorus of 'He's delicate'. At nine, he moved to Newcastle-under-Lyme High School, where he did his best to 'wrestle and lark about and generally take my place in the world of boys'. But fear still gripped him – not so much during school hours as on the way there and home again. 'The main danger was Penkhull School, [full of] working-class children . . . Most of the pupils . . . seemed to live in the Sutton . . . The problem . . . was to get past Penkhull School without being mobbed.'

In his autobiography, *Sprightly Running*, he particularly dwells on one episode. Walking home with a group of High School boys, he was suddenly set upon by a Penkhull pupil, who knocked him to the ground so that he injured his knee. What really hurt (he writes) was that his own schoolfellows failed to come to his rescue. He declares that his first novel, *Hurry On Down*, reflects this experience:

My hero tried one job and one adjustment after another, veering wildly up and down the social scale in the process . . . The book was . . . taken as . . . illustrating social changes [in postwar Britain]. I am far from disputing . . . this . . . [But] its deep motivation is somewhere else . . . the mood at its centre was born that afternoon in 1935, as I scrambled to my feet, dazed, nursing my knee, and saw, on the one hand, the glowering faces of the elementary-school boys, and on the other the aloof backs of my schoolfellows – and wondered how, between the two of them, I was ever going to live.

* *

He writes that at school he was 'backward and unteachable', labelled as a dunce and put in a class with children younger than himself. There was a further setback when, at the age of sixteen, the retina of his left eye became detached, leaving him with only rudimentary sight in it. This led, two years later, to his rejection for military service. Nevertheless he was able to go to Oxford.

In later years he would see himself described in print, 'by journalists who have never met me', as a typical product of the scholarship system which brought grammar-school boys to Oxbridge. This was nonsense. 'Nobody suggested that I should read for a scholarship'; his school record made the idea seem absurd. On the other hand his father could afford to pay the university fees and support his son there, and Wain had sufficient academic ability to pass the undemanding entrance exam for fee-payers. Consequently he arrived at St John's College in January 1943 feeling distinctly uncomfortable. He had not '*earned* Oxford' – as had Larkin and Amis – through intellectual achievement; nor did he come from the upper-class milieu 'where boys grew up to think of Oxford as something that comes along naturally'. Between these two worlds, 'I lacked both available kinds of confidence.'

But this swiftly ceased to matter. He fell in love at once with the university and its surroundings. 'Everything was new, everything was unknown, everything was beautiful. Oxford has won a good many hearts, but never did it make so complete and immediate a conquest as of mine.' And, perhaps because he was happy, he immediately 'expanded' intellectually, and 'became a star pupil'.

Like Larkin and Amis, he was reading English, but unlike them he was enthusiastic about most of the syllabus. In particular he quickly developed a passion for Samuel Johnson, whose eloquent pessimism echoed his own fraught childhood and adolescence. Moreover, by a happy chance, he found himself being taught by a man 'whose attitude to life, both in great matters and small, was more Johnsonian than that of anyone I have met before or since'.

Not all C. S. Lewis's pupils felt affectionate about their tutor's hectoring teaching methods – John Betjeman had been a notable failure nearly twenty years earlier – but Wain coped with Lewis's rhetoric by turning himself into 'a miniature Lewis . . . a quick-fire debater'. Nor did he have a problem with Lewis's proselytizing Christianity: 'My parents were Christians of the extreme Low-Church variety . . . my mother at one time toyed with the idea of becoming a Quaker.' During student days Wain described himself as a Christian.

Adolescence had brought him no sexual experience. At home, he had developed an idolizing passion for a neighbour's daughter, and the fact that this was unrequited convinced him that 'sexual fulfilment was one more of the things that were not for me'. He may have been thinking of Kingsley Amis when he wrote of his Oxford days: 'Most of us were nerve-ridden little virgins, but there were one or two who had been kicked in at the deep end . . . You could pick out these youths immediately; they were less worried by life, more pleased with themselves . . .'

He met Larkin before he came to know Amis. When Wain arrived at St John's, 'Philip . . . was just finishing his undergraduate course that spring, and vanished in the summer'. He found the twenty-one-year-old Larkin 'quiet, rather aloof . . . no roaring student companion . . . But even so,' Wain continues,

he was important to me . . . His literary self-training had already begun and had already borne some fruit; and this, combined with his quietness, his slight stammer, and (perhaps) the impression of giant intelligence produced by the fact of his having a large dome-like head and wearing very thick glasses, all helped to make him 'the college writer'.

He sensed, behind Larkin's ironic self-effacement, 'a rock-like determination to do whatever it might be necessary to do in order to write well'.

On his side, Larkin had no recollection of meeting Wain while they were both still undergraduates, but did recall hearing that 'a man called Wain' was among the more interesting freshmen. 'Years afterwards,' he writes, 'John told me that our acquaintance at this time was limited to a brief bitter exchange at lunch about Albert Ammons's "Boogie-Woogie Stomp" and the poetry of George Crabbe. If so, it was a great opportunity lost.'

Though Larkin soon decamped to his library job in Wellington, he would occasionally reappear at St John's for festive weekends, when (writes Wain)

we urchins were ready to come to blows for the privilege of entertaining him . . . It took the trumpet-call 'Philip's coming up!' to bring together a motley crew who did not associate at any other time, and who were connected simply by a common admiration for one whom we already considered a Flaubertian saint of letters.

Among this group was Amis, when he was able to get to Oxford on leave. 'My first casual meetings with him,' writes Wain, 'came about because we were both, so to speak, swimming in the thin fluid that solidified only when Philip Larkin arrived.' He recalls that it was Amis who 'sold me my copy of Philip's first novel, *Jill*' – presumably because Caton of the Fortune Press had failed to get any copies into Blackwell's bookshop. But if the Wain–Larkin–Amis friendship began with Wain paying homage to Larkin's achievement and potential as a writer, he himself now began to move steadily towards a position of power and influence in the literary field.

* *

His first step, during his second year at Oxford, was to launch *Mandrake*, the 'little magazine' in which Amis reviewed *A Girl in Winter*. Besides printing verse and prose by undergraduates – including Kenneth Tynan, then at Magdalen – it spread its net into the London literary world, collecting contributions from such luminaries as C. Day-Lewis. *Mandrake* continued to appear intermittently until the mid 1950s, with Wain often writing reviews for it, but he handed over the editorship (to Arthur Boyars)* before taking his finals at Oxford – in which he received a First Class.

He was immediately given a junior research fellowship at St John's, but from 1947 most of his time was spent not at Oxford but in Reading, where he worked as a lecturer in the English department (St John's allowed this plurality of employment). Still only twenty-two, he embarked on a marriage to another young Reading lecturer, Marianne Urmstom, and they set up home in a bungalow on the edge of the town. Kingsley Amis, visiting him there, thought him prematurely middle-aged:

He . . . seemed, though three years younger than the twenty-five-year-old me, to comport himself like somebody in his forties . . . His walking-stick, among the able-bodied surely a warning signal in the same category as facial hair, and a tendency to tweed hats, made me uneasy.

Yet Wain's determined, focused attitude to building a literary and academic career rubbed off on Amis. He recalls that it was Wain who 'pushed me in the academic direction myself, inciting me to go for my

---

* Then an undergraduate at Wadham College, Boyars later achieved some reputation as a translator of Russian poetry. He married American-born Marion Lobbenberg, who as Marion Boyars became one half of the innovative British publishing house Calder & Boyars, which dared to publish such writers as Henry Miller and William Burroughs at a time when such books could be suppressed for 'obscenity'.

First, pointing me towards a provincial college lectureship and away from the suburban schoolmaster's job I had vaguely envisaged'.

The train journey from Reading to London was very short, and Wain gradually began to make himself a public niche as a critic. During 1950 he had an article on the poetry of William Empson published in John Lehmann's widely read *Penguin New Writing*. Soon he was reviewing books about poetry for the BBC Third Programme. Some of his own poetry had already been published in *Mandrake*, and in 1951 his first collection, *Mixed Feelings*, was printed by the Reading University School of Art, Wain collecting subscriptions and distributing copies to such friends as Amis and his old tutor C. S. Lewis. Two years later, he arranged for the Reading University School of Art to print Amis's own second collection of poems, *A Frame of Mind*.

Meanwhile Wain was dutifully doing the sort of academic work that Oxford and Reading expected of him – writing a study of early nineteenth-century literary criticism – and was also (as he puts it) 'employing odds and ends of time in writing a novel'. He claims that he had no great ambition in this sphere; it was 'not . . . from any wish to "be a novelist", but simply to see if I could write a novel that would succeed in getting into print. My avowed aims were to get the book published and make a hundred pounds from it.' Although he said he had caught the bug of novel-writing from the enthusiasm that Amis displayed while writing 'The Legacy' ('Kingsley . . . spoke of [it] with such enjoyment,' writes Wain, 'and seemed to be having so much fun writing it'), Amis remembers it the other way round in his own memoirs, where he alleges that Wain 'encouraged me to be some sort of proper writer instead of the dabbler I had largely been'.

Wain's progress with his own novel was slow – the book 'lay for long spells in my drawer, was written in fits and starts, and didn't get finished for three years' – but by 1953 it was done, and was accepted for publication by Secker & Warburg. Almost at the same moment, Wain's career as a man of letters took a leap forward of a different sort. The Third Programme had been giving John Lehmann* a monthly

---

* In his heyday – now ending – Lehmann had been immensely influential; Amis wrote that many people saw him as 'a sort of spider of the Ivy [restaurant], organizing, with the aid of Mr Stephen Spender and the head of the Third Programme, the metropolitan literary racket'.

slot to present a radio version of *New Writing*, under the title *New Soundings*, but by the end of 1952 it was decided to drop him (partly because he had failed to discover new young writers), and Wain was offered a six-month contract to edit and introduce a revamped programme of the same sort. Possibly punning on the name of his workplace, he decided to call it *First Reading*.

Wain now found himself 'hurled into the midst of . . . the "metropolitan literary world"'. He claims that he did not enjoy assembling the programme: 'I have not the temperament of an editor and dislike spending my days and nights among other people's manuscripts; if they are bad they depress me, and if they are good they make me want to go away and start writing something myself.' But there was no need to hunt for contributions. 'They came to me, shoals of them, and from every part of the literary spectrum. It gave me an idea of what was happening to that vague but powerful abstraction, "the mind of the age".'

He was determined to make the programme more controversial than Lehmann's *New Soundings*, seeing it as 'a chance to move a few of the established reputations gently to one side and allow new people their turn, people whose view of what should be attempted was roughly the same as my own'. He was soon under attack for this. Indeed the very first item in the first programme brought criticism, which Wain thought undeserved: 'I didn't deserve to be savaged for such exploits as presenting an excerpt from *Lucky Jim*.'

5

Dixon and Christine

For a long while Amis did not give up trying to get 'The Legacy' published, but in August 1949 he told Larkin: 'I . . . have re-started "my second novel".' He feared it was 'probably another "slight" one' – a criticism that had been made of its predecessor – but at least this time he had 'worked out the point of it'.

He believed that novels should have 'points'. He had been reading 'the greater part of *Ulysses*', and felt that much of Joyce's narrative was aimless: 'All the thought-stream business strikes me as a sodding bore . . . I think novels ought to tell a story . . . and have a theme . . . and give you a sense that a problem has been propounded and solved . . .'

The 'point' of his own new book was still largely to vent his fury with his father-in-law, 'Daddy B', who frequently imposed his company on the newlyweds. 'I hate him; I *hate* him; I HATE him; I *HATE* the old *APE'S BASTARD*,' Amis told Larkin after one of these visits. 'I shall swing for the old cockchafer unless I put him in a book, *recognisably* . . .' Meanwhile Hilly was pregnant again, and on 27 August 1949 Amis reported the birth of his second son, telling Larkin: 'Martin is really extraordinary – one of the most protesting faces I ever saw.'

Kingsley was trying for university lectureships. He applied unsuccessfully to Durham, to Bristol, and to a 'cunt-only place' (women's college) in London, finally getting a job at the University College of Swansea ('Swonzy'). He was depressed at the prospect of 'Welch life', but when he began to teach there in the autumn term of 1949 he found most of the 'stew dunce' pleasant enough, especially the girls. However, lecturing was certainly a sweat:

I've had to work hard at my lectures in advance – reading up all about *filthy Pater* . . . Still, nothing like a good full week's work, is there? No, there isn't, except possibly migraine combined with psoriasis, or a grinding hangover without having been drinking, or catching syph off a lavatory seat. I want to write down what I want to write down, not fart to and fro with other men's *stupid* ideas.

At first he had to live by himself in uncomfortable digs – 'the bathroom and shithouse *can only be reached through my bedroom* (a common Welch arrangement)'. He incorporated a reversed version of this (a bedroom only reachable through the bathroom) into the new novel. Hilly and the children soon joined him in Swansea, but he pined for Larkin:

I wish I could see you. I find even a couple of days with you does me a lot of good for quite a long time; I leave you feeling much cleverer and funnier than before you arrived, and more of a writer, even if you've crapped on my poems, and more isolated than I was before, but glad about it instead of depressed.

He wrote to Larkin as frequently as ever, pouring out the comic invective – 'HORRIBLE SMELL OF ARSE' was now a frequent curse – and using terms like 'craps' (for people he disliked) and 'in a pig's arse' (a blunt way of saying no), both of which Larkin eventually incorporated into one of his best-known poems.*

Though Swansea life was tolerable, he longed for London – apart from anything else, the women there were far more attractive – and he felt that the best way to get there was 'to keep on shutting myself up on my own and writing poems and a novel'. Even to have 'rather a crappy book' published would be a step forward, and in this mood he worried far less about the quality of 'Dixon and Christine' – the working title of the new novel – than he had about 'The Legacy'. (The surname of the hero, university lecturer Jim Dixon, had been suggested by Larkin's current address in Leicester, 12 Dixon Drive.)

* 'My wife and I have asked a crowd of craps / To come and waste their time and ours: perhaps / You'd care to join us? In a pig's arse, friend.' ('Vers de Société' in Larkin's *High Windows*, 1974.)

'I don't think it's as good or so verbally funny as The legacy,' he told Larkin in August 1950, 'but it may be more publishable and perhaps some of the things that happen are funnier.' Meanwhile the Amises were seriously short of money; Kingsley had to spend his summer marking Higher Certificate exam papers to earn cash, and for a while Hilly took a part-time job as a washer-up in a café. Not infrequently, Kingsley sent an SOS for a loan to Larkin, who invariably obliged.

Among new books then being reviewed was the second collection of short stories by the thirty-seven-year-old Angus Wilson, *Such Darling Dodos* (1950), and Amis read it and its predecessor, *The Wrong Set* (1949), with anxiety, fearing 'lest they shd. be exactly like me, but it seems they aren't,' he told Larkin. 'I thought him quite good, but not very funny ... And everything seemed a bit inconclusive.' Now approaching his own thirtieth birthday, he felt so afraid of continuing failure that 'I'm too frightened to send "Dixon" on the rounds'. And when in the spring of 1952 he tried it on the publishing house of Michael Joseph, the result was once again rejection. Meanwhile when he contemplated John Wain's steady progress in the literary world – Wain was now reviewing for the *Sunday Times* – Amis felt 'a pang of sincere grief'.

Following the Michael Joseph rejection, he parcelled up 'Dixon and Christine' and sent it to Belfast, Larkin having left Leicester for a job in the library of Queen's University. 'When I read the first draft,' Larkin has recalled, 'I said, Cut this, cut that, let's have more of the other. I remember I said, Let's have more "faces" – you know, [Jim Dixon's] Edith Sitwell face, and so on.' Larkin's letters with his suggestions have not survived, but it is evident from Amis's replies that some of them were radical. Apparently Larkin felt that Dixon should take a more active part in reorganizing his love-life – abandoning his awful girlfriend and pursuing the desirable Christine – than he did in the first draft. 'I wanted to tell the reader that if chaps in the shit climb out of the shit, it's by good luck, not by their own efforts,' Amis explained to Larkin, 'but I quite see that that's not very interesting and what's needed is a ... monstrous offensive by Dixon against the others.' Larkin also asked that the awful girlfriend be re-named. Amis had called her 'Veronica Beale', and this made her too obviously a caricature of Larkin's Monica Jones, whose full Christian names were Margaret Monica Beale. Amis modified it to 'Margaret Peel'.*

Amis began radical revisions of the novel in the light of Larkin's criticisms,† and discussed the changes in his letters to Larkin, just as he had with 'The Legacy'. He remarked that there were now 'so many threads' to the narrative that it was becoming as complicated as a detective story. During September 1952 he sent Larkin what he described as 'a summarized complete synopsis for final checking', which listed all the events of the plot. The checking proved not to be final, since a few weeks later he began a completely new draft.

His letters at this period make it clear that he believed fiction should be entirely realistic and totally credible. After reading a novel by the American writer Nathanael West, he remarked to Larkin: 'What a stupid *liar* the man is; I feel when reading him as I do with Virginia Woolf: I want to keep saying "No, he didn't", "No, it didn't happen as you describe it", "No, that isn't what he thought", "No, that's just what she didn't say."' One author whom he did admire for accurate realism was Graham Greene. After reading *The End of the Affair*, which was published during 1951, Amis remarked: 'I know the miracles are piss . . . but the rest was fine.'

Only a very few comic novels won his approval. They included Cyril Connolly's *The Rock Pool* (1936), and, even more so, Anthony Powell's *From a View to a Death* (1933), a satire on the aimlessness and dishonesty of British country life – 'as funny as anything I've ever read'. However, he was disappointed by *A Question of Upbringing* (1951), the first volume of Powell's 'A Dance to the Music of Time', judging it

---

* Amis usually avoided telling Larkin what he thought of Monica, but in a couple of letters he does complain that she wears the 'wrong make-up', and that 'her make-up would have to be scraped off with a cold chisel for an adequate examination to be made of the more detailed lines on her face'.
† There was briefly a danger that it might lapse into the 'Willow Gables' genre; in February 1950 Amis told Larkin: 'Am working like a bastard on my novel: 250 pp of last draft now, but a lot more to say. I go on writing chapter after chapter without seeming to get any nearer the end. My heroine gives me the horn a lot and as I think I told you I keep writing little supernumerary scenes about her. Later today I shall be working on the bit where a Lesbian pass is thrown her way and I shall be hard put to it not to sprawl ejaculating over the typewriter.'

the most inconclusive book I have ever read. *A question of upbringing? Whose* upbringing? *What* question? *Who's* asking it? *What's* the answer? . . . It is the sort of book where you wonder whether someone has torn the last quarter out. It travels imperceptibly on its way, steadily losing direction, shedding feeling and discarding tension for the end.

Turning to a 'light' novelist who had recently become popular, Amis remarked to Larkin: 'We've settled it that Nancy Mitford's no good, haven't we?' She reciprocated after the publication of *Lucky Jim*, calling it 'evidence . . . of declining civilization'.

As to the two giants of twentieth-century English comic fiction, Amis hugely admired the early Evelyn Waugh of *Decline and Fall*, *Vile Bodies* and *A Handful of Dust*, while despising (as we have seen) the lush romanticism of the much later *Brideshead Revisited*; and he admitted – in a 1953 *Spectator* book review – that, while as an adolescent he had found P. G. Wodehouse powerfully funny, the Wodehouse magic no longer worked on him. In this review (written soon after the completion of *Lucky Jim*) he remarked that, unlike American humorists such as James Thurber, British comic writers generally chose to create situations very far from real life. They should remember the old adage that 'it takes a serious writer to be a really funny writer'.

Larkin was very impressed by a dryly comic novel published in 1950, *Scenes from Provincial Life* by 'William Cooper' (Harry Hoff), and felt it achieved what Amis was aiming for in 'The Legacy' and 'Dixon and Christine'. Amis was offended: 'I got hold of *Scenes life**' 'a couple of weeks ago and read it with great attention. I found it, on the whole, *very good*, but not particularly funny, and I can't under-stand how you came to compare it with *The legacy*. I liked it rather [for] the exact transcription of an environment.' And later that month: 'Re *Scenes*: you must be mad, man, if you think every sentence is *funny*. Mildly and pleasantly amusing, yes; but nothing *really funny*, surely, as we understand it . . .'

It is probably a mistake to look for literary influences on *Lucky Jim*.

---

* In his letters to Larkin, Amis usually referred to books by the first and last words of their titles; for example *A Girl in Winter* became 'A winter'.

Amis did not have to turn to existing novels to find his voice as a comic writer, since it had already been found, and perfected, in the letters to Larkin. For example (in February 1950):

... this afternoon I have to boil down [Matthew Arnold's] *Culture and Anarchy* for the honours people oh little girls' penholders oh boy scouts' underpants. I don't want to do that: I want to let the first crisp, *trenchant*, glittering pages of a new novel or the first leisurely, irresistible stanzas of a new long poem flow from the ends of my hands, or begin my book on Mozart, or entice some pretty innocent, with long gleaming plaits or fiercely strained pullover, in from the street and play old Harry with her modesty, the dear little thing.

All that was needed was to clean it up for public consumption.

Quite a lot of cleaning went on. Jim Dixon in *Lucky Jim* is far more of an innocent than Amis himself, whose letters to Larkin bulge with sexual aspirations; for example: 'On Friday I am giving a little coffee-party for six of the students which shd. be quite amusing. I am inviting the one I want to bugger and the two I most want to fuck.' Sometimes it was more than just aspirations. 'I am getting a trifle implicated with a lady student,' he reported in October 1950. Larkin requested details, and got them:

The lady student, since you ask, is ... thin, very dark, hairy, intelligent, very funny and lively, twenty-two, reading English, sexually experienced, rather sado-masochistic. How am I getting involved with her? *Sexually*, dear man. She will go on if I go on, but I haven't yet decided whether to do that or not.

He did not make it clear whether Hilly was aware of this affair, but another letter to Larkin alleged – possibly as a justification of his infidelity – that Hilly herself had a 'boyfriend'. A little later Amis wrote: 'No, my wife's boyfriend isn't anyone you know. He has very nearly stopped being it now. They don't seem to last long with Hilly.' And, despite his unbridled expressions of lust when writing to Larkin, he regarded extramarital relationships as a source of trouble as well as pleasure: 'That old winged boa-constrictor, sex, still has me in his coils, and is flying around with me looking for a good shit-marsh to drop me into.'

* *

He cared as much about getting his poetry into print as his fiction. 'I've started sending my poems round to the papers ah-HAGH-hagh-hagh,' he reported to Larkin in February 1950,

starting with the *Listener* and the *N[ew] S[tatesman] & N[ation]*. Much hope I've got, but I can't just sit here waitin' and hopin' any larnger. You won't get anywhere if you don't try, you know; NO, nor if I try. You can't expect other people to make your name for you, you know; NO, not unless I change it to 'I let men get up my back passage for nothing'.

At first, the response from these and other magazines was negative – 'The lissner sent my poems back in the minimum possible time.' Nevertheless his poetry did gradually begin to creep into print. F. W. Bateson, an Oxford don who had taken over the supervision of Amis's ill-fated B.Litt., selected a poem for his newly-founded journal *Essays in Criticism*, and Amis was also asked to contribute to a PEN anthology called *New Poems 1952*. In an autobiographical note in the latter, he mentioned that he was 'currently engaged on a novel', and this caught the eye of a publisher, Hilary Rubinstein, nephew and employee of Victor Gollancz. Four years younger than Amis, Rubinstein had known him slightly at Oxford. He wrote to him and asked to see the novel.

By 1952, the firm of Gollancz badly needed some new blood. Founded in 1927, its heyday had been in the Thirties, when its list ranged from Dorothy L. Sayers to the celebrated Left Book Club. Describing himself as 'very nearly a Marxist', Victor Gollancz (the son of a London jeweller and an alumnus of St Paul's School and Oxford) had appointed two left-wing intellectuals, John Strachey and Harold Laski, to help him choose such radical-minded authors as George Orwell. The Club's books were offered at slashed prices to anyone who guaranteed to buy the chosen title each month. Membership boomed, discussion groups were set up around the country to meet the books' authors and debate the latest titles, and the Club – which continued during the war – undoubtedly played a part in the electoral landslide that brought Labour to power in 1945. However, by 1952, with Labour out of office again, Gollancz had been obliged to turn to foreign fiction (especially American) to keep afloat.

Amis replied to Rubinstein on 8 December 1952:

Yes, of course I remember you, and it was very pleasant to get your letter. I shall be very glad to send you my novel when the time comes. It would never make an author's or a publisher's fortune, but I think it is quite funny; that, at any rate, is its aim. Still, it's not much use going on about it; I'm on the final draft now and should be able to get it to you in February or March . . .

It was a good guess; on 3 March 1953 he told Larkin that the retyping of the latest version of 'Dixon' was nearly finished.

It wouldn't be any use giving it to you to look at again, except for your entertainment, because the bloody thing will just cease to exist if it gets any more structural tinkering. What I will do, if the occasion arises, is to get you to go through the MS saying what you think isn't funny, so that such bits can be cut out and not annoy the reading public. If the occasion doesn't arise, i.e. if no bugger will have it, then I'll present you with both versions and you can wipe your arse on them for all I care . . .

I've called it *Lucky Jim* now,* to emphasize the luck theme – epigraph Oh, lucky Jim, How I envy him . . . I'm afraid you are very much the ideal reader of the thing and chaps like you don't grow on trees, course not . . .

The typing was finished by the end of March, and Amis told Larkin he was 'sweating now on John Wain taking an episode for his [radio] programme; if he does it will be a great stroke towards getting the thing published, I think . . . Jolly good about the John Wain programme isn't it? What are you sending him?' On 15 April he parcelled up the corrected typescript for Rubinstein, with a covering letter: 'As you'll see, serio-comedy is the formula really, though if it gets by at all I imagine it'll get by chiefly on the score of the comic angle.' He wrote again next day with news from the BBC

---

* Which Larkin apparently disliked, since Amis wrote to him: 'Don't worry about *Lucky Jim* as a title; most people will have forgotten about the title by the time they see the ironical application of it in the first 7/8 of the book. I think. I hope.'

that they're going to broadcast some of my novel in the 'First Reading' programme on the Third in ten days' time. It'll be a 15-minute affair, about 2000 words. Since I still believe (in the face of much contrary evidence) that acceptance by the BBC is a recommendation rather than the reverse, I pass this information on in the hope that someone at your end shares my belief.

Passing on the same news to Larkin, Amis said that the BBC letter had come from the Corporation's 'Wain Division'.

* *

Wain had done Amis proud, picking the *Lucky Jim* excerpt as the opening item in the very first edition of *First Reading*, to which a large proportion of the literary world would be listening. The hour-long programme went on the air at 9.10 p.m. on Sunday, 26 April 1953, and Wain began with a general statement of intent: he was going to 'use these programmes as a means of putting over a certain point of view about contemporary letters'. He said he intended to feature the work of younger writers who were 'suspicious of anything that suggests sprawling and lack of discipline', and went on:

Kingsley Amis has published both poetry and criticism: but as far as I know, none of his work in fiction has yet seen the light. So I thought it would be pleasant to open the proceedings with a slice of the novel he is at present engaged on.

The title is *Lucky Jim*, and the particular episode we are going to hear opens with the hero, Dixon, suffering from a hangover and a bad conscience.

Actor Alan Wheatley then read the scene in which Dixon encounters Christine at the Welches' breakfast table, and takes her upstairs to show her the damaged sheets.

Meanwhile Hilary Rubinstein had been reading the typescript. The day after the broadcast, he sent Amis the Gollancz verdict. 'I think it is a really brilliant book and got more fun out of it than anything else I have read for a long time.' He had put off telling Amis until his own opinion had been confirmed by the firm's chief reader, J. R. Evans. 'I am happy to say that he shares my great enthusiasm for the book. Now everybody in the firm is itching to read it.' Amis wrote back by return: 'I was overjoyed to get your letter this morning and read all the nice things you had to say about my book. Somehow, the thought of anyone actually liking it came as a great surprise . . .' In fact Victor Gollancz himself had not yet read it, and when he did he was far from keen, describing it as 'vulgar and anti-cultural'. Rubinstein and another director, Gollancz's daughter Livia, nevertheless got his agreement for an offer to be made to Amis – an advance on royalties of £100.

On 5 May 1953, Amis wrote to Larkin: 'Not a proper letter, this ("I CAN SEE THAT"); just a wee note to say that Victor Gollancz Ltd, of Covent Garden, have taken *Lucky Jim* for it to be printed. They think it will be out in November. Good, isn't it? It will be dedicated to you.'

6

Nice things are nicer than
nasty ones

Hugh Massingham, radio and television critic of the *New Statesman*, did not share Hilary Rubinstein's enthusiasm for *Lucky Jim*. In an article published some weeks after *First Reading* had begun, he quoted two sentences from the *Lucky Jim* excerpt as samples of the 'deplorable' work that Wain was promoting:

In spite of the ravages wrought by his headache, Dixon felt happier as he wondered what foods would this morning afford concrete* proof of the Welches' prosperity.

He remembered his father, who until the war had always worn stiff white collars, being reproved by the objurgatory jeweller as excessively 'dignant' in demeanour.

Massingham had liked some things in the programme: 'The first broadcast was partly redeemed by two poems from Mr G. S. Fraser and the second by Mr Alvarez, who came out with a fresh and angry piece of criticism.' Was this the first application of the word 'angry' to any of the Fifties poets and novelists?

Alfred Alvarez ('A. Alvarez' or 'Al Avarez' in print) was an Oxford undergraduate whom Wain had taken under his wing. Born into a London Jewish family that had made its money in the rag trade, and sent to Oundle public school, Alvarez had founded a Critical Society at Oxford, and was outspoken and irreverent. He says he was 'very flattered' to be asked to contribute to *First Reading*. For it, he wrote a

---

* Changed to 'visible' in the published text.

ten-minute script attacking those contemporary poets who used private symbols – 'the mess,' as he put it, of which 'about half modern verse is made up'.

In his memoirs, Alvarez writes that Wain

was an inspiring figure in those early days, quick-witted and funny, shivering with energy and ambition . . . He saw himself as a mixture of Dr Johnson, George Orwell and J. B. Priestley, a plain man full of common sense, a plain-speaker who had no truck with pretension. He talked about books brilliantly, but only in pubs over a constant stream of pints, and preferably to an admiring audience. Perhaps he had picked up this habit from his mentor at Oxford, C. S. Lewis . . .

With hindsight, Alvarez also feels that there was a fundamental weakness in Wain's character, the result of his having been pampered in boyhood, 'his parents' golden child, the one who could do no wrong and whose every utterance was treasured'.

In the linking script for the opening edition of *First Reading*, Wain scarcely waved a revolutionary flag. His underlying argument was that it was time to take stock of the consequences of modernism:

Having got as far as the middle of the twentieth century, we ought to be looking both back and forward. Looking back, we see that we have passed through a period of frontier expansion. Daring pioneers, often proceeding by guess-work and with equipment they had designed and built themselves, pushed out into the unknown and established some kind of foothold there . . . But a period of expansion has to be followed by a period of consolidation . . . The question is no longer, 'how much further can we press on?' It is rather, 'what shall we do now we are here?' . . .

What I hope to present, then, is the work of writers who are pre-eminently qualified to administer this huge territory and reduce it to order . . .

Yet Massingham had taken this as a battle-cry: 'Mr Wain['s] implication, I think, is fairly clear. Our brave new world is over at last and the old fogies can be led off to the slaughterhouse . . . Mr Wain and his fledglings can move in and establish the new dispensation.' He added there was 'something faintly ridiculous in treating young men, whom some of us have never heard of, with the solemnity that should be reserved for Mr Eliot or Mr Empson'.

Rather surprisingly, Amis drew Hilary Rubinstein's attention to Massingham's insults: 'Did you see that atrocious write-up of 1st Reading in the New S & N to-day? It seems a bit hard to be condemned on the strength of two sentences.' But, writing to Larkin (who had had a poem included in one of the programmes), he agreed that Massingham's criticisms of *First Reading* were generally justified: 'JBW . . . *is* portentous you know . . . And he *does* stuff the programme with his friends, and bloody awful . . . they mostly are.'

Massingham continued to attack the programme, calling it 'amateurish' and the writing it featured 'impoverished'. The BBC lost its nerve, and as soon as Wain's contract for *First Reading* had expired, he was replaced by Ludovic Kennedy. In his memoirs, Wain is unrepentant, defending what he had done with the programme: 'If I drew up a list of the writers who first reached a wide public through *First Reading*, it would be a fairly comprehensive roll-call of the younger established writers of today.' And he claimed that 'the result was the birth of what later became known as "The Movement"'.

* *

In the summer of 1950, Amis sent Larkin some of his newly-written poems, and Larkin evidently commented that the overall tone was drab, for Amis replied:

Sorry about the drabness . . . but . . . I feel it's *so important* to be correct in diction and sentiment that I don't mind being a bit flat . . . I feel the time for originality has gone by; what we want to do is to purge English po[etry] of offences against metre, decent humility, meaning (i.e. stop verbal music bum* and inchoate image bum), and the eternal law that you are only entitled to speak for yourself. Above all, let there be no *self-indulgence* . . .

Amis regarded Dylan Thomas as a particular offender against these rules; he described Thomas's 'A refusal to mourn the death, by fire, of a child in London' as 'a very good example of Thos. using his verbal

---

* As remarked earlier, 'bum' was usually how Amis concluded his letters to Larkin.

alchemy to dress up a trite idea in language designed to prevent people from seng [*sic*] how trite it is . . . I wish he'd GROW UP.'* John Wain agreed, voicing (in an essay published after Thomas's death) 'the suspicion that his writing, in the more "difficult" poems, is quasi-automatic . . . The gnawing doubt remains as to whether [he] really *cared* whether it meant anything precise or not.' Other criminals among older poets included, in Amis's opinion, Gerard Manley Hopkins ('trying to treat words as if they were music') and post-*Waste Land* T. S. Eliot – 'I . . . read the cocktale farty [*The Cocktail Party*], which struck me as stale gobbets of auden-isherwood boiled up in "mysticism" on the Grgr [Graham Greene] level . . .'

Amis's willingness to be drab was maybe partly a reflection of the atmosphere of Britain in the early 1950s. Alvarez writes that it was a period when life was 'grim and impoverished. Meat was rationed, the cooking was dreadful . . . and to keep warm you bundled yourself up in sweaters and hurried from one pathetic electric fire to another . . . Luxury meant a steak or a banana or a cup of genuine coffee.' This austerity was the result of the war's vast drain on the country's resources. It also reflected a national depression that was psychological as well as economic; as Alvarez puts it, 'the country was exhausted by the battering it had taken and demoralized by the loss both of its empire and of its status as a world power'. This was not an environment that nurtured radical or rebellious ideas among the young. 'I was twenty when the Fifties began,' Alvarez writes,

and the young in the Fifties were a pusillanimous bunch, careful with their emotions, respectful of their elders . . . a generation of good children, maybe the last of them . . . We may have squabbled with our parents, but we didn't disagree with them fundamentally about how life and society were ordered . . . I was determined to live my life in my own way and on my own terms, but it never crossed my mind that I wouldn't finish up a good citizen, obeying most of the rules, paying my taxes and fathering children who would also turn out to be good citizens . . .

---

* There is a parody of *Under Milk Wood* in Amis's second novel, *That Uncertain Feeling* (1955): 'I was Bowen Thomas, tailor of Llados . . . I was talking a mouthful of grass under the still hornbeam.'

Alvarez remarks that even Amis's Jim Dixon, for all his rebelliousness, ends the novel by getting himself a nice girl and a good job.

It is true that Britain had flirted briefly with Socialism, electing the Labour Party to power in 1945; but Alvarez observes that this was not so much a change in the country's political climate as a reaction against the war's underlining of the British class system – 'a vote against the officers by the enlisted men'. It soon appeared that Labour's social reforms (nationalization and the inauguration of the Welfare State) mattered less to the voters than the hope of economic prosperity. There might be a National Health Service, but there was still no prospect of an end to rationing, and in 1951 the country returned the Tories to power under the leadership (once again) of Winston Churchill, who by then was aged seventy-seven.

Amis went public with his attack on 'verbal music bum' in the July 1952 issue of *Essays in Criticism*, when he responded to another critic's defence of an image in one of Edith Sitwell's poems, 'Emily-coloured primulas'. Amis asserted that it meant nothing to anyone except Sitwell herself, who was merely allowing her readers to eavesdrop on 'her personal fantasies'. In the same magazine's issue for October 1953 he sneered at another contemporary poet, W. R. Rodgers, saying that his verse could only appeal to an 'inattentive' reader – 'Attention to the meaning is disastrous.' Yet he felt more confident about poetry than fiction as the genre for literary clarity. Soon after *Lucky Jim* had been accepted by Gollancz, he wrote to Larkin:

Yes, you told me about the Burton your novel had gone for . . . I should think poetry would be your best line for a few decades now. There isn't that *going-on-ness* about poetry which makes novels so horrible, both to read and write. I've begun another [*That Uncertain Feeling*], but might easily stop it soon. Everything that has happened in it so far is boring, rather than not boring.

Though Wain was making a similar attempt at clear speech in his own poetry, Amis thought that the results were very mixed. In June 1952 he asked Larkin: '. . . did you see those poems of ole Johnny Wain's in the N S & N and Listener? I thought a lot of the book he wrote was quite good . . . but these routine terza-rima things . . . just go on and on, what? He doesn't say anything you couldn't say in half the time, does he?' And a few months later: 'I was reading old Wain's poems again the other day; the flaw is diffuseness and slackness . . .'

The 'book' was Wain's slim 1951 collection *Mixed Feelings*. Few of the poems in it make much impression today. It opens with 'In Memory of Henry Payne', a tribute to a recently dead porter at St John's College, Oxford:

> Silence? no hint of a chant from the
> bards acknowledged, birds of the college? Then
> bear with a tongue untuned, a book-choked brain
> fumbling and faltering, for somehow a word must be said.
> No one was glad when the grim good man lay dead.
>
> Grim? he hung a frown on his face like
> a watch on his wrist, but his mien was a mask;
> he smiled at his ease with his eyes, his nod was a jest;
> like a bright brass knocker he guarded the gate for his bread.
> No one was glad when the grim good man lay dead . . .

John Betjeman was able to do this sort of thing so much better in his memorial poem to another Oxford character, an ancient Pembroke College don, in his 1954 collection *A Few Late Chrysanthemums*: 'Dr Ramsden cannot read *The Times* obituary today / He's dead.'

The Fifties was actually Betjeman's final decade as an active poet – he had begun in the 1930s and wrote little verse after the appearance of his *Collected Poems* in 1958; but that book's publication was one of the literary events of the decade, proving that there was still a vast audience for poetry which had flavour and above all clarity. Amis's huge admiration for Betjeman went back to his undergraduate days. Devoting an entire chapter to him in his memoirs, he praises Betjeman's skill at

taking us from the reassuringly familiar, sometimes bland, surface of things to the unpleasant underlying facts of death, loss, pain, illness, grief. In that his work resembles that of Philip Larkin, despite great differences in other respects . . .

In due time, Larkin was to achieve the same level of clarity – and almost the same level of popularity – as Betjeman. But it took him a very long while, and Wain never got there at all.

One poem in Wain's *Mixed Feelings* refers to 'the era of the mushroom cloud', and another appears to be about the threat of the 'hydrogen bomb' (as it was then called) – an early attempt at what the Sixties called a 'protest song':

> I hope to feel some pity when it comes,
> Before the burning instant that devours,
> Before the final flash when terror numbs.
>
> Time to seek out a field with grass and flowers
> And minutes eat like cherries, one by one,
> Will be my single prayer to those grim Powers . . .
>
> I hope to feel some pity when it comes.

Otherwise the collection has no flavour of the period in which it was written; whereas Wain's first novel conveys just as much of the Fifties as *Lucky Jim*.

* *

Amis did not care for it. 'John Wain read me a lot of his novel: like a detective story without any crime or detection', he told Larkin in August 1952, not long before completing the final version of *Lucky Jim*. Wain's *Hurry On Down* is named after a 1947 hit record by jazz singer and pianist Nellie Lutcher. The song is seductive ('Hurry on down to my place, baby,/Nobody home but me'), but Wain used the title to suggest the element of social descent in the adventures of his hero.

Charles Lumley has just come down from Oxford with 'a mediocre degree in History', and, having no aim in life, has chosen to live for a few weeks in lodgings in the Midland town of Stotwell, a 'dingy huddle of streets and factories', while considering his next move. He determines to call on his fiancée, Sheila, who lives nearby, but at her house he comes into conflict with her rigidly conventional sister and brother-in-law, Edith and Robert Tharkles. Just as Jim Dixon would do, Lumley imagines a brutal revenge on them for not listening to his point of view:

Speech would never work with these people. Indeed, it was inconceivable that anything could be got across to them by means of language, unless one overpowered them and left them gagged and bound in the presence of a gramophone record endlessly repeating a short, concise statement. It would have given him pleasure to begin the composition, then and there, of such a statement; to have outlined in a few simple sentences the nature of the crime against humanity that they and their kind were committing by the mere fact of their existence.

However, unlike Dixon, Lumley does something about it. First he speaks his mind to Robert – 'I was just wondering why no one's ever found it worth while to cut off that silly moustache of yours and use it for one of those brushes you see hanging out of windows next to the waste pipe' – and then he throws a bowl of washing-up water over Robert and Edith, before walking out of their lives.

It seems to have been a wise move, since we now learn that his fiancée Sheila closely resembles Margaret in *Lucky Jim*. Summoning up her features in his mind, Lumley recalls 'the ivory bald patches behind her ears, the quivering of her pointed chin as she had raised her face to be kissed for the first time', and he realizes that by marrying her he would in effect have married her whole detestable family. Indeed he now becomes aware that he is 'running away from everything that, up to that moment, had been his life'. He feels 'imprisoned' in the middle class, the victim of a traditional-style upbringing which has left him ill-prepared for 'the jungle of the nineteen-fifties'.

What are the features of this jungle? At the back of Lumley's mind (we learn) lurks a 'mushroom-shaped cloud' – another reference to the threat of nuclear war. Yet he feels that his rebelliousness is different from that of the left-wing intellectuals of the 1930s: 'He thought . . . of all the expensive young men of the thirties who had made . . . a gesture somewhat similar to his own, turning their backs on the setting that had pampered them; and how they had all failed from the start . . .' He ascribes this failure to 'their idiotic attempt to look through two telescopes at the same time: one fashioned of German psychology and pointed at themselves, the other of Russian economics and directed at the English working class'. Unlike the Auden generation, the ideologies of Freud and Marx are not for him.

Nevertheless he decides impulsively to join the working class, and becomes an itinerant window-cleaner: 'With one bound he had leapt clear of the tradition of his class and type.' Though the stuffy-minded headmaster of his old school – whose mannerisms are much like those of Welch in *Lucky Jim* – refuses to employ him, he picks up enough jobs to contribute financially to a strange ménage where he makes his home, a shed that has become the dwelling-place of a drop-out novelist called Froulish and his slatternly girlfriend Betty.

Like Amis's Bertrand in *Lucky Jim*, Froulish represents the pretentiously posing 'Bohemian' artist. When he reads from work in progress to a gathering of the Stotwell Literary Society, we discover that his supposed magnum opus is just a piece of sham Joycean modernism:

'A king ringed with slings,' began Froulish without more ado, 'a thing without wings but brings strings and sings. Ho, the slow foe! Show me the crow toe I know, a beech root on the beach, fruit of a rich bitch, loot in a ditch, shoot a witch, which foot?'

No sooner has Lumley embarked on working-class life than – like Dixon – he falls in love with an apparently unattainable woman, Veronica, supposedly the niece of a rich man* (but in reality his mistress). Becoming crazily obsessed with this dream-girl, of whom he has initially caught a mere glimpse – like John Kemp in Larkin's *Jill* – Lumley immediately determines to increase his earning power, in the hope that he can buy his way into her company. Falling in with the wrong sort of people, he soon becomes knowingly involved in drug-smuggling, and is witness to a murder. (His morals are thoroughly tangled, since he walks out on the Froulish–Betty ménage as soon as he discovers that Betty is helping to support them all by working as a part-time prostitute.)

Nearly meeting his own death, Lumley retreats again into manual labour, working as a hospital orderly and then a chauffeur. By now

* Like Christine in *Lucky Jim*.

his determination to reject his own social class is arousing furious accusations from its members that he is 'letting the side down'. Yet it is evident that middle-class existence in 1950s Britain is even less attractive than life at the bottom of the pecking order.

Working-class life is certainly dingy, characterized by greasy cafés selling 'chipped mug[s] of dark brown swill', and funereal pubs: 'A few old men sat staring with red-rimmed eyes into their pints, making the beer look like tears they had dripped into their glasses and were saving for some purpose.' Everything is clouded by the fumes of cheap Woodbine cigarettes, and an old man in a pub nearly suffocates Froulish and Lumley with a pipe stuffed with strong shag: 'Dense blue smoke gathered around Froulish . . . Charles started back before he, too, should be overwhelmed.' Violence erupts unpredictably: a huge 'rough' seizes Lumley and threatens him with a brass knuckle-duster, on the spurious grounds that he is 'takin' the bread out of other folk's mouths'. Yet when Lumley, rejected by Veronica, begins to 'walk out' with a working-class girl, Rosa, another hospital orderly, he finds reassurance in her family's way of life:

This was Rosa's father's Sunday afternoon, and he had been spending it as he always did, in his armchair by the fire with the *News of the World* on his knee, fast asleep . . . Stuffed with ham, cake, bread and butter, and pints of dark tea, they moved from the table . . . Charles felt that his search was over . . . his demands on life had grown smaller and smaller, until that stuffy, cosy room contained everything that he needed to fulfil them.

Wain does note that the English working-class milieu is already being invaded by America; he mentions that girls are now leaving villages to get jobs in 'milk-bars within striking distance of American airfields', and that the teenagers who frequent the provincial town-hall dances on Saturday nights choose their clothes and style their hair 'to make them look like their own conception of Americans'.

Nevertheless the British working class is still confident of its own identity, while by comparison the middle class seems precariously positioned – one of its members remarks nervily on 'the way the working class have got above themselves since the war'. Moreover the bourgeoisie live in uglier surroundings than the lower orders, in trolley-bus-ridden suburbs, lit by 'horrible white light from concrete lamp-standards'; while their own drinking-places are either sleazy 'gin palaces' whose Saloon Bars* are frequented by prostitutes, or pretentious hotel bars like the Oak Lounge of the Grand Hotel in Stotwell, where Lumley first sees Veronica (Dixon in *Lucky Jim* drinks with Margaret in 'the Oak Lounge in a large roadside hotel'). Moreover the middle-class-ridden countryside is just as unsatisfactory, a two-dimensionally unreal 'Technicolor landscape'; Lumley perceives that 'real actions' are only undertaken in towns (a theme first aired in Anthony Powell's *From a View to a Death*).

Furthermore the lives of the middle class have a far less strong moral framework than those of the working class. Many of them inhabit the edge of crime – a legacy, maybe, from the wartime black markets. A typical specimen of this type announces to Lumley his intention of 'squeezing you into the racket, old boy'. Such people use smoking not for pleasure but for style: Lumley notes that a college acquaintance who likes to be thought intellectual 'had his pipe at the ready in case it should be necessary to put on his don's act at short notice'. Even the less devious members of the middle class have unnecessary-sounding jobs, live brash lifestyles in London flats, and talk too loudly. When Lumley goes to one of their parties, he notes that 'the sounds he could hear were made by people who had assembled to have a good time, but they might easily have been cries of anguish'.

Given that Lumley soon perceives the hellish falseness of this milieu, the surprise at the end of *Hurry On Down* is that he chooses not to remain in the working class but takes a highly-paid job writing scripts 'for some of the top rank radio shows' – in other words, he joins one of the most superficial and valueless strata of London life. 'The runaway fight between himself and society had ended in a draw,' writes Wain, who in the final chapter also improbably reunites Lumley with Veronica. But then as Veronica herself remarks of Daniel Defoe's *Moll Flanders*, which (even more improbably) she claims she has just been reading, 'It doesn't end, it just stops'; and the same might be said of

---

* In the 1950s most pubs were divided into a 'Public Bar' for working men and a 'Saloon Bar' for the middle classes, plus a 'Jug and Bottle' counter, accessed through a separate door, from which drink could be bought to take away.

Hurry On Down. Moreover it stops in exactly the same place as *Lucky Jim*, with the hero getting the girl and a promising job in London.

* *

Wain's allusion to Defoe's picaresque novel suggests that he regarded *Hurry On Down* as belonging to the same genre. Making an effort to praise it in a letter to Wain, Amis remarked that it 'does succeed above all in getting across a grotesque and twisted view of life (which is what I try to do, though it's not the same view – this I think is where we're similar)'. To Larkin, however, he described it as a failed comedy: 'all *right* in a *way*, but *not funny enough* . . . I thought it very overwritten: people are always slumping and choking and feeling searing pain exploding all over their bodies and all that.' His dislike of the book seems to have been partly motivated by financial jealousy; in his memoirs he recalls Wain boasting that he had received an advance of £250, as against the £100 Gollancz was giving Amis for *Lucky Jim*. But in September 1953, the month before *Hurry On Down* appeared in the shops, Amis's novel also found an American publisher, and he reported gleefully to Larkin that the combined British and American advances 'come to nearly twice John's – ho ho'.

Hurry On Down had mixed reviews; the *Spectator* praised it as 'inventive, impulsive, cogitative', but the *Manchester Guardian* thought it an odd mixture of moods, and *The Times Literary Supplement* called it 'clumsy in conception'. In his autobiography, Wain makes no great claims for it, describing himself as lacking 'the power of sustaining large structures'; he said he would be a short-story writer 'if it weren't so impossible to make a living by it'. He also revealed that at first *Hurry On Down* was unplanned: 'I [was] improvising, writing one scene after another with no idea of what was coming next, expressing a mood (and very much my own mood, of course) rather than telling a plotted story. [Later] I took the work in hand, and the second half was written . . . with a plan setting out what is to happen in each chapter.' Actually the improvised, dream-like opening chapters are more memorable than the carefully planned remainder. *Lucky Jim*, in contrast, is the result – as we have seen – of intense planning and protracted rewriting. Virtually nothing is there that does not belong to a conscious scheme.

In a letter written many years after the novel was published, Amis denied that there was 'any social statement or . . . social attitude' in *Lucky Jim*. 'I was trying to tell some truths about human nature in a contemporary setting . . .' So what were those truths?

The book has its starting-point in Amis's own schizophrenia. By nature, he was (in Jim Dixon's words about himself) 'the boredom-detector . . . a finely-tuned instrument'. But this real self could only emerge in his letters to Larkin; and Dixon is an Amis without his Larkin. He can only express boredom and rage by making faces to himself: 'his Chinese mandarin's face', 'his Eskimo face', 'his Edith Sitwell face',* 'his Evelyn Waugh face'. At the outset of the story he has to keep his true feelings entirely private. When Christine remarks that Bertrand is 'such a queer mixture', Dixon responds by 'naming to himself the two substances of which he personally thought Bertrand a mixture' – but only to himself. When Margaret histrionically asks him 'Do you hate me, James?' he wants 'to rush at her and tip her backwards in the chair; to make a deafening rude noise in her face, to push a bead up her nose'; but all he actually does is to ask her: 'How do you mean?'

As well as hiding his objections to other people, Dixon – for the first part of the novel – does his best to give priority to their feelings and needs, rather than to his own. Although the reader can see from the outset that Margaret is a selfish manipulator ('Throw her a lifebelt and she'll pull you under,' as another character puts it), Dixon naively fails to perceive the full extent of her dreadfulness, and consistently tries to be fair to her, far more than she ever deserves. Meanwhile the book's three other objectionable main characters, Professor Welch, his wife, and their arty-poseur son Bertrand, ride roughshod over everyone else's needs. Compared to them, Dixon is (at this stage) pure altruism, acutely sensitive to his fellow human beings.†

---

* Despite this, and an attack on Sitwell's poetry in the *Spectator*, in which Amis participated (at first pseudonymously), she wrote to the magazine saying how much she had enjoyed *Lucky Jim*.

† At one point Amis decided to call the book 'The Man of Feeling'; he told Larkin rather vaguely that this was because 'D[ixon] has more to feel about than he had before', but what prompted it was surely Dixon's capacity for empathy and his honesty towards his own emotions.

Welch is not merely selfish; he seems to be neurologically unable to recognize the existence of any other person. This of course is a caricature of 'Daddy B' – or rather, not a caricature but a coolly precise and accurate portrait of a totally self-absorbed individual:

Dixon . . . asked in his flat northern voice: 'How's Margaret?'

Welch's clay-like features changed indefinably as his attention, like a squadron of slow old battleships, began wheeling to face this new phenomenon, and in a moment or two he was able to say: 'Margaret.'

Similarly, the portrait of Margaret herself is built up of precise, accurately observed details, chiefly relating to her appearance, such as 'the green Paisley frock in combination with the low-heeled, quasi-velvet shoes', 'the tufts of brown hair that overhung the ear-pieces of her glasses', and the wrong choice of lipstick.

Amis observes men just as closely too:

Dixon looked again at Bertrand's eyes. They really were extraordinary: it seemed as if a sheet of some patterned material were tacked to the inside of his face, showing only at two arbitrary loopholes.

Even objects are described with the same degree of precision: the self-starter on Welch's car sounds at first like 'the ringing of a cracked door-bell'; then comes 'a treble humming that seemed to involve every component of the car'; then 'the effect . . . of beer-bottles jerkily belaboured'. When the car finally moves, the engine gives out 'a loud lowing sound'. This is a demonstration of Amis's incredibly accurate ear – the key to his skill as a mimic, here recalled by Larkin: 'Kingsley's masterpiece, which was so demanding I only heard him do it twice, involved three subalterns, a Glaswegian driver and a jeep breaking down and refusing to start in Germany. Both times I became incapable with laughter.'*

* Like Amis, Dixon is a brilliant mimic; his 'Merrie England' lecture brings the house down because – all inhibitions obliterated by alcohol – he delivers the first part of it as an impersonation of Welch, and then of the college principal. The lecture seems to have been Larkin's suggestion, after he had read the first draft of the novel. 'He'd have to be drunk, I think,' was Amis's response to the idea.

Language comes up for close observation too. When Bertrand concludes a remark with 'if you'll pardon the expression', Dixon thinks to himself: 'Why shouldn't they pardon the expression? . . . Why?' Most memorable in this department is his analysis of one of Bertrand's verbal mannerisms:

'. . . And I happen to like the arts, you sam.'

The last word, a version of 'see', was Bertrand's own coinage. It arose as follows: the vowel sound became distorted into a short 'a', as if he were going to say 'sat'. This brought his lips some way apart, and the effect of their rapid closure was to end the syllable with a light but audible 'm'.

The book does superficially appear to be, in Victor Gollancz's words, 'anti-cultural'. (Anthony Powell has written that 'in certain quarters *Lucky Jim* was looked on quite simply as a shower of brickbats hurled by a half-educated hooligan at the holiest and most fragile shrines of art and letters, not to mention music'.) Dixon dreads Welch's arty weekend, and tells Margaret: 'He wants to test my reactions to culture.' But *Lucky Jim* is actually not attacking culture itself, but the way people use the idea of culture to achieve mastery over others. As Amis once put it in an interview: 'Culture's good, but not the way the Welches did it.' When Welch sings in the bath, the music is 'recognizable to Dixon as some skein of untiring facetiousness by filthy Mozart'. But Amis adored Mozart,* who only becomes 'filthy' because Welch insists on imposing him on other people. ('One wants to annoy Mozart lovers,' Amis explained, 'not denigrate Mozart.') Bertrand goes much further than whistling Mozart; he uses his self-conferred status as an artist to justify his enormous aggression – despite claiming to be a pacifist, he is always threatening to knock Dixon down. Dixon thinks of countering this with another abuse of culture: 'For a moment he felt

* 'I'm sorry to have to tell you this,' Amis wrote to Larkin in 1950, 'but of late I've been getting very keen on that billiard-playing Austrian's stuff. It strikes me that he did all Bach is supposed to have done . . . and all that Beethoven did *that was worth dong [sic]* . . .' And in 1951: '. . . I have just bought 3 more Mozart piano concertos . . . The trouble with Mozart is really his intolerable pessimism, his loading of the ordinary allegro with more blisteringly tragic content than it'll stand . . .'

like devoting the next ten years to working his way to a position as an art critic on purpose to review Bertrand's work unfavourably.'

Like Froulish in *Hurry On Down*, Bertrand claims that being an artist releases him from the obligation to behave properly. Christine – who starts out as Bertrand's girlfriend – remarks that 'Having a relationship with an artist's a very different kettle of fish to having a relationship with an ordinary man'; but Dixon rightly finds this 'repugnant'. Meanwhile Dixon himself is constantly proposing his own, alternative ideas of culture. The novel's real mark of distinction is the superb language in which he describes his own feelings. Metaphor is allowed, but it has to be very precise. The *tour de force* is the passage which Wain chose for *First Reading* – the description of the hangover:

The stuff coming from the light seemed less like light than a very thin but cloudy phosphorescent gas; it gave a creamy hum . . . His face was heavy, as if little bags of sand had been painlessly sewn into various parts of it, dragging the features away from the bones, if he still had bones in his face . . . Someone seemed to have leapt up nimbly behind him and encased him in a kind of diving-suit made of invisible cotton-wool . . . His mouth had been used as a latrine by some small creature of the night, and then as its mausoleum.

We are told that Dixon 'sometimes wished he wrote poetry or something', since this would give him the feeling of being 'a developed character'; but of course this sort of language *is* poetry.

The novel has a political stratum, but this tends to disguise its real nature. We are told that Dixon was at a grammar school, has taken his degree at a redbrick university (Leicester), and has a north-country accent. He appears to be Socialist in outlook, telling Bertrand: 'If one man's got ten buns and another's got two, and a bun has got to be given up by one of them, then surely you take it from the man with ten buns.' He starts to like Christine when, to his surprise, he sees her heartily eating a working-class-style fried breakfast with lashings of tomato ketchup. A medieval historian by profession, he rejects the upper-class assumption that society is in decline:

Those who professed themselves unable to believe in the reality of human progress ought to cheer themselves up . . . by a short study of the Middle

Ages. The hydrogen bomb, the South African Government, Chiang Kai-Shek,* Senator McCarthy himself, would then seem a light price to pay for no longer being in the Middle Ages.

The enemy is essentially Conservative: Mrs Welch funds her husband's arty goings-on and Bertrand's self-indulgent lifestyle from a private income, and she has right-wing views – Dixon mentions her 'advocacy of retributive punishment'.

Yet Amis himself was no longer committed to left-wing politics by the time he came to write *Lucky Jim*, and it would be risky to take all this at face value. Dixon is not really a provincial left-winger. From the beginning of the novel, he hopes to 'leave the provinces for London', and when he finally receives and accepts Gore-Urquhart's offer of a job there, he luxuriates in the prospect of metropolitan life: '... he pronounced the names to himself: Bayswater, Knightsbridge, Notting Hill Gate, Pimlico, Belgrave Square, Wapping, Chelsea. No, not Chelsea.' (Chelsea would be the haunt of the likes of Bertrand.)

Fundamentally, the book has the essentially selfish (and non-socialist) moral that you should take care of your own feelings before you consider other people's.† Dixon states the truism that 'nice things are nicer than nasty ones', and in a 1972 letter Amis explained what he meant by this: 'The phrase is ... aimed (by the novel rather than by the character) against a whole moral and aesthetic system, that which embraces self-realization through suffering...' Moreover Dixon admits that the distinction between what you find 'nice' or 'nasty' is ultimately a subjective and therefore selfish one: he tells Christine that there are 'two great classes of mankind, people I like and people I don't'. Even halfway through the book his philosophy has become totally hedonist: 'Doing what you wanted to do was the

---

* Nationalist Chinese leader, an odd inclusion in this list of supposedly objectionable features of life in the 1950s.

† An amoral moral that Amis repeated in many of his later books, albeit putting it into the mouths of blatantly self-centred characters. For example in *One Fat Englishman* (1963): ' "Human life is so horrible," Macher said ... "that the only thing to do is what you want." ' And in *You Can't Do Both* (1994): 'Jeremy smiled and said ... "If you really want something you should have it, you ought to have it, you must do it or take it if you can." '

only training, and the only preliminary, needed for doing more of what you wanted to do.' He has learnt to manipulate the enemy as skilfully as they manipulate him, making hoax phone calls, commandeering other people's taxis, and doing everything that is needed to get the girl of his choice. Consequently he has also closed the gap between feeling and words. If you go for what you want, irrespective of other people, you can speak your mind about it:

The bloody old towser-faced boot-faced totem-pole on a crap reservation, Dixon thought. 'You bloody old towser-faced boot-faced totem-pole on a crap reservation,' he said.

7

Getting to be a movement

Only one reviewer, Walter Allen* in the *New Statesman*, perceived the intensely selfish undercurrent in *Lucky Jim*. After summarizing the plot, Allen said that his synopsis made Dixon sound something of a Charlie Chaplin figure, 'the *naïf* who, from his very innocence, exposes the sham'. But this was not the case:

Jim Dixon is far from that: he is, in his anxious way, playing the racket. If he were less anxious, he would play it better: the impossible situations arise from the fact that he can never wholly kid himself that the racket is worth playing. He is not the dumb ox with the heart of gold at all . . .

Other critics who liked the book entirely failed to spot this. *The Times*'s anonymous reviewer made Amis's hero sound like Bertie Wooster – 'Dixon . . . has no chip on his shoulder but instead a mischievous imp whose irresistible impulses get him deeper and deeper into the mire of official disapproval' – while Sean O'Faolain in the *Observer* judged him (quite wrongly) to be one of those principal characters like Paul Pennyfeather in Waugh's *Decline and Fall* or J. D. Salinger's Holden Caulfield who are not so much protagonists as people to whom things happen: 'Mr Amis['s] hero, or anti-hero . . . is . . . fated . . . to suffer every sort of deserved and undeserved discomfiture . . . He is a grown-up version of *The Catcher in the Rye*.' John Betjeman reviewed the book in the *Daily Telegraph*, saying

---

* Literary journalist, critic, academic and novelist (1911–1995). Allen was the son of a Birmingham silversmith, and proud of his working-class origins.

that he had not laughed so much at 'a new funny book' since Evelyn Waugh's *Decline and Fall* in 1928; and he too treated Dixon as essentially a nice guy in a nasty world. He told Amis privately that he felt the happy ending was a mistake, a Wodehousian evasion: 'Much better to have left him in the dark-brown stuff . . .' But this assumes that the shit is of other people's making. Amis defended his decision crisply: 'I'm fed up with novels where the hero doesn't get the girl. Of course he gets the girl . . . If he didn't . . . it would leave the reader feeling . . . "Oh, he's trying to give it profundity, is he?"'

The book's two unfavourable reviewers came closer to what Amis had actually created when they admitted to disliking Dixon. Julian Maclaren-Ross* in the *Sunday Times* described him as 'an ignoble buffoon', and Frederick Laws in the *News Chronicle* said it was 'a relief to learn that he is finally removed from the educational world'.

Walter Allen, as well as being the sole critic to decode Amis's book correctly, was also the only one to observe – in the opening paragraph of his review – that a covertly selfish go-getter like Dixon was symptomatic of an emerging *Zeitgeist*:

A new hero has risen among us . . . He is consciously, even conscientiously, graceless. His face, when not dead-pan, is set in a snarl of exasperation. He has one skin too few, but his is not the sensitiveness of the young man in earlier twentieth-century fiction: it is the phoney to which his nerve-ends are tremblingly exposed, and at the least suspicion of the phoney he goes tough. He is at odds with his conventional university education, though he comes generally from a famous university: he has seen through the academic racket as he sees through all the others.

Allen was a little wide of the mark with 'phoney'. Certainly there are examples of the bogus in *Lucky Jim* – Margaret's emotional play-acting, and of course Welch's and Bertrand's falsification of culture. But Dixon's real enemy is altruism, and the gracelessness and exasperation which Allen identified in Dixon is the impatience of

* Maclaren-Ross (1912–1964), uncrowned king of Fitzrovia and author of *Memoirs of the Forties* (1965), was the model for the eccentric writer X. Trapnel in Anthony Powell's novel-sequence 'A Dance to the Music of Time'.

the go-getter when confronted with the restraints of conventionally altruistic society.

Allen's review then attempted to explore the origins of this impatience in the new type of hero. He guessed that 'the Services' (wartime military service and postwar National Service)* had played a part in it – and there is indeed plenty of evidence that young men's experiences in uniform both during and after the war were contributing to the steady erosion of deference to elders and social superiors during the Fifties.† Allen also suggested that there were intellectual influences on the new hero: 'George Orwell, Dr Leavis and the Logical Positivists – or, rather, the attitudes these represent – all contributed to his genesis.' But where, besides *Lucky Jim*, was this new hero to be found? 'In fiction I think he first arrived last year,' wrote Allen, 'as the central character of Mr John Wain's *Hurry On Down*.'

Another reviewer – no less than Anthony Powell – sensed that something different was arriving. 'Mr Amis is the first promising young novelist who has turned up for a long time,' Powell told readers of *Punch*. Either he had not read Wain's novel, or he did not rate it as highly as Walter Allen. Meanwhile Wain himself was spreading the rumour that the best bits of *Lucky Jim* had really been written by Philip Larkin. When Larkin passed this on to Amis, he received the ready agreement that 'more than a few *Jim* cracks was your doing'.

The first Gollancz printing of the novel – which went on sale on 25 January 1954 – was a modest 750 copies. After a mere three weeks it was constantly being reprinted and had sold ten times that number. Before publication Amis had joked to Larkin that when it was filmed

---

* Wartime conscription had continued when peace came, so that at the age of eighteen every male in the country was required by law to register with the military authorities. Call-up for the two years of compulsory military service could be deferred until after an apprenticeship or university course, but most boys chose to get it over without delay.

† See the Prologue in the present writer's *That Was Satire That Was* (2000); for example: 'Dennis Potter, who did part of his National Service as a clerk in Whitehall, recalls having to bawl "Permission to speak – SAH!" every time he wanted to ask one of his superiors something. "That little phrase seemed to me to sum up the whole of English life at that time."' Nicholas Luard, who from 1961 to 1963 ran The Establishment Club with Peter Cook, says of the early 1950s: 'Authority was everything: you disobeyed any form of it, from a schoolmaster to a doctor, at your peril. You didn't even think about it.'

he wanted Alec Guinness as Dixon, Boris Karloff as Welch, Orson Welles as Bertrand and Alfred Hitchcock directing – 'Just pipe-dreaming dear.' Real bids for the film rights soon began, and for a while there was an idiotic plan to cast the highly unsuitable 'cheeky chappy' Norman Wisdom in the title role. Meanwhile the book won a Somerset Maugham Award, though Maugham himself (who despite providing the cash was not on the judging panel) hated *Lucky Jim*, and was not seduced by its hero as most reviewers had been; he described Dixon as 'mean, malicious and envious'.*

* *

In the very month of publication of *Lucky Jim* – January 1954 – Amis was identified as one of a group of young poets called the 'University Wits'. This occurred in the course of a *Spectator* poetry review by Anthony Hartley, a literary journalist in his late twenties, who had been at Oxford and was slightly acquainted with Amis, Wain and Larkin. Only two University Wits were actually named by Hartley: Amis and Donald Davie, who was the same age as Amis and lecturing at Trinity College, Dublin; and Hartley said little about their poetry. Contrasting it with another (nameless) group, which took Yeats, Ezra Pound and Dylan Thomas as its model, Hartley identified the Wits as descendants of the Thirties poets, 'especially Auden and Empson'.

Vague and slight as Hartley's remark was, it reflected a growing feeling in the London literary community that some sort of new group of writers was in the process of emerging. A few weeks later, on 8 March 1954, Amis remarked to Larkin that he had been 'flanked by you and Alvarez' in an edition of a BBC Third Programme series called *New Poetry*, and he added: 'There's no doubt, you know, we are getting to be a movement, even if the only people in it we like apart from ourselves are each other.'

Larkin's contribution to the broadcast had been his poem 'Fiction and the Reading Public', a sour comment on the banal demands that readers make on novelists ('Give me a thrill, says the reader, / Give me

---

* This remark was made by Maugham in the *Sunday Times* at Christmas 1955. Claiming that Dixon was representative of a new 'white-collar proletariat' who were entering universities on government grants, Maugham went on: 'Charity, kindliness, generosity, are qualities which they hold in contempt. They are scum.'

a kick . . .'). This was followed by an Amis poem which might have been intended as a sequel to Larkin's. Called 'Something Nasty in the Bookshop', it opened by remarking how young poets have to struggle to be noticed in the middlebrow world of modern bookselling:

> Between the GARDENING and the COOKERY
> Comes the brief POETRY shelf;
> By the Nonesuch Donne, a thin anthology
> Offers itself.

> Critical, and with nothing else to do,
> I scan the Contents page,
> Relieved to find the names are mostly new;
> No one my age . . .

The poem goes on to observe sardonically that the sort of indifferent poets who contribute to such forgettable anthologies 'divide by sex', the men writing about intellectual subjects, the women about love-affairs. Males try to keep love at a distance, but 'Girls aren't like that', which leads to the conclusion that 'Women are really much nicer than men; / No wonder we like them'. Moreover male poets *do* try to write love-poetry; they're just not so good at it as the women.

This, of course, was an example of the stylistic drabness which Amis had defended in his letter to Larkin four years earlier, and which characterizes virtually all of *A Frame of Mind*, Amis's second collection of poems, which Wain had printed for him at Reading University in 1953. Al Alvarez – who as Amis remarked had one of his own poems read in the same broadcast – compares this drab style to 'a well-made essay; it had a beginning, a middle and an end, and it made a point. It was carefully rhymed, rhythmically inert and profoundly complacent.' Amis reciprocated by expressing (in the same letter to Larkin that suggests they are 'getting to be a movement') his dislike of what Alvarez, Donald Davie and Wain were trying to do with poetry: 'I don't give a pinch of salt for old Al's "stuff", nor Davie's, nor old John Barry Wain's really much.'

So there were divisions in the ranks of this new 'movement' even before it had established itself. Nevertheless the idea that there *was* a movement began to gather pace – simply because it made the dull literary scene of the mid-1950s seem a bit livelier. In the *Spectator* on 27 August 1954, Anthony Hartley had another go at identifying it.

This time it was in an article called 'Poets of the Fifties', and Hartley named Amis, Larkin and Wain among those he considered to be developing a tone of voice that he called ' "dissenting" and non-conformist, cool, scientific and analytical' (the others included Donald Davie, Thom Gunn and George MacBeth). He warned of the dangers of their style – 'elimination of richness, of dryness pushed to the point of aridity' – but concluded that they amounted to 'the only considerable movement in English poetry since the Thirties'.

Hartley might have claimed to be part of the movement himself, since his own poetry had appeared alongside that of Amis, Larkin, Wain, Davie, Gunn, and two poets not mentioned in his article, Alvarez and Elizabeth Jennings, in a 1953 anthology called *Springtime*. The introduction, by co-editors G. S. Fraser and Iain Fletcher, described the prevailing tone of the poems as 'a level conversational tone of voice'. This was certainly the case in the six Larkin poems in the book. They included 'Coming', which contains his now famous description of his own childhood as 'a forgotten boredom'.

A few weeks after Hartley had identified 'the . . . movement', it became 'The Movement'. The story of how the capital letters arrived is told by the man who in 1954 was editing the *Spectator*'s literary pages, J. D. (John) Scott. 'The circulation was not behaving as it should,' he recalls,

and one day in the autumn [of 1954], the editor, Walter Taplin, gave the staff a pep-talk. What could we do to liven things up . . . ? Sensational journalism: not an easy product for a literary editor, whose main job is to arrange for reviews; you can review sensational books in a sensational way, but what can you do if people are not producing sensational books?

Well, you can look again to see whether those already in your hands are not capable of generating a deeper or more widespread interest.

Where Scott looked was Anthony Hartley's piece on 'Poets of the Fifties'. Could anything sensational be squeezed out of it? Scott felt that it could – that he might even light 'a box of fireworks' if he took this alleged movement in poetry, and tried to see how far it extended beyond poetry, and specifically into the novel, and to consider the extent to which it represented some historic change in society. Two of the poets named in 'Poets of the Fifties' had then recently published first novels; Kingsley Amis's *Lucky Jim* and John Wain's *Hurry On Down*. Not very much, but I used it as the basis for my attempt.

The result, which appeared in the *Spectator* on 1 October 1954, was an unsigned article by Scott called 'In the Movement'. He says that it was 'designed to grab the attention of any casual reader . . . on his way from the political pages ("The End of Bevanism?") to the financial column ("Sterling Convertibility Deferred")', and was therefore 'written in a tone brisk, challenging and dismissive'. It began with a vivid, dramatic vignette of some of the visible social changes that Britain had experienced in the last few years: 'The bus service has made the village into a suburb; the gaunt moorland produces a glittering factory; the angry slagheaps sink and melt greenly into the landscape, and the long dull High Street flowers with the black tulip of Montague Burton, the Tailor of Taste.' By comparison (Scott went on) the Fifties literary scene was stagnant.

The last 'movement' of note (he argued) had been in the Thirties, a period notable for 'fierce cold-bath Marxists' led by W. H. Auden. Its leading figures, including Auden himself, were still on the scene, but they had now become elder statesmen, 'acclaimed by Public Orators and applauded at princely Venetian first nights' – a reference to the facts that one of the Auden gang, C. Day-Lewis, had now risen to the height of Professor of Poetry at Oxford, while Auden himself had turned opera librettist; his and Stravinsky's *The Rake's Progress* had been premiered in Venice.

The Second World War had produced no 'movement' (Scott continued), 'not even a distinctive, central mood' – other than 'what might be called the 1984 mood' of the late Forties (Orwell's novel *Nineteen Eighty-Four* had been written in 1948), which was a reaction to what Lionel Trilling had described as 'the baffled wonder and shame that there is no way of responding to Belsen and Buchenwald'. So far, the Fifties had failed to come up with a voice or mood of their own. 'For years now,' Scott complained, 'there has been no coherence in the literary scene.'

Yet now, he went on, there was 'this new Movement of the Fifties' which Anthony Hartley had spotted among the younger poets. Moreover, 'three novels have been published – Mr John Wain's *Hurry On Down*, Mr Kingsley Amis's *Lucky Jim*, and Miss Iris Murdoch's *Under the Net*, which have been widely taken to represent the Movement'.

When he wrote his recollections of the circumstances behind his 'Movement' article more than thirty years later, Scott seems to have forgotten that he mentioned Iris Murdoch's first novel alongside Amis and Wain. It is true that Jake Donaghue's dream-like odyssey around London and Paris in *Under the Net* has a certain resemblance to the grotesque adventures of Charles Lumley, but it is motivated not by social restlessness but by Jake's desire to find the two people whom he loves, Anna Quentin and Hugo Belfounder; and, far from sharing Jim Dixon's rage at those who get in his way, the only person with whom Jake is angry is himself.

Al Alvarez recalls Murdoch in the early Fifties, when she was a young Oxford don: 'the lone Existentialist among all the Logical Positivists, a handsome young woman, with a bell of blonde hair, a broad face and a gruff, forthright manner, like one of Eisenstein's peasants'. Amis had known her since they had both belonged to the Communist Party at Oxford, but he never claimed any literary affinity. In a letter to Larkin, he made some comments on her second novel, *The Flight from the Enchanter* (1955), which he might well have applied to *Under the Net*: 'All seems very *unreal* to me. I can't believe that the chaps in it are real or doing things that real people do . . . The characters all seem abnormal, somehow.'

Having identified the three novelists whom he believed to exemplify the Movement, Scott went on to define its principles:

It is bored by the despair of the Forties, not much interested in suffering, and extremely impatient of poetic sensibility, especially poetic sensibility, about 'the writer and society'. So it's goodbye to all those rather sad little discussions about 'how the writer ought to live', and it's goodbye to the Little Magazine and 'experimental writing'. The Movement, as well as being anti-phoney, is anti-wet; sceptical, robust, ironic, prepared to be as comfortable as possible in a wicked, commercial, threatened world which doesn't look, anyway, as if it's going to be changed much by a couple of handfuls of young English writers.

It was shrewd of Scott to recognize the element of self-seeking in Amis and Wain's novels – that their heroes were 'prepared to be as comfortable as possible'. And he concluded by observing that fiction which was 'not openly on the side of social responsibility' seemed 'shocking and improper' after the left-wing doctrine of the Thirties.

And it is true that, in the newest novels, almost everything is made fun of with an off-handed toughness which might make one imagine that the authors . . . don't approve of anything. That remains to be seen. But the Movement is interesting . . . And small as it is, it is nevertheless a part of the movement of that tide which is pulling us through the Fifties and towards the Sixties.

* *

Scott says that the article caused as much of a stir as his editor could have hoped. 'It struck a nerve in the body of people interested in literature, and this nerve vibrated. Some of the vibrations were odd.' These included an uncharacteristically mild letter to the *Spectator* from Evelyn Waugh, who observed that it was unhelpful to treat writers as a group. He added: 'I have read two of the three novels which [the article] identifies as symptomatic of the new trend. I enjoyed them both greatly . . .' Waugh did not say which two, but if they included *Lucky Jim* he would have encountered Dixon making his 'Evelyn Waugh face'. According to Anthony Powell, Waugh retaliated by pronouncing its author's surname as 'Ames' and referring to him as 'Little Kingsley'.

Two weeks after Scott's article was published, Amis wrote to Larkin: 'Well, what a lot of bullshit all that was in the *Spr* about the new movt. etc. Useful up to a point, but the point is nearly here, I feel . . .' Yet a year before Hartley and Scott had identified the Movement, Amis had given some indication to Larkin that he regarded them both as members of some sort of emerging literary group. In undergraduate days he had frequently written to Larkin fantasizing how some of the great names in English literature might be re-cast as the personnel of a jazz band; in November 1953 he returned to this 'old gag', telling Larkin it was 'more for my amusement than yours, I imagine':

JACK WAIN AND THE PROVINCIAL ALL-STARS

Wain (tpt, voc) directing Phil Larkin (clt), 'King' Amis (tmb), Don Davie (alto), Al Alvarez (pno), Tommy Gunn (gtr), George 'Pops' Fraser (bs), Wally Robson (ds).

Wallace Robson, an Oxford don, had introduced Wain to Alvarez, who describes him as 'Oxford's young literary guru'.

Did the Movement exist? The question is purely academic, since Hartley's and Scott's articles meant that those mentioned in them would in future be treated as a group, whether or not they had anything truly in common. Moreover, in the wake of the *Spectator* publicity, two anthologies were published which gathered its supposed members together between the same set of covers, giving some sort of historical veracity to the Movement. D. J. Enright's 1955 collection *Poets of the 1950s* included poems by Amis, Larkin, Wain, Davie, Elizabeth Jennings, Enright himself, John Holloway and Robert Conquest. The last-named – an Anglo-American polymath who became a great friend of Amis's – edited his own anthology of the group, *New Lines* (1956), adding Thom Gunn to Enright's list. By 1958 Amis, writing to an inquirer who was at work on a book about the Movement, no longer dismissed the whole thing as 'bullshit'. He admitted that

we ... have in common ... a desire to write *sensibly*, without emotional hoo-ha; this boils down to saying that we all try to write poems that are intelligible in the sense that they can be paraphrased; there may be obscurities but no answerless riddles. John Wain put it best when he said that my verse wasn't really much like his, but it seemed like it to some people because 'they can make head or tail of both of us' – unlike so many contemporary poets. If extended to cover the whole group, I think that remark would be pretty fair. It doesn't make us a 'movement', of course ... all the 'movement' thing came from critics and reviewers.

Amis might have observed that in his poetry, he was trying for the same accuracy of speech that he had achieved triumphantly in prose in *Lucky Jim* – and which he could manage effortlessly in his mimicry. A friend (James Michie) recalls how 'he once came up to me and asked me to do a cow mooing. I did it. He said, "No, not like that. I've just discovered we are all wrong. It doesn't go from down to up. Listen. It goes from up to down – moo-oo-ooo." Detail. That was his forte. He loved to get the details right.'

There were no poems by Al Alvarez in the Enright or Conquest anthologies, and in his memoirs he expresses his disgust at the anti-modernist element in the Movement. Recalling Amis pulling one of his absurd faces whenever such modernist giants as Eliot or Pound were mentioned, Alvarez comments: 'The first few times he went through this routine were funny; after that it was just depressing. For Amis & Co., Modernism was a plot by foreigners . . . to divert literature from its true purpose; and their business was to get it back on its traditional track . . .' The trouble (observes Alvarez) was that all the Movement could offer to replace the melodrama and showmanship of modernism was 'a tetchy vision of postwar provincial England populated, like a Lowry painting, by stick figures united, above all, by boredom'.*

Alvarez does, however, make an exception of Larkin, whom he regards as the one Movement poet 'who was able to make something out of the restrictions of the style . . . a master of the wry, self-deprecating put-down and slangy half-rhymes'. Moreover (he says) Larkin wrote out of 'genuine depression and anger', though he had the wisdom to 'keep them at an ironic distance'. Amis agreed with this valuation. 'Larkin is easily the best of us all,' he remarked in 1958. This was the year in which Larkin – who had already found his distinctive voice in such mid-Fifties poems as 'Church Going', 'Mr Bleaney' and 'An Arundel Tomb' – wrote 'The Whitsun Weddings'.

Amis, too, was finding his poet's voice. Reviewing Amis's 1956 collection *A Case of Samples* in the *Manchester Guardian*, Larkin remarked that the best things in it would 'exasperate only those who cannot see when a poem is being funny and serious simultaneously'. A fine example of this is Amis's 'A Dream of Fair Women', a comic-erotic fantasy in which he imagines a 'squadron' of lightly-clad young ladies throwing themselves at him, one by one:

---

* For a full-length study of the Movement, which argues that it did indeed exist, and was significant and influential, see Blake Morrison, *The Movement* (Oxford University Press, 1980).

> Speech fails them, amorous, but each one's look,
> Endorsed in other ways, begs me to sign
>   Her body's autograph-book;
> 'Me first, Kingsley; I'm cleverest' each declares . . .

At the end of the poem he confesses that it is, of course, 'all a dream'. But according to Alvarez, it wasn't.

'I spent a weekend at Kingsley Amis's house in Swansea,' Alvarez writes in his memoirs.

During a long, drunken Saturday evening, Kingsley disappeared into the garden with each of the women in the party. While they were gone the rest of us sat around trying to make conversation and pretending not to be embarrassed. Half an hour later our host and whatever lucky lady had gone with him sauntered back in, smoothing their clothes and hair but not quite able to conceal the wild furtive triumph in their eyes.

8

A literary Teddy boy

By the time that the critics had begun to talk about the Movement, the war had been over for nearly ten years. Life in Britain was still rather drab and austere compared with the pre-war era; John Wain's second novel, *Living in the Present* (1955), describes a typical Fifties restaurant, with 'blousy waitresses' dumping 'platefuls of twice-cooked inferior food' in front of customers:

They had even given up crossing out from the menu the dishes that were 'off ', but . . . Edgar . . . knew by long experience that there would be, at this hour, nothing 'on' but corned-beef rissoles, a spoonful of greens boiled to rags and tasting of soda, and perhaps a chunk of waxy ice-cream to follow . . .

London was full of places like this; so were the provinces; while as for the country towns and villages, they did not rise even to this parody of communal feeding; in any town with less than ten thousand inhabitants, there was, after eight o'clock, nothing to put in your belly except the lukewarm beer of the local pub.

Food rationing had continued until 1954; the cookery writer Elizabeth David recalls 'the deadly boredom of queuing and the frustration of buying the weekly rations'. Yet by 1955, in the preface to a new edition of her handbook of Mediterranean food,* she was able to write:

So startlingly different is the food situation now as compared with only two years ago that I think there is scarcely a single ingredient, however exotic,

---

* First published in 1950 by John Lehmann; another of his contributions to the cultural life of the period.

mentioned in this book which cannot be obtained somewhere in this country, even if it is only in one or two shops.

In the years immediately after the war, few Britons had ventured abroad for holidays, and those who did had very little money to spend there. The American author Raymond Chandler, writing to his British publisher Hamish Hamilton in 1949, passed on a story he had been told by some fellow countrymen who had been to Luxembourg:

The atmosphere was cheerful, people from all the countries of Europe, almost, were there, having their ease. At two tables were English people, only two. At one sat an elderly couple, formerly well-to-do, now not so well-to-do. At the other a demobbed tank officer with his mother. On all the tables of the hotel dining-room but these were bottles of wine. This is a true story. The English could not afford wine. Those who had never surrendered drank water in order that those who had surrendered might drink wine.

British visitors to the Continent had certainly switched to wine by 1955; the Foreign Office restricted the amount of cash they could take abroad, but the *Spectator* advised would-be travellers that in Paris it was better value to order wine by the carafe than by the bottle, while those who went to Italy were recommended to drink local wines rather than waste money on Chianti. An advertisement by the South African tourist board pointed out that currency restrictions did not apply to Britons travelling to their country, and mentioned 'the fascinating native life' as another of the attractions (apartheid had been introduced in 1948).

Meanwhile Britain was not taking care of its own tourist attractions. John Betjeman's weekly column in the *Spectator* largely consisted of such news as the closure of the Kennet and Avon Canal, and the destruction of fine Georgian and Victorian buildings to create contemporary-style shopping arcades. Those eighteenth- and nineteenth-century mansions which survived were largely being divided and subdivided to cope with the housing shortage: *Ideal Home* magazine ran a feature on 'Making a four-room flat from one room'.

Winston Churchill finally gave up the office of prime minister in April 1955, and was replaced by Sir Anthony Eden, who led the Tories to a comfortable general election victory the following month. Kingsley

Amis voted Labour, but he admitted in a *Spectator* article that at present, in comparison with the Thirties, 'the *chic* attitude is a Right-wing one'. With Hilly and their youngest child, eighteen-month-old Sally, he took part in a demonstration against capital punishment, during a visit to Swansea by the Home Secretary; Amis hoped the minister had been caused 'a small passing twinge' by seeing them with their banners, but he wrote the episode up in a jokey *Spectator* article which suggests that he did not take the issue very seriously.

There was a general feeling that ordinary people were powerless, and that the country was run by a clique – 'the Establishment', as the *Spectator* political columnist Henry Fairlie dubbed it:

. . . what I call the 'Establishment' in this country is today more powerful than ever before. By the 'Establishment' I do not mean only the centres of official power – though they are certainly part of it – but rather the whole matrix of official and social relations with which power is exercised . . . The 'Establishment' can be seen at work in the activities of not only the Prime Minister, the Archbishop of Canterbury and the Earl Marshal, but of such lesser mortals as the chairman of the Arts Council, the Director-General of the BBC, and even the editor of *The Times Literary Supplement*, not to mention divinities like Lady Violet Bonham Carter.

There was remarkably little public discussion about the pros and cons of the nuclear deterrent.* In a Christmas 1954 radio programme, Bertrand Russell pointed out that the millions that Britain was spending on defence were probably wasted, since the country could be knocked out in a moment by a mere handful of thermo-nuclear bombs. But as yet this prospect failed to spark off passionate arguments or campaigns.

In the cinema, there was a pronounced mood of nostalgia for Britain's days of wartime glory, exemplified in *The Dambusters* (1955), with Michael Redgrave as Dr Barnes Wallis, the inventor who worked out how to bomb the apparently impregnable Ruhr dams, and Richard Todd as the dauntless RAF pilot Guy Gibson, who led the raid; and

---

* Following the atomic bombing of Hiroshima and Nagasaki by the United States in August 1945, the USSR began the testing of nuclear weapons four years later, followed by Britain in 1952.

Reach for the Sky, based on Paul Brickhill's 1954 biography of Douglas Bader (played by Kenneth More), who loses both legs in a flying accident but still manages to become a war hero. The trend for such films continued as late as 1957, with *Ill Met by Moonlight*, in which Dirk Bogarde portrayed Major Patrick Leigh-Fermor capturing a German general in wartime Crete. The lid was only finally put on this genre in 1960 when Peter Cook and his colleagues in *Beyond the Fringe* satirized it in a sketch called 'The Aftermyth of War'.

As to the state of British theatre in the early and mid-Fifties, Anthony Hartley wrote in the *Spectator*, rounding up the year's plays at the end of 1954, that he was

appalled by the lack of standards among those fabricating material for actors and actresses to perform. It is not easy to recall one English play in this last year which even suggested that there might be a new playwright behind it . . . The [leading playwrights] of 1954 were, of course, Charles Morgan and Christopher Fry . . . It seems to be the fact that the best writers . . . are . . . not concerning themselves with the theatre . . . The English stage is passing through a singularly barren period. Shaw must be turning in his grave.

* *

Amis had promised Gollancz the manuscript of his second novel, *That Uncertain Feeling*, by the end of July 1954, but he soon fell behind schedule. 'I've really been doing far too much journalism and such,' he told Hilary Rubinstein. He was now reviewing novels regularly for the *Spectator*, often writing the week's lead review. He did not hesitate to hit out at literary lions. Of J. B. Priestley's latest novel, *Low Notes on a High Level*, he wrote: 'I tried hard to work up some emotion as positive as boredom'; and of Evelyn Waugh's *Officers and Gentlemen*: 'A great deal of what is obviously offered as comedy is not quite funny enough . . . [Guy] Crouchback is really a terrible fellow.'

He did not review John Wain's new novel. Wain had told him that he was thinking of giving up his Reading University job and becoming a full-time writer. 'He explained,' Amis reported to Larkin,

that while he only had a 4th-rate scholarly career, at best, ahead of him, he had a first-rate literary one. When he said this I nodded slowly, my eyes fixed on my glass of gin and tonic in a manner that suggested I had detected in it some unusual but harmless chemical reaction.

Wain's *Living in the Present*, published in the summer of 1955, is the story of Edgar Banks, an unsuccessful schoolmaster who decides to commit suicide – and, just for the fun of it, to murder someone with the same poison. His choice of victim is a poet called Rollo Philipson-Smith, who belongs to something called the Movement. 'You can't get into it,' Philipson-Smith tells Banks, 'because at this stage we're not looking for recruits – and when we do we'll hand-pick them. And as for opposing it, you might as well realize from the start that it's going to be irresistible – utterly irresistible.' In fact this Movement is not a literary trend but Fascism in thin disguise.

Isabel Quigly was the *Spectator* reviewer of the book:

If *Living in the Present* were John Wain's first novel, one would most likely greet it with critical whoops ... Like it or not, that scratchy voice, that disgruntled view of the universe ... have power. [But the book] must be called a setback, because it is not an advance ... All that was fresh, because new, in *Hurry On Down*, seems trite because said again in exactly the same idiom ... a series of rather unadventurous adventures ...

When Wain sent him a copy, Amis confided his own opinion of the book to Larkin:

It isn't so much that it's a bad book ... no, [it] goes further than that, in not *seeming to be by a writer* ... You feel the chap hasn't got hold of the fact that first you want to get hold of something you want to say, and then you sort of fudge up a plot ... Nor does he realize that a novel ought to remind you of life occasionally ... And now what the hell am I going to say when I write to thank him for it?

His own new novel followed *Living in the Present* into the shops a few weeks later. *That Uncertain Feeling* is the story of John Lewis, a Welsh librarian who risks destroying his happy marriage by having a fling with a local *grande dame*. Far less iconoclastic than *Lucky Jim*, it still seemed ground-breaking – or maybe window-breaking – to the

New Statesman reviewer, 'Richard Lister', whom Amis's friend Robert Conquest identified as V. S. Pritchett in disguise:

There are two classes of novel which have for some time divided between them the commendation of the literary reviewers – the sensitive and the posh. But Mr Kingsley Amis has made his name by loudly belonging to neither. He is brashly, vulgarly, aggressively unsensitive, and the world his characters inhabit is the world that has succeeded the posh. It is the world of the Welfare State in all its crudity, and Mr Amis is a literary Teddy boy. This is a world far too common for the sensitive to survive in, and it is one from which the posh beat a hasty retreat to those square Georgian houses behind those creepered walls. Of course, it is bound to catch up with them in time. Mr Powell's upper-class thrusters will soon be in the post office queue . . . to draw their children's allowances: Miss Bowen's complicated heroines will be getting their treatment or their sleeping tablets 'on the health': and Mr Waugh's Officers and Gentlemen will, before they are much older, be feeding in canteens or cafeterias . . . But meanwhile the horror is postponed for their creatures; they set their novels in the privileged pre-war.

Mr Amis sets his in the utterly unprivileged present . . . [He] brings into contrast the old world and the new, to the advantage of neither. The new world is sitters-in,* and nappies and half-washed tea-cups, and multiple stores and mass-producing tailors . . . [It] is painted with a mixture two parts disgust and three parts farcical comedy.

Conquest was amused at the description of Amis as a 'literary Teddy boy' – a phrase which reminds us that, while the early and middle Fifties in Britain were a time of conformity and conservatism for the middle-class and middle-aged, a distinctly rebellious attitude was surfacing in the lower levels of society. The 'Teds' were associated in the public mind with violent crime, and with the dance-halls which purveyed the latest American musical import, 'rock and roll' (later 'rock 'n' roll'). In 1954 the American singer Bill Haley recorded 'Rock Around the Clock'. Initially only a modest success, it spread worldwide following its use in *The Blackboard Jungle*, a movie about a key issue of the Fifties, juvenile delinquency. Another American movie about

* The current term for baby-sitters.

young delinquents, *Rebel Without a Cause* (1955), starred the twenty-four-year-old James Dean. Loosely inspired by *Romeo and Juliet* (like the 1957 musical *West Side Story*, another drama about delinquency), *Rebel* was based on an actual case study of a delinquent, teenage psychopath; but its fame came less from its content than from Dean's death in a road accident shortly after it was released, which confirmed his status as an idol for the would-be rebellious younger generation.

A year after *Rebel Without a Cause* had been shown in British cinemas, the literary world suddenly woke up to the existence of a young man who was the same age as James Dean, and who seemed to be an intellectual and cultural counterpart to the rebellious youth Dean had portrayed on screen. Kingsley Amis was among the first to comment on him.

* *

On 15 June 1956, Amis reviewed in the *Spectator* a book which had been launched at the end of the previous month by his own publisher, Victor Gollancz. 'One of the prime indications of the sickness of mankind in the mid-twentieth century,' his review began,

is that so much excited attention is paid to books about the sickness of mankind in the mid-twentieth century. The latest of these books is more readable than most; it is more compilation than original work, and the worst it can do is to make you feel a little overwhelmed at its author's erudition. Here they come – tramp, tramp, tramp – all those characters you thought were discredited, or had never read, or (if you are like me) had never heard of: Barbusse, Sartre, Camus, Kierkegaard, Nietzsche, Hermann Hesse, Hemingway . . . The Legion of the Lost, they call us, the Legion of the Lost are we, as the old song has it. Marching on to hell with the drum playing – pick up the step there!

The book was *The Outsider*, by a young discovery of Gollancz's called Colin Wilson. Amis's review was by no means hostile, but it provoked an immediate and prickly response. 'Had an incredible letter from Capitaine C. Wilson of the Légion Etrangère,' Amis wrote to Conquest four days after the review had been printed. He supplied Conquest with excerpts from Wilson's complaints, which were not just about the review but a response to Amis's own novels:

This anti-culture stuff gets you nowhere . . . I believe I represent a new trend in English literature . . . not having time myself, I persuaded my girlfriend to read your 2 books and tell me what she thought . . . your fault seems to me to be the same as Auden's . . . I feel you'd better know the worst . . . I have a lot of things I want to establish – vital things for the course of modern history – and knocking you and other misplaced figures off their pedestals will be the first step . . .

Amis commented to Conquest: 'Good stuff, eh? I give him 2 years before paranoia closes over his head.' But if he had known more about Wilson's background and personality, he would not have been so astonished.

9

I hadn't the faintest doubt of my genius

On Christmas Day, 1954, a young man of twenty-three with horn-rimmed glasses and short dark hair was alone in a chilly rented bed-sitting room in south London, looking out at the icy grey weather, and cooking for himself. 'I recall that I had tinned tomatoes and fried bacon for Christmas dinner.'

His girlfriend had gone back to her family for the holiday, and he did not have the money to return to his own parents in Leicester. Moreover his relations with them were strained; his father felt he had wasted the chance to settle down in a steady office job, and was prophesying that he would come to no good.

'I felt at a loose end. So I sat on my bed, with an eiderdown over my feet, and wrote in my journal.'

Though he had left school at sixteen, with minimal qualifications, and had been doing low-level menial work ever since, he was widely read in European literature, and he began to consider his predicament in the light of it. 'It struck me that I was in the position of so many of my favourite characters in fiction: Dostoevsky's Raskolnikov, Rilke's Malte Laurids Brigge, the young writer in Hamsun's *Hunger:* alone in my room, feeling totally cut off from the rest of society.'

He picked up the journal he had been keeping, and started writing about this. 'And then, quite suddenly, I saw that I had the makings of a book. I turned to the back of my journal and wrote at the head of the page: "Notes for a book *The Outsider in Literature*".'

During the past months he had been writing a novel, based on Jack the Ripper. But he now felt that its narrative was becoming weighted down with too many intellectual references and meditations. 'The sensible thing, I decided, was to write a separate book about the ideas.'

In little more than an hour, 'I had outlined *The Outsider* in the back of my diary – chapters on Sartre, Camus, Hemingway, Hermann Hesse (whose work was then almost completely unknown in the English-speaking countries), Dostoevsky, Tolstoy, William Blake, Rama-krishna, Gurdjieff, and so on.'

He fell asleep that night with a sense of deep inner calm. 'It seemed one of the most satisfying Christmas Days I'd ever spent.'

* *

Colin Henry Wilson was conceived out of wedlock and born in Leicester on 26 June 1931, three months before the marriage of his parents. 'My background was working-class, but I do not feel that this is of any particular importance . . . In my case, it was simply a nuisance that I wanted to escape and then ignore.' The ordinariness of Leicester was what bored and irritated him, rather than his place in the class system – 'the feeling that life is rather dull and rather predictable, and that "that is all there is" '.

Colin's father, Arthur Wilson, was a worker in one of Leicester's many boot and shoe factories. Arthur's own father had been killed in the First World War and, as the eldest male in the family, Arthur had taken over the role of protector to his sisters and brother. 'It made him rather a dominant character who liked his own way,' says Colin.

My mother told me that she was attracted by him because he seemed more grown up than the other men she knew. When she was nineteen, she went on holiday to an aunt in Doncaster with her elder sister, my aunt Connie, and with Connie's boyfriend Frank and my father. She and Connie slept in a double bed. On the first night, Connie got out of bed and announced that she intended to go and join Frank, who was sharing a double bed with my father. So my father was obliged to get into bed with my mother, who was a virgin at the time. A few weeks later, I was on the way.

Although the Wilsons had three more children, Arthur possibly resented the existence of Colin, whose accidental conception had forced him into what Colin describes as 'not basically a happy marriage, although it could have been worse'. When war broke out in 1939, Arthur went into the army, and for a few months we missed him ... After six months or so, he was discharged ... they discovered he had duodenal ulcers – and we were delighted. But he had only been home a day or two when we remembered how much we disliked him and slipped back into the old routine of trying to avoid him.

One of Colin's methods of keeping out of his father's way was to immerse himself in words:

I learned to read fairly late – at about seven or eight – but [then] began reading everything I could lay my hands on – comics, my mother's 'True Romance' and 'True Detective' magazines, the *Just William* books, Leslie Charteris's 'Saint' and P. G. Wodehouse ... I spent most of my time in a dream world.

Staying with an uncle, he was ticked off for reading *Weird Tales* and other pulp magazines that he had discovered in a cupboard. 'My uncle was furious and gave me a long talking-to. He didn't seem to understand that I didn't particularly like the physical world, and found most of the grown ups I knew unutterably boring.'

He soon graduated from pulp fiction to encyclopaedic information, acquiring at a church bazaar a book called *Practical Knowledge For All*, which contained not only courses on subjects from aeronautics to philosophy, but also a selection from the great poets. 'I ... had this desire to know everything.' Moreover, when he was absorbed in words and information, 'I experienced [a] "magical" sensation ... a sense of *leaving behind* my personal identity, of becoming simply a perceiving mind.'

Science was his first love; and he was determined not merely to read about it, but to write it all down.

At the age of thirteen I had a girlfriend ... But just before my fourteenth birthday she 'chucked' me for my best friend. That August, feeling miserable and at a loose end, I began to write my first book. It started simply as an attempt to write a brief summary of all I knew about physics and chemistry ... Then I grew more ambitious, and decided to include astronomy and geology ... I had originally believed that it could all be compressed into one pocket size notebook; by Christmas it had swollen to six.

He turned to philosophy, which at first he found 'completely baffling
. . . But when I read Joad's* account of the ideas of Bishop Berkeley, I
suddenly became interested . . . a frightening experience for a thirteen-
year-old who had always taken it for granted that the universe rests
on solid foundations.' He also struggled with expositions of the theory
of relativity; he scarcely understood it, yet 'I wanted to become a
second Einstein'.

Having crammed his head with so much knowledge, he began to
experience intellectual vertigo; and he also felt profoundly out of touch
with ordinary life. 'At the age of thirteen, I had come very nearly to
"the end of thinking" and had not even started to live . . . I felt that I
was carrying around an intolerable burden of knowledge, a burden
that seemed far too heavy for someone of my age.'

Yet his performance at school did not reflect the breadth of his
reading. Thanks to the 1944 Education Act, which greatly increased
the opportunities for British working-class children to receive secondary education, he was able to obtain a place (by sitting a scholarship
exam) at the Gateway Secondary Technical School in Leicester,† but
says he 'came bottom of the class in my first year there' and 'left school
at sixteen'. Nevertheless 'I hadn't the faintest doubt of my genius'.

He was 'vaguely intending to become a scientist and work for ICI',
but was inadequately qualified. 'So I took a job in a small local factory,
where a couple of dozen women wound wool from hanks on to
bobbins – my job was to weigh the wool when it came in, weigh it
when it went out, and keep the women supplied with hanks and
bobbins.' He loathed this treadmill life, and once again retreated from
daily reality into the consolation of words. 'In the evenings I retired to
my bedroom and read poetry – Spenser, Milton, Cowper, Byron,
Shelley, Wordsworth, Poe, Tennyson.'

---

* C. E. M. Joad (1891–1953), writer of popular books on philosophy, and a star of
the BBC radio *Brains Trust*.
† From 1944, secondary state schools in Britain were divided into Grammar, Technical
and Secondary Modern, the latter providing for those children who failed the 'Eleven
Plus' exam. Technical Schools were intended to have the same status as Grammar
Schools, and specialized in scientific and technical subjects. However, they tended to
be regarded as inferior to Grammar Schools, and comparatively few of them were built
or opened.

After a while his old school offered him a job as a laboratory assistant. He took it, 'but it was a mistake to try to return to science. The months of poetry had made me determined to become a writer.' He had now soaked himself in George Bernard Shaw, and was writing his own play, heavily influenced by *Man and Superman*; also a journal:

I bought a huge notebook and just began pouring my thoughts and feelings into it . . . I particularly poured my depressions into it, and one day when I'd been writing about my absolute fury with this bloody physics master, I suddenly decided to commit suicide . . . I would go straight to the reagent shelves, take down the bottle of potassium cyanide, and drink it straight down. When I walked into the classroom . . . I ignored the crowd gathered around the master's desk and went and took down the cyanide. As I pulled out its stopper, I could suddenly *see* myself raising it to my lips, and feel the agonizing pain in the pit of my stomach . . .

He resigned from the school job and found work in a local income tax office. 'Again, it was a bad choice – a return to more boredom and frustration.' He continued to write, sending off stories to magazines, and experiencing 'days of anger and despair' when they came back.

At eighteen, National Service suddenly offered new opportunities. 'I decided to enter the Royal Air Force, hoping to learn to fly.' Basic training was surprisingly enjoyable – 'It was exhilarating to get out of bed at 6.30 in the morning and march up and down a parade ground' – but he was soon assigned to an office job as a junior clerk. 'Once again, I sank into the old condition of disgust and resentment.' His typing was so poor that the adjutant sent him to the medical officer for an assessment.

On my way to see the M.O., I had an inspiration. I told him that I was homosexual, and that I was finding it a dreadful strain to have to undress at night among all those splendid male bodies. In fact, one of my closest friends in Leicester had been homosexual, although I had never experienced the slightest inclination in that direction.

The medical officer was sympathetic, but the military police demanded that he reveal the names of other homosexuals in the camp.

'They spent hours questioning me until I decided to co-operate. A few weeks later I had to see a senior medical officer . . . who told me that the best thing would be to discharge me from the RAF.'

Back in civilian life, he opted for labouring rather than office jobs, and began to practise meditation ('a reference in T. S. Eliot led me to buy the *Bhagavad Gita*'). He started a love-affair with a girl of fifteen, and life grew much more attractive. 'My only minor problem was that Sylvia was determined to marry me, and I had no intention of marrying anyone. Ever since I was nine or ten years old, I had been convinced that I was a "genius", and was destined for great things.'

He abandoned Sylvia and set off to visit a pen-friend in Strasbourg. Getting as far as Paris, he called on Raymond Duncan, brother of the dancer Isadora, who dressed in a toga and ran a Left Bank 'academy' teaching a philosophy which he called 'Actionalism'. Wilson explains this as 'the conviction that man can only contact reality through action, not through mere thinking. Since I had already arrived at the same conclusion myself, we found ourselves in warm agreement, and he offered to let me stay in the Akademia Duncan and to teach me printing and hand-loom weaving.' However, Wilson soon tired of learning these skills, set off for Strasbourg, failed to hit it off with the pen-friend, and returned to Leicester, 'half-inclined to become a Catholic so I could enter a monastery'.

It was back to clerking, and labouring in a steel factory. Meanwhile, 'I was trying to write my first book, a novel called (at that time) "Ritual of the Dead", based on the Jack the Ripper murders; I also wrote a series of essays on subjects that interested me – Hemingway, Eliot, the Diary of Vaslav Nijinsky.'

He was now having an affair with the staff nurse at the steelworks, who was nine years older than him. She became pregnant. 'We talked half-heartedly about getting an abortion. But when my parents heard about it, they took an unexpectedly moral stance, and demanded to meet Betty. After that first meeting, my mother seemed shocked. "But she's a *lady*." And they ordered us to get married.'

Colin Wilson, aged twenty, married Dorothy Betty Troop in 1951, and they decided to begin married life in London. But when the baby, Roderick, was born, it became increasingly difficult to find a home there – 'in those days,' recalls Wilson, 'landladies didn't like babies or pets'. (Margaret Drabble writes of 1950s landladies: 'These were the days of No Blacks, No Irish, No Students, No Women, and a shilling extra for every bath.')

After only eighteen months, the Wilsons had lived at four different London addresses. 'Finally, in January 1953, we separated "temporarily" while I looked around for another flat; meanwhile, Betty returned to Leicester.' The marriage was never resumed.

Colin had taken a job as a hospital porter. After Betty's departure he made another trip to Paris, this time earning a little money as a salesman for a literary magazine, the *Paris Review*. 'I had hoped to stay . . . and finish my novel; but by November, it was clear that I would probably starve . . . Reluctantly, I returned once again to Leicester.'

This time he found work selling carpets in a department store. There he met and began a relationship with a girl called Joy Stewart, a graduate of Trinity College, Dublin, who joined him in London when he returned to the capital soon after. Again he took a series of dead-end jobs; but now at last he began to find kindred spirits.

* *

He later wrote a thinly fictionalized account of this in his 1961 novel *Adrift in Soho*. Its hero, Harry Preston, leaves his navvying job in the provinces and sets off for the capital with a manuscript in his suitcase:

I was working on a ten-volume work on the nature of freedom . . . The first volume would deal with the basic problem of whether life is worth living, or whether it would be more sensible to commit suicide. It would range from Greek and oriental pessimism to the modern German romantics; I should attempt to show that pessimism is the basic reaction of all thinking men to human existence.

He rents a room from a typically ferocious landlady, who has her own approach to the race issue. 'You'll notice there are negro tenants in the house,' she tells him.

'Some landladies won't have them, but I don't hold these prejudices. But I think the white people in the house should try to set them an example of good manners and tidiness. They can easily be taught with a little patience . . . So if you notice any of the black tenants breaking the house rules, I hope you'll remember to mention it to me.'

Fleeing from this awful lodging-house, he is drawn into a bohemian group that drifts around the Soho pubs and coffee-bars in grubby clothes and duffle coats. He starts rooming with them, in an atmosphere of free love. 'Some of them are art students,' explains one of the residents.

'The bloke in the bed . . . is a freelance journalist. He makes quite a lot of money at it . . . He just likes this kind of life. He likes sex and drink and marihuana . . . The others don't mind having him around because he pays the rent . . . The girls sleep with anybody they want to – so do the men.'

In reality, Wilson's first contact with London bohemia was in a markedly less romantic part of the capital, the distant northern suburb of Dollis Hill, where a middle-aged Hungarian émigré who called himself Alfred Reynolds convened a vaguely anarchist gathering of drifters and would-be philosophers known as 'The Bridge'. Wilson attended a few meetings, but says he soon turned his back on this 'wishy-washy' gathering. However, he did form a friendship with one of its members, a young man from the north of England called Stuart Holroyd, two years his junior.

Born in Bradford in 1933, Holroyd describes himself as one of the 'kids who ungratefully rejected the boons of Mr Butler's [1944] Education Act', because he had taken A-levels at school but refused to go to university, and had headed for the capital at the age of nineteen. He found that London was still recovering from the war:

It was scarred and dingy and there were still extensive bomb sites. Rubble, greyness, smog, poverty, garish whores on the streets in Soho, trams still running along Kingsway, tramps sleeping on the Embankment and under the Arches: it was a run-down city by today's standards, but for me it was romantic and exciting and just what I had expected from my reading of Dickens.

Living off the dole, Holroyd spent much of his time keeping warm in the city's most famous all-night café, Lyons Corner House in the

Strand. Here he had met Alfred Reynolds and been invited to Dollis Hill to sit at his feet. Now he transferred his discipleship to the amazingly self-confident Colin Wilson:

Colin . . . would assert of other writers that they were fools or mediocrities and claim that he was the greatest living English writer, but he was not at all condescending . . . He retained something of the look of the school 'swot': high brow, thin mouth, small eyes behind thick glasses, short back and sides haircut; and when he moved or shook hands he did so jerkily, as one not quite at ease with his body. He was quite tall, but no one would ever take him for a sportsman.

Holroyd was soon introduced by Wilson to another admirer he had acquired, a Welshman in his mid-twenties named Bill Hopkins. 'Bill . . . was . . . from a theatrical background,' writes Holroyd,

and in conversation was dramatic, entertaining, eloquent and combative. He chain-smoked thin hand-rolled cigarettes, was usually unshaven and tousle-haired and had a kind of ravaged look which went well with his wild genius image but was probably produced by malnutrition, sleeplessness and excessive smoking.

Wilson says that Hopkins 'declared that he never read other people's books because he preferred to be completely original', and that he was 'the first man I had met who was as conceited and as assured of his future greatness as I was myself '.

Hopkins himself fills in more details of his early years:

My father Ted Hopkins was the outstanding music hall star of Wales. But shortly after my birth in Cardiff in 1928, he lost all his money in the Depression, and when he died of pneumonia in 1937 we became totally destitute. My mother, a theatrical beauty who had been a Cochran girl, brought us five children (I was the youngest) to London, and we lodged in a couple of bleak rooms in Kennington. When war broke out, my mother joined ENSA, forming an act with my sisters to entertain the troops. I sometimes appeared in it too, but my mother was so against my entering the theatre professionally that she bullied the editors of south London newspapers to take on me and my brother as junior reporters.

It was a magic key! I soon found myself in Fleet Street, joining the *New York Herald Tribune* as a rewrite man. And when I did National Service, it was as an Air Ministry news correspondent. After that, for a while, I edited a magazine called *Across Frontiers*, for the Crusade for World Government – a very idealistic movement, with people like Einstein, J. B. Priestley and Albert Camus. We aimed to make everyone 'citizens of the world', so that national governments could no longer quarrel and make war. But there was no money, and I'm afraid I soon fled back to Fleet Street.

I was earning good money, and meanwhile my poems were being published in literary magazines. Then I tried to launch a magazine of my own, *The Saturday Critic*, but it used up every penny I had, even before the first issue could come out. Then I met Colin Wilson. We became bosom friends at once – we talked without stopping for literally twenty-four hours.

They exchanged manuscripts – Hopkins was writing a strange novel called *The Divine and the Decay*. He returned Wilson's Jack the Ripper manuscript, now titled *Ritual in the Dark*, with a note which read: 'You are a man of genius.'

Holroyd says that what the three of them had in common was 'a shared conception of man as a creature with spiritual hunger . . . We held that mystical experiences, visionary states of consciousness, moments of ecstasy . . . should be the chief object of man's endeavour. "Religious Existentialists" we called ourselves.* "Spiritual Fascists", we were called by our critics.'

There is certainly a touch of Fascism in the attitudes of Harry Preston, Wilson's fictionalized self-portrait in *Adrift in Soho*. At one moment he glances through an evening paper and learns of the death of James Dean; his reaction is brutal: 'It seemed to me that one film actor less in the world could only be a good thing . . . If a far-sighted destiny would arrange enough accidents of this sort, the world might be left in the hands of really intelligent people . . .'

Encouraged to believe in himself intellectually by Holroyd and Hopkins ('a bunch of geniuses', as Holroyd modestly puts it), Wilson

---

* Hopkins dissents from this, saying he never agreed with Holroyd's tendency towards mysticism.

now took a step which would later pay big dividends in terms of publicity:

I decided to try to save rent by buying a tent and sleeping outdoors. The first night, I erected the tent on a golf course in north London, but it was too obviously conspicuous. Then a friend suggested the obvious solution: a waterproof sleeping bag. It was, in fact, a kind of rubber envelope that went over the ordinary sleeping bag. When it rained, I could pull up a hood over my head . . .

Learning of Wilson's alfresco sleeping arrangements, Bill Hopkins (who was giving Wilson some financial support from his earnings as a journalist) commented approvingly – and shrewdly: 'That's right, Col, build up the legend.'

Wilson chose Hampstead Heath as his outdoor home:

I usually woke up at about eight o'clock, and packed my belongings on the back of my bicycle. Then I cycled down Haverstock Hill to a busman's café, where I could get a huge mug of tea and a slice of bread and dripping for a few pence. I arrived at the British Museum for opening time around ten o'clock – I had started using the Reading Room in the last year of my marriage, no doubt inspired by romantic tales of Marx, Shaw and Samuel Butler writing masterpieces there. I left my haversack and sleeping bag in the cloakroom, then spent the day working at my novel.

Ritual in the Dark was still based on Jack the Ripper, but as Wilson now rewrote it ('for perhaps the tenth time', he says) it developed into

a study in three 'outsiders' (a word I had borrowed from Bernard Shaw). One was an 'intellectual outsider', like Nietzsche, one an 'emotional outsider', like Van Gogh, one a 'physical outsider', like the ballet dancer Nijinsky. The 'physical outsider' expresses his frustration through sadistic violence, like Jack the Ripper.

Wilson had decided to give the book a 'mythological' structure, like Joyce's *Ulysses* – in his case the mythology came from the ancient Egyptian *Book of the Dead* – and one day, in the British Museum, he wanted to look up T. S. Eliot's review of Joyce's novel, 'Ulysses, Order and Myth'. Failing to find it, he consulted a staff member, who in turn had no success, and put the matter in the hands of one of the senior officials of the Reading Room. This was Wilson's namesake, Angus Wilson, who like Philip Larkin had chosen librarianship as a day job to support his writing career. Just turning forty in 1953, he had already made a substantial name with the two volumes of waspish short stories that had slightly disappointed Kingsley Amis, and had recently published his first novel, *Hemlock and After*.

Helping Colin Wilson to track down the Eliot essay, Angus Wilson – who was homosexual, and may have been attracted by the intense-looking young man with floppy dark hair and horn-rimmed glasses – asked what he was writing, 'and when I told him it was a novel, he offered to read it. Christmas [1954] was only a few weeks away, and I rushed to complete the first part, so Angus could read it over the holiday. I handed it to him just before he left.'

By this time, the winter weather had made Wilson pack up his sleeping bag and rent a room in New Cross, supporting himself by labouring at a local laundry. But the work was exhausting, and ate into his library hours, 'and when my journal was stolen out of my pocket one day, I gave in my notice'. Next, he took a job as a washer-up for a coffee-house in the Haymarket. 'I worked every evening, from half past five until midnight, so I could spend my days in the Reading Room.'

As good as his word, Angus Wilson read the opening section of *Ritual in the Dark* over Christmas, and when the British Museum reopened at the beginning of January 1955 he was encouraging to Colin – 'He told me to go ahead and finish it, and then he would show it to his publisher.' But Colin had now diverted himself on to his book about the Outsider in literature, and decided to finish this first.

Angus Wilson genuinely liked his namesake, but later caricatured him cruelly as the pretentious young autodidact 'Huggett' in the title story in his 1957 collection, *A Bit Off the Map*. It tells how Kennie, a young psychopath, drifts into the group of Huggett's disciples (mod-elled, of course, on Holroyd and Hopkins). 'Huggett's a genius . . . a sort of philosopher and a mystic too,' says the hero-worshipping Kennie. 'Huggett's writing a book that's to go a long way for finding out the Truth . . . it's not only religion he's taking in but philosophy. So he works in this shipping office, but he has poems published and he's got all these followers – The Crowd they're called.'

They meet at an Italian coffee-bar, standing out from the regular clientele there, who wear jeans and listen to the skiffle group playing in the corner. The men of The Crowd, who do almost all the talking, are dressed in 'tired suits . . . stained flannels and grubby corduroys', the women, who say next to nothing and seem to be listening devotedly to the men, in 'jumpers and skirts . . . pathetically dim brooches and ear-rings'.

They treat Kennie as 'our twenty-one-year-old Teddy boy', and he has ambitions to be a star in the coffee-bar culture: 'I could sing, if only I could stop smoking. There's Elvis Presley's got all these cars and Tommy Steele started just in a skiffle group like in one of the coffee-bars that I spend most time in. (You have to learn to make one coffee last.)'*

All of the men in The Crowd are writing 'plays and novels and stories' whose characters have 'strange-sounding surnames like Gorfitt, Sugden, Burlick and Rawston' (a sharp bit of observation: the hero of Colin Wilson's *Ritual in the Dark* is called Sorme, and other characters in the book include Callet, Gowdie, Vannet, and Glasp; Bill Hopkins's *The Divine and the Decay* has a central character named Plowart, and includes people called Buffonet, Lumas and Stollet).

Kennie describes what Angus Wilson evidently perceived as the Fascist inclinations of his namesake's gang:

'We've got to breed a new race with real Will Power. It's Will Power that'll get you to the top . . . Reg that's the next to Huggett . . . says . . . Shit in the face of humanity – if millions have to be liquidated what's it matter? Most people are never alive anyway but Huggett believes in Power and Leadership for the Regenerations [sic] of the World.'

---

* Tommy Steele, Britain's first home-grown rock'n'roll star, was spotted in his late teens singing skiffle – a cheery British version of American folk-blues, played largely on home-made instruments – in a trio which also included the future writer of musicals Lionel Bart. Steele (whose real surname was Hicks) was propelled into the Top Twenty during 1956 with 'Rock with the Cavemen', co-written by Bart.

Kennie takes this a little too literally, for at the end of the story he murders a half-crazy old man.

* *

One day in the spring of 1955, while he was writing *The Outsider*, Colin Wilson took his girlfriend Joy down to see Canterbury Cathedral. 'We wandered into a secondhand shop and I came across a book by Victor Gollancz called *A Year of Grace*, which was a religious anthology.'

In 1943, eleven years before publishing *Lucky Jim*, Gollancz had had a breakdown, largely brought on by guilt over an extra-marital affair – one of his symptoms was the belief that his penis was retracting into his body. Recovering, he turned to religion (a personal fusion of Judaism, in which he had been brought up, with aspects of Christianity), and in 1950 published the anthology of spiritual writings which Wilson stumbled across.

Though he did not share Gollancz's religious beliefs, Wilson sensed an affinity. 'I decided to type out the first chapter of *The Outsider*, and to send it to Gollancz, together with an outline of the rest of the book. To my delight and astonishment, he wrote back an encouraging letter, saying he liked it, and would be glad to read it when it was finished.'

They eventually met for lunch. Wilson describes Gollancz as 'a large man with a bald head, bushy eyebrows and a booming voice. The first question he asked me was how I had succeeded in reading so much; I told him that I'd had nothing else to do since I was about thirteen.'

Wilson's completed typescript was accepted by Gollancz in the autumn of 1955, its author receiving an advance of £75. At this stage the book was titled 'The Pain Threshold'; it was one of Gollancz's staff, Jon Evans, who came up with the clever idea of borrowing – indeed, plagiarizing – the title of the English translation of Albert Camus's 1942 novel *L'Etranger*. Gollancz also sent proofs to Edith Sitwell, who had turned out to be an unlikely champion of *Lucky Jim* (despite Jim Dixon's 'Edith Sitwell face'), and she duly responded with a declaration – emblazoned by Gollancz across the dust-jacket – that *The Outsider* was an 'astonishing' book and that Wilson would be 'a truly great writer'. Nevertheless Gollancz was taking a gamble in ordering a first printing of as many as five thousand copies.

* *

Wilson had now moved to Notting Hill, where he was sharing a battered house (24 Chepstow Villas) with Bill Hopkins and other like-minded males. Various girls drifted in and out of the beds, but – as Angus Wilson had spotted – were discouraged from participating in the intellectual ferment. Holroyd quotes Wilson on this: 'Women get in the way of a man's thinking, particularly so-called intelligent women with their bright chatter.'

The Outsider was due to be published at the end of May 1956. 'I'd already had some signs that it was likely to be successful,' recalls Wilson.

I'd been sent along to be interviewed by some nice journalist, and he immediately went for this whole business about sleeping on Hampstead Heath . . . I spent an evening at his flat talking into his tape recorder – which struck me as a fabulous device – and listening to a record of the latest hit show, *My Fair Lady*.*

Gollancz had persuaded the *Evening News* to carry a feature on Wilson on the Saturday before publication, 26 May. It was headlined 'A Major Writer – and He's 24', and its author predicted that *The Outsider* 'will shock the arid little academic philosophers a good deal, and one or two of the more fashionable critical mandarins may wince at his coming'. In fact the chief of those mandarins, Cyril Connolly,† did quite the opposite, the very next day.

On the Sunday morning (Wilson remembers) he and Joy 'got up at about eight o'clock, hurried down to the corner and bought the two leading Sunday posh newspapers, the *Sunday Times* and the *Observer*, and both turned out to have rave reviews of *The Outsider*. One by

---

* Grundig portable tape recorders became available in the shops during the mid-1950s. The original Broadway cast album of *My Fair Lady* reached Britain during 1956, ahead of the show's London opening, and was one of the first LP records (which were replacing 78 rpm discs) to become a bestseller.

† Who himself coined the term 'mandarin' in the literary sense in his book *Enemies of Promise*: 'I shall christen this style the Mandarin, since it is beloved by literary pundits, by those who would make the written word as unlike as possible to the spoken one.'

Cyril Connolly and the other by Philip Toynbee, both the major reviewers of those papers.'

Connolly's piece began:

I feel a quickening of interest in this extraordinary book because I suggested *The Outsider* as the English title of M. Camus's *L'Etranger*,* on which Mr Wilson extensively draws. He is a young man of twenty-four who has produced one of the most remarkable first books I have read for a long time, a blending of the philosophic approach with literary criticism . . .

His book is far from being an anthology or a collection of appreciations of favourite authors wired clumsily together round an uncertain theme, like an ill-made bouquet . . . He has read prodigiously and digested what he has read . . . His faults are . . . a succession of minor inaccuracies in quotations and titles,† a general gracelessness and a hurried pontificating manner inclined to repetitions . . .

Referring to a passage in which Wilson had mentioned typing the book, Connolly concluded: 'You should keep an eye on Mr Wilson, and hope that his sanity, vitality and typewriter are spared.'

Philip Toynbee's review was headed 'UNLUCKY JIMS'. He praised *The Outsider* as lavishly as Connolly:

It is an exhaustive and luminously intelligent study of a representative theme of our time – and what makes the book truly astounding is that its alarmingly well-read author is only twenty-four years old. I know that such extraneous information ought not to affect one's judgement, but . . . it is pointless to deny that this fact has coloured my reading of this remarkable book. Who is Colin Wilson? How did he have *the time*? Is he an outsider himself?

* Connolly also wrote the introduction to the English translation, in which he interpreted Camus's bleak novel and its hero in a strikingly positive light: 'Mersault . . . is sensual and well-meaning, profoundly in love with life . . . He lives without anxiety in a continuous present . . .'
† A correspondent to *The Times Literary Supplement* (14 December 1956) said he had found '86 major errors . . . and 203 minor errors' in Wilson's quotations from other authors.

There are many hasty and superficial judgements ... But when all this is said *The Outsider* remains a most impressive study ...

Nearly fifty years on, the praise heaped on Wilson by Connolly and Toynbee (and other reviewers who followed them) is one of the puzzles of literary history, since a great many people find *The Outsider* to be exactly what Connolly said it was not, 'a collection of appreciations of favourite authors wired clumsily together round an uncertain theme, like an ill-made bouquet'.

Wilson admits that he found it difficult to write 'the links between the various sections' – in other words, what ought to have been the central, binding argument of the book. He recalls that it took 'two weeks' hard work to write the link between Wells and Sartre in the first chapter; it finally came to me in a flash of inspiration as I was hitch-hiking on the back of a lorry near Oxford'. The result of this 'inspiration' reads as follows: 'In his early novel, *La Nausée*, Sartre skilfully synthesises all the points we have already considered in connection with Wells ...' Whereupon Wilson launches into yet another of the plot-synopses or summaries, heavily larded with quotations, which characterize *The Outsider*.

At times, the book amounts to little more than an anthology, with Wilson's commentary rarely rising above the level of a first-year under-graduate essay; for example (to take three typical, consecutive links):

The reader cannot fail to be struck by the similarity between Camus's work and Franz Kafka's ...

Camus's *L'Etranger* reminds us of another modern writer who has dealt with the problem of freedom, Ernest Hemingway ...

At first sight, Hemingway's contribution to the Outsider would seem to be completely negative. Closer examination shows a great many positive qualities ...

This sort of writing leads Harry Ritchie, in his book on the Angry Young Men, to heap scorn on *The Outsider* – 'puerile pontification masquerading as analytical expertise . . . fatuous polemic which lack[s] the attractions of either an objective critique or a personal manifesto'. Ritchie complains of 'the absence of any coherent development in the argument – indeed, the absence of any argument whatsoever', and suggests that Wilson's sole aim in *The Outsider* is simply 'to show off how many books he has read'. Ken Tynan came to the same conclusion in a 1958 article:

As one ploughed through its inconsistencies, repetitions and flights of paranoid illogic (an experience rather like walking knee-deep in hot sand), all one could state with any certainty was that an 'outsider' was anyone whose books happened to have been on the author's recent library list.

Wilson himself admitted, not many months after the publication of *The Outsider*: 'I have no capacity whatever for abstract thought.'

So why were Connolly and Toynbee so enthusiastic? In his cultural history of the Fifties, Robert Hewison points out that *The Outsider* bears a certain resemblance to Connolly's own wartime journal-with-quasi-philosophical-aphorisms, *The Unquiet Grave* (1944). Connolly's biographer Jeremy Lewis offers another reason:

Abstract thought – as opposed to highly personalised musings on the human condition – was never one of Connolly's strong points . . . As A. J. Ayer remarked, 'What originally led reviewers like Connolly and Toynbee astray was their unfamiliarity with abstract ideas combined with middle-class guilt provoked by the work of an autodidact.'

Lewis points out that Connolly gave up philosophy at Oxford and switched to history because 'the whole area known as metaphysics was completely over my head, or rather outside it'. Toynbee, too, had read history at Oxford, and was no metaphysician, but a journeyman author and reviewer with a soft spot for religion (he moved gradually from agnosticism to Christian belief before his death in 1981).*

* After reading my account of *The Outsider*, Colin Wilson wrote to me: 'You are welcome to this view, if it is what you really think after reading the book. But if it is really just an anthology of quotations put together by a literary jackdaw, how do you explain the fact that it has never been out of print in England, America and Japan for

The two reviews had immediate effect. When *The Outsider* went on sale the following morning, Gollancz's first printing of 5,000 copies was sold in a few hours. So was a second printing three days later. Meanwhile at Wilson's Notting Hill hang-out

the phone was ringing nonstop. First my editor from Gollancz saying an awful lot of people wanted my phone number – well, I hadn't got a phone, but the people in the basement had, and they agreed to take calls, and they must have quickly regretted it, because all kinds of people rang up: *Life* magazine rang up wanting to do an interview, television rang up wanting me to appear on TV, and so on, all day long.

On publication day, the *Evening News* ran yet another feature about Wilson, 'The Inside Story of the Outsider', in which he talked about the nights he had slept rough on Hampstead Heath. By the end of the week the *Daily Mail* diary reported that he had been so busy giving interviews to the press that he had only had time to eat chocolate bars. The next day's *Sunday Times* announced that Wilson would be writing regularly for the paper, and the 'Pendennis' gossip column in the *Observer* carried a pair of portrait photographs by Jane Bown. One was of Wilson, and the accompanying paragraphs stated that 'after a hard week, in which [he] has been hotly pursued by publishers, press, and public relations manipulators, he goes home to Leicester, to see "how Leicester has taken it"'. The other was of a young playwright, whom the columnist described as

pleasant, unassuming, unselfconscious and sensitive . . . a bit surprised to find

---

forty-five years, and that it was translated into at least thirty languages (the most recent being Chinese)? How come nobody has rumbled me before this?' He has also supplied me with a brief summary of his intention in the book: 'The existentialism of Sartre, Camus, Heidegger, *et al.*, ends in gloom and pessimism. In *The Outsider* I ask: "Is this inevitable, or is there a flaw in their logic?" Both in *The Outsider* and subsequent work, I set out to show that THE PESSIMISM IS UNNECESSARY – indeed, a kind of schoolboy howler – and that if you take into account mystics like Ramakrishna and Blake, you end up with quite different conclusions.'

Whatever one's view of *The Outsider*, it can certainly claim to be the first popular book to have made many British readers aware of such European writers as Hesse, Rilke and Sartre.

himself regarded as a critic of society or as a reflector of the attitudes to society of his generation ... 'What moves me is people,' he says. 'I wish people understood each other better, had more care for each other, more concern.'

This was John Osborne, whose *Look Back in Anger* had opened at the Royal Court three weeks before publication of *The Outsider*. 'I went to see it,' writes Colin Wilson, 'and hated it – it seemed to be self-pitying verbiage.'

10

Man in a Rage

After his brief taste of being a performed playwright, the young
Osborne had continued to scrape a living in the lowest, most eccentric
echelons of professional theatre. During 1950 – shortly after his twentieth birthday – he had answered an advertisement for actors inserted
in the *Stage* by the Saga Repertory Company, Ilfracombe. It could pay
no salary, but offered a share of the takings. Arriving in Devon, he
found himself in the company of some young performers straight out
of drama school, who had been rounded up by a gay former wartime
airman called Anthony Creighton. 'Anthony . . . had toured extensively in an RAF drag show directed by Terence Rattigan . . . He
showed me a photograph of himself with Rattigan [who], dressed in a
tutu, had sung his own show-stopper, "I'm just about the oldest fairy
in the business."'

The Saga company scraped a living in the West Country, then
moved to Hayling Island Holiday Camp, where the campers provided
a 'literally captive audience'. Osborne persuaded Creighton to let him
play Hamlet, and cut the running time to two hours by removing most
of the text except his own lines – 'I just went through it like a butcher's
knife.' His mother, Nellie Beatrice, came to see the final performance,
and gave away the plot to her neighbour: 'I've seen it before. He dies
in the end.'

Then it was back to the West Country, and an acting job with a
little company in Bridgwater. His first appearance was in a comedy
called *My Wife's Family*. 'I had naturally been cast as the lovely
boy who opens the play being discovered with his arms round the
housemaid and kissing her.' This actress was a local girl called Pamela
Lane, who had trained at RADA. After a few months she and Osborne

were married – in another town, so that Pamela's parents should not know about it. However, the vicar tipped them off. Too late for the ceremony, Pamela's father came to the theatre,

more weary than angry, insisting that Pamela and I should have lunch with them at whatever hostelry catered for the town's Masons and Rotarians. We had pilchard salad and light ale in almost complete silence apart from an occasional wracking sob from the mottle-necked Mrs Lane. In the afternoon, we had a matinée and after the evening performance I saw Pamela back home. To my relief, I was not invited in.

He and Pamela fled from Bridgwater to London, where they lodged with Anthony Creighton. In the intervals of scraping a living with various low-grade theatre companies, Osborne wrote another play, inspired by the theology of Dante and heavily indebted to T. S. Eliot's verse dramas. Pamela read it, and declared it 'dull and boring'. She became pregnant, but managed to abort by taking pills and gin. Some while later, away from home and working in repertory at Derby, she began an affair with a dentist, and the marriage to Osborne petered out.

Anthony Creighton, meanwhile, had been doing various non-theatrical jobs. One was as a night-time telephone exchange operator – 'something of a sinecure for unemployed homosexuals,' writes Osborne sardonically – and another at a firm of debt collectors in Oxford Street. Two middle-aged women at the company had taken a fancy to him, and this gave him the idea for a play.* Osborne supplied the title, *Epitaph for George Dillon*, and they wrote it together in less than three weeks. Creighton undertook what Osborne calls 'the more tedious playmaking passages', while he himself concentrated on the big verbal set-pieces – such as Dillon, a young would-be actor and playwright (largely a self-portrait by Osborne), mocking the middle-aged couple who have given him free board and lodging because the wife is besotted with him:

---

* He and Osborne had already collaborated on a play about the McCarthy trials in the USA, which was never performed.

Look at that wedding group. (*Points to it.*) Look at it! It's like a million other grisly groups – all tinted in unbelievable pastels; round-shouldered girls with crinkled-up hair, open mouths, and bad teeth. The bridegroom looks as gormless as he's feeling lecherous, and the bride – the bride's looking as though she's just been thrown out of an orgy at a Druids' reunion. Mr and Mrs Elliot at their wedding. It stands there like a comic monument to the macabre farce that has gone on between them in this house ever since that greatest day in a girl's life thirty-five years ago.

Osborne admits that the collaboration with Creighton was a fairly slapdash affair. Although *Epitaph for George Dillon* crackles into life whenever its eponymous hero goes into a rant, its actual theme is ill-focused, so that we never know whether the authors see Dillon as an exploiting sponger or a thwarted genius or both. Creighton and Osborne sent it out to all the leading agents and managements, but it was invariably returned, usually without comment.

This was towards the end of 1954. On 4 May 1955 Osborne noted in his pocket diary: 'Began writing *Look Back in Anger.*'

* *

'I was working in an absolute vacuum,' he recalled. 'It was simply something I wrote for myself, I suppose. I don't really think I seriously thought that anyone would put it on.' He wrote Act One in three days, then landed a one-week acting job in Morecambe, where he rented a deckchair on the pier and continued writing in the May sunshine. Some years later, a critic of the play mistakenly alleged that it had originally been titled *On the Pier at Morecambe*. In fact there were a number of working titles, written – and crossed out – on the front page of the handwritten first draft:

BARGAIN FROM STRENGTH

CLOSE THE CAGE BEHIND YOU

MY BLOOD IS A MILE HIGH

MAN IN A RAGE

ANGRY MAN

FAREWELL TO ANGER

1. *The young Kingsley Amis. 'For the first time,' wrote Philip Larkin, 'I felt myself in the presence of a talent greater than my own.'*

2. *Philip Larkin in his role as librarian: 'I spend most of my time handing out tripey novels to morons.'*

3. *The Amis family at Swansea in 1956; Martin is the younger of the two boys.*

4. John Osborne, who emerged from 'a childhood of Dickensian richness and oddness'.

5. John Wain. His first novel, Hurry On Down, *was described by Kingsley Amis as 'all right in a way, but not funny enough'.*

6 & 7. Two characteristic images of the Fifties: working-men's food (described by John Wain as 'corned-beef rissoles, a spoonful of greens boiled to rags and tasting of soda, and perhaps a chunk of waxy ice-cream to follow') . . .

. . . and one of the skiffle groups that could be found playing in the new Italian-style coffee bars.

8. Colin Wilson in his sleeping-bag on Hampstead Heath – 'I decided to try to save rent.'

9. (a) Bill Hopkins and (b) Stewart Holroyd, acolytes of Colin Wilson. "Religious Existentialists", we called ourselves. "Spiritual Fascists", we were called by our critics.'

10. *Colin Wilson and Joy Stewart in their London bedsitter.*
'*A Major Writer – and He's 24,*' *trumpeted Fleet Street.*

11. *A cartoon by Cecil Keeling on the front of* Twentieth Century
*magazine (November 1957), showing the evolution of the literary
man through three generations of writers; the youngest wears the
Colin Wilson uniform.*

12. Kenneth Haig (left) as Jimmy Porter, and Alan Bates as Cliff, having his trousers ironed by Mary Ure as Alison in the Royal Court production of Look Back in Anger.

13. Colin Wilson (right) *doing a Jimmy Porter.*

14. The Daily Mail's *Flook* (below) *becomes an AYM.*

15. *Sir Laurence Olivier as Archie Rice in* The Entertainer, *John Osborne's response to the Suez crisis.*

16. *The young John Braine. His agent Paul Scott 'obtained for me a BBC audition which to my surprise resulted in my being asked to make two broadcasts'.*

17. *John Braine trying to look like Joe Lampton in* Room at the Top.

18. Doris Lessing (above), *the only female contributor to Declaration – 'This is how I became an Angry Young Man.'*

19. John Osborne and Mary Ure protesting about the Bomb in 1959.

20. *John Braine buys a new house in stockbroker country, with a car to match. It was handy for the weekly London meetings of the Fascist Beast Luncheon Group.*

21. *Kingsley Amis in 1986 – one of 'England's Angry Old Men'.*

Returning to London, he finished it in less than three weeks from his starting date, and immediately began sending out copies. Kitty Black, principal play-reader for one of the leading agencies, Curtis Brown, returned it with a not totally discouraging comment: 'I feel like the head-mistress of a large school in which I have to tell its most promising pupil that he must think again.' Pat Desmond, who had put on Osborne's first attempt at a play, wrote that he could make nothing of the new script. However, the act of writing *Look Back in Anger* had left Osborne in a 'happy state of grace', and he spent the summer painting an old Rhine barge, tied up at Chiswick, on which he and Anthony Creighton were now living. 'Something, I felt, was going to turn up.'

It did, in the form of a man in a rowing-boat. The *Stage* had been carrying an advertisement from something calling itself the English Stage Company, requesting new plays by new writers. Osborne had sent his in, expecting months of silence. Instead, 'I heard within days.' They would pay him £25 for an option, and their artistic director George Devine would like to meet Osborne. When he arrived at Chiswick, the tide was in, and he had to commandeer a small boat and row it himself in order to get on board *Egret*, the Osborne-Creighton floating home.

Osborne already knew George Devine by sight, having watched him act in a recent production of *Hedda Gabler*. But as yet he was aware neither of the years of struggle that Devine had been enduring to get a cherished project under way, nor that *Look Back in Anger* had been the answer to Devine's prayers.

Now in his mid-forties, Devine had been a prominent but quirky figure in the professional theatre since before the war. The son of a bank clerk, he had been educated at a public school owned by an eccentric uncle, and at Wadham College, Oxford. He became president of the OUDS, and persuaded John Gielgud to direct a *Romeo and Juliet* in which he and other undergraduates acted alongside Peggy Ashcroft as Juliet and Edith Evans as the Nurse. Leaving Oxford without a degree, he had teamed up with the French theatrical inno-vator Michel Saint-Denis, with whom he created the experimental London Theatre Studio. Their work was interrupted by the war, in which Devine fought in the army and was twice mentioned in dis-patches. In 1945 his collaboration with Saint-Denis was resumed at the Old Vic Centre, where they provided superb training for a generation of young actors who performed under Devine's direction in the Young Vic touring company.

Disgracefully, this entire enterprise was closed down in 1952 by the Old Vic governors, fearful that Saint-Denis might end up in charge of the National Theatre, which was soon to be inaugurated at the Old Vic – 'We cannot have it run by a Frenchman.' Devine then went freelance (occasionally appearing as an actor as well as directing), and transferred his energies to the foundation of a company which would be as radical as his Young Vic work, but would put the emphasis on new writing. After many vicissitudes the English Stage Company was constituted, and a lease taken on an off-West-End theatre, the Royal Court in Sloane Square, which had recently come back to life after a period of neglect.

Devine told a potential patron: 'I want to have a contemporary theatre. I have been all my life in the classical theatre. I want to try to make the theatre have a different position and have something to say and be part of the intellectual life of the community.' But where was he to find the scripts?

British theatre in the mid-1950s was truly in the doldrums. 'Shakespeare, Sheridan, Maugham and Wilde were keeping the new playwrights out,' writes Robert Hewison in his cultural history of the period, and Peter Ustinov, then chiefly known as a young playwright, complained: 'There is very little reason for the dramatist to be confident these days. Like Ibsen's Mrs Alving he is haunted before he begins to work by ghosts – ghosts of the past.'

The problem was largely caused by ownership. An organization known as 'The Group' had its claws on twenty-one of the West End theatres, with the feline Hugh 'Binkie' Beaumont of the H. M. Tennant management at the centre of the web. In February 1948 a Theatre Conference had been called to discuss the crisis, but Beaumont and his cronies smeared it with the allegation that the organizers were Communists. 'The theatres remained in the hands of the managers,' writes Hewison, 'and by the end of 1948 hopes that wartime enthusiasms could be built on had evaporated.' T. C. Worsley, in his capacity as *New Statesman* drama critic, complained: 'The postwar theatre . . . is still addressing itself to the left-overs of the old audiences . . . Being naturally conservative, it relies on the conventions that succeeded in the immediate past.'

The dominant names among British playwrights were Terence Rattigan (*The Deep Blue Sea* was among his postwar hits, in 1952), T. S. Eliot (*The Cocktail Party* was premiered in 1950), and the Eliot imitator Christopher Fry, best known for *The Lady's Not for Burning* (1949). The mood of conservative nostalgia was reflected in two British musicals which arrived in the West End in 1954 and 1955 respectively, and remained for long runs: Julian Slade's tuneful but effete *Salad Days*, and Sandy Wilson's Twenties pastiche *The Boyfriend*, which John Osborne went to see while writing *Look Back in Anger*.

There was no shortage of would-be new playwrights; George Devine received more than 600 scripts in response to his *Stage* advertisement, but he complained that they were all awful – ' "phoney" drama – phoney "poetry"; phoney "theatrical situations"; turgid wallowings in the mud of the "poetic soul" '. All except *Look Back in Anger*.

It is much to the credit of the English Stage Company that somebody spotted Osborne's script among the slush-pile. Devine passed it to Lord Harewood, who was on the Company's board. 'Most train journeys,' recalls Harewood,

involved devouring a couple of scripts. An early example came from John Osborne . . . George was keen on it and I read it with mounting excitement on the way up to Harewood [his Yorkshire mansion] one evening. Dicky Buckle [the ballet and art critic Richard Buckle] was staying with us over the weekend and I told him we had had a script from an unknown playwright, brilliantly written and enormously exciting . . . He took it away and said next morning that he had found it a thrilling experience, but that we could never put such a thing on in the theatre. One could not insult an audience in this kind of way . . .

Other board members agreed that it was 'a very promising find', but 'a difficult play to swallow'. Nevertheless they gave approval to Devine buying an option from Osborne.

When Devine stepped out of his rowing-boat and climbed aboard the *Egret* that summer afternoon, Osborne found himself facing a man who looked more like a public-school housemaster than a leading figure in the theatrical avant-garde ('If I didn't have white hair and smoke a pipe, no one would listen to me,' Devine used to say). Osborne happened to be wearing a blue blazer and flannels, bought 'for all-purpose use in Home Counties comedies', and fervently wished he could 'go below and change my absurd costume into some Left-Bankish outfit, stale with pastis and Gauloises'.

He expected Devine to give him a 'quick merciless viva' on *Look Back in Anger*, followed by a 'merciful dismissal'. Instead, it was the state of British theatre that had Devine 'growling his irritation to the tides'. Osborne admitted that he had enjoyed Rattigan's *The Browning Version*, but back-pedalled hastily when Devine dismissed the entire Rattigan *œuvre* as 'homosexual plays masquerading as plays about straight men and women'. There was a similarly blunt dismissal of Christopher Fry's verse dramas – 'absolute shit'. Osborne found this 'a little breathtaking. I was only accustomed to this kind of throw-away vehemence from myself.'

Having dismissed the reigning monarchs of the West End, Devine turned to questioning Osborne about his own life, in and out of the theatre. 'It was strange to be examined in this encouraging manner.' Eventually Devine confirmed the £25 purchase of a year's option on *Look Back in Anger*, and a few days later invited Osborne to his Hammersmith house. There he introduced him to his associate director, a sexually ambiguous young man fresh from television called Tony Richardson, whose opening words to Osborne were: 'I think *Look Back in Anger* is the best play written since the war.'

* *

How had the twenty-five-year-old Osborne made the leap from the gauche, ill-patched-together *Epitaph for George Dillon* – not to mention his crude earlier efforts at play-writing – to a play which would be regarded as recording and reflecting the voice and experiences of a whole generation?

He himself confides, in his autobiography, that *Look Back in Anger* was partly sparked off by the absconding of his wife, Pamela Lane: 'Perhaps Jimmy Porter did owe a glancing debt, though not much, to my first wife.' He wrote it while still deluding himself that 'Pamela would come back', that she would return to him from her 'Jewish dentist in Derby':

I didn't feel liberated from Pamela. The prospect of divorce never entered my sometimes wild projections of the future . . . during those shocked, brooding months after we separated. Writing *Look Back in Anger* presented no purge or lasting comfort . . . [But] I had addressed myself to events in some way.

Jimmy Porter's wife Alison is not Pamela, nor are her parents Pamela's; Osborne emphasizes that 'Mr and Mrs Lane were much coarser characters than Alison's mother and father', though he admits that 'their tactics were similar'. But while conceding that the play's mood was conditioned by his personal life, he emphasizes that its implicit subject-matter was 'not confined to the hulk of my marriage'. It was a reaction to the sluggish and defeated character of the times he found himself living in.

'If one word applied to that postwar decade,' he writes of the Fifties,

it was inertia. Enthusiasm there was not, in the climate of fatigue . . . The country was tired, not merely from the sacrifice of two back-breaking wars but from the defeat and misery between them. The bits of red on the map were disappearing as the flags came down and the names we knew on mixed packets of postage stamps were erased. Like so much else, it all happened without people being very aware of it. The leaping hare of the Victorian imagination had begun to imitate the tortoise even before 1914, but in the summer of 1955 it was still easy enough to identify what we regarded as a permanent Establishment. The continued acceptance of hanging, the prosecution of homosexuals, and censorship in film and theatre made life easy for the liberal conscience. The Conservative Party could still be stigmatized as figures of fun on their grouse moors; Etonians dominated the Cabinet.

This might lead one to suppose that *Look Back in Anger* is a left-wing play, a protest against the unloosening grip of the Conservatives, and against upper- and middle-class nostalgia for the great days of the now fast-disintegrating British Empire. It is nothing of the sort.

This is how Osborne describes his hero in the opening stage direction:

He is a disconcerting mixture of sincerity and cheerful malice, of tenderness and freebooting cruelty, restless, importunate, full of pride, a combination which alienates the sensitive and insensitive alike. Blistering honesty, or apparent honesty, like his, makes few friends. To many he may seem sensitive to the point of vulgarity. To others, he is simply a loudmouth. To be as vehement as he is is to be almost noncommittal.

Jimmy's captive audience consist of his wife Alison, who spends most of Act One at the ironing board, and his friend Cliff, who helps him run a sweet-stall in the local market. Jimmy teasingly brands them both as dolts – Alison 'hasn't had a thought for years', and Cliff is an 'ignorant . . . Welsh ruffian' – and constantly demands that they make him cups of tea. When he is not abusing everyone verbally, he slips into mock music-hall routines, or plays jazz on the trumpet. 'Anyone who doesn't like real jazz,' he asserts, 'hasn't any feeling either for music or people.' Alison mentions that he used to run a band. (Colin Wilson was photographed playing jazz trumpet as part of the publicity for *The Outsider* – he owned a trumpet, and played along to records in the hope of sounding like Bix Beiderbecke – and one of the reviewers of *Look Back in Anger* described Jimmy's music as 'all that "in the movement" trumpet playing'.)

Alison comes from a conservative family, and when Cliff reads out a news story from the Sunday papers about the Bishop of Bromley issuing an 'appeal to all Christians to do all they can to assist in the manufacture of the H-Bomb', Jimmy's comment to her is: 'You don't suppose your father could have written it, do you? . . . Sounds rather like Daddy, don't you think? . . . Is the Bishop of Bromley his nom de plume . . . ?'

Jimmy's anger is initially directed at the boredom of a rainy Sunday evening in a Midlands town:*

God, how I hate Sundays! It's always so depressing, always the same . . . Reading the papers, drinking tea, ironing. A few more hours, and another week gone. Our youth is slipping away . . . Oh heavens, how I long for a little ordinary human enthusiasm . . . Why don't we have a little game? Let's

* Osborne said in 1982: 'I've always thought . . . the provinces [is] where real life happens . . . It's no accident that one of our greatest novelists, like Jane Austen, or indeed the Brontë sisters, lived in the provinces . . . I find no pleasure in London at all now.'

pretend that we're human beings, and that we're actually alive . . . Oh, brother, it's such a long time since I was with anyone who got enthusiastic about anything . . . Nobody thinks, nobody cares. No beliefs, no convictions and no enthusiasm. Just another Sunday evening.

He complains that the two 'posh' Sunday papers* always offer the same pretentious cultural commentaries: 'Even the book reviews seem to be the same as last week's. Different books – same reviews . . . I've just read three whole columns on the English Novel. Half of it's in French.' He grumbles of an article by J. B. Priestley that it, too, might have been written by Alison's father: 'He's like Daddy – still casting well-fed glances back to the Edwardian twilight from his comfortable, disenfranchised wilderness.' But he has some sympathy for the breed:

I hate to admit it, but I think I can understand how her Daddy must have felt when he came back from India, after all those years away. The old Edwardian brigade do make their brief little world look pretty tempting. All home-made cakes and croquet, bright ideas, bright uniforms . . . Phoney . . . Still, even I regret it somehow, phoney or not . . . I must say it's pretty dreary living in the American Age . . . Perhaps all our children will be Americans.

Alison's brother Nigel is a Conservative MP; Jimmy mocks not just his politics but his lack of vigour:

The Platitude from Outer Space – that's brother Nigel . . . But somewhere at the back of that mind is the vague knowledge that he and his pals have been plundering and fooling everybody for generations . . . He's a patriot and an Englishman, and he doesn't like the idea that he may have been selling out his countrymen all these years, so what does he do? . . . Seeks sanctuary in his own stupidity.

Later, we learn that Jimmy's father died as a result of fighting Fascism in the Spanish Civil War, and that Jimmy and a friend 'went

---

* The *Observer* and the *Sunday Times*; possibly not named for fear of offending their drama critics.

to some of Nigel's political meetings' with 'bunches of their Poplar cronies', and 'broke them up'. Alison describes Jimmy as having 'declared war on . . . sections of society'. Yet some of his attitudes are far from left-wing.

True, he has chosen – despite being a graduate of a provincial university – to do a working-class job (running the market stall). Indeed he claims to be working class himself, but Cliff remarks that 'some of his mother's relatives are pretty posh'. Moreover, while some of his attacks on Alison imply a left-wing stance ('Nigel and Alison,' he mocks, 'sycophantic, phlegmatic and pusillanimous'), they are underpinned by a misogyny which today would be labelled politically incorrect.

'Have you ever noticed how noisy women are?' he sneers – quite unjustly, since Alison's usual response to his jibes is to keep silent. Later, he seems to disclose a visceral fear of women, telling Alison's friend Helena:

You'll end up like one of those chocolate meringues my wife is so fond of. My wife . . . sweet and sticky on the outside, and sink your teeth in it, (*savouring every word*) inside, all white, messy and disgusting.

And when, in the play's most often quoted passage, he attacks the flabbiness of the Fifties, and the absence of idealism, he does so in the context of another misogynist outburst:

Why, why, why, why do we let these women bleed us to death? Have you ever had a letter, and on it is franked 'Please Give Your Blood Generously'? Well, the Postmaster General does that on behalf of all the women of the world. I suppose people of our generation aren't able to die for good causes any longer. We had all that done for us, in the Thirties and the Forties, when we were still kids. (*In his familiar, semi-serious mood.*) There aren't any good, brave causes left. If the big bang does come, and we all get killed off, it won't be in aid of the old-fashioned, grand design. It'll just be for the Brave New nothing-very-much-thank-you. About as pointless and inglorious as stepping in front of a bus. No, there's nothing left for it, me boy, but to let yourself be butchered by the women.

Left alone with Alison, Jimmy tries to justify his behaviour by claiming that his aggression is provoked by love:

There's hardly a moment when I'm not – watching and wanting you. I've got to hit out somehow. Nearly four years of being in the same room with you, night and day, and I still can't stop my sweat breaking out when I see you doing – something as ordinary as leaning over an ironing board.

Alison accepts this unquestioningly, kisses him, agrees to go to bed with him, and lets him initiate the private childish game of 'squirrels and bears' which evidently sustains the marriage

Alison, in other words, is a male dream of the ideal wife: tireless domestically (slaving at the ironing board), sexually compliant, and passive in the face of insults. Indeed, as several critics have remarked, she scarcely exists as an individual – she (and Helena) are just shadows of Jimmy, which is why both women are seen wearing one of his shirts.* And in his book on Osborne's plays, Ronald Hayman shrewdly points out that 'neither of [Jimmy's] relationships with the two girls is made anything like so warm or so real as [his] relationship with Cliff' – as Hayman puts it, there is a 'rough-and-tumble tenderness' in the verbal and physical horseplay between the two men. Kenneth Tynan goes further in a 1958 article: 'Jimmy has a pathological pull towards bisexuality.' Cliff superficially appears to be attracted to Alison, but his real love (says Tynan) is for Jimmy, and vice versa. (In his memoirs, Osborne remarks that he and Anthony Creighton, with whom he was living when he wrote the play, were frequently assumed to be lovers. Creighton has claimed that he and Osborne had a physical relationship, and Osborne's letters to him are sufficiently affectionate for this to be true.†)

Alison confides in Cliff that she is pregnant; but before she can give Jimmy this news he lets fly with another extraordinary attack on her:

---

* Mary McCarthy points this out in John Russell Taylor (ed.), *Look Back in Anger: a Casebook* (Macmillan, 1968).
† 'I love you,' Osborne wrote to Creighton on one occasion, 'inadequately for your needs and almost without physical passion, but my passion is far stronger than they (the world) could ever know.'

If only something – something would happen to you, and wake you out of your beauty sleep. (*Coming in close to her*.) If you could have a child, and it would die . . . If only I could watch you face that. I wonder if you might even become a recognizable human being yourself. But I doubt it.

It is at this point that Helena, an upper-middle-class actress, joins the ménage. 'That bitch' is Jimmy's initial reaction, and indeed she initially conforms to his stereotype of her, sending Alison's father a telegram telling him to come and rescue Alison from Jimmy. Yet once again Osborne frustrates the political expectations he has set up.

When 'Daddy' (Colonel Redfern, recently returned from a lifetime of service in India) actually arrives, he proves to be essentially in sympathy with Jimmy (the two of them never meet on stage). 'I can't help feeling that he must have had a certain amount of right on his side,' the Colonel tells Alison. 'Your mother and I weren't entirely free from blame' (he means in their hostile reaction to the marriage). Indeed Alison herself suggests to her father that he, with his nostalgia for the old social order, and Jimmy, with his rage at the stagnation of Fifties society, have something in common: 'You're hurt because everything is changed. Jimmy is hurt because everything is the same.' Again, our view of Jimmy as a left-wing rebel is subverted.

Having packed Alison off home, Helena (too) changes political tack, and throws herself at Jimmy, becoming his mistress (she also does Jimmy's ironing, just like Alison). Equally improbably, she makes a graceful departure when Alison, who has had a miscarriage, returns to her husband. One can see here how the writing of *Look Back in Anger* gave solace to the cuckolded Osborne, who not only imagines the return of Pamela but awards himself a socially superior mistress during her absence.

The play also has another layer of personal meaning for its author. Jimmy's invective reaches its height when he turns his rage on Alison's mother (whom we never meet):

Mummy may look over-fed and a bit flabby on the outside, but don't let that well-bred guzzler fool you . . . She's as rough as a night in a Bombay brothel, and as tough as a matelot's arm . . . She's an old bitch, and should be dead!

... My God, those worms will need a good dose of salts the day they get through her!

Strikingly, in his memoirs Osborne follows his account of writing the play with a diatribe against his own mother, Nellie Beatrice. 'So much malice directed at innocence,' it begins. 'Those eyes which missed nothing and understood nothing.' Yet she comes over in the autobiography as essentially comic. Why was Osborne in such a sustained rage with her?

In the play, Jimmy puts much of his own anger down to the loss of his father, and his mother's emotional coldness during this tragedy:

For twelve months, I watched my father dying – when I was ten years old ... My mother looked after him without complaining, and that was about all. Perhaps she pitied him. I suppose she was capable of that ... But *I* was the only one who cared! ... Every time I sat on the edge of his bed, to listen to him talking or reading to me, I had to fight back my tears. At the end of twelve months, I was a veteran ... All that that feverish failure of a man had to listen to was a small, frightened boy ... You see, I learnt at an early age what it was to be angry – angry and helpless.

The published text of *Look Back in Anger* has the dedication: 'For my father'.

As for being an up-to-the-minute young person, an archetypal youth of the Fifties, Jimmy (at twenty-five, Osborne's own age) is already tarnished with middle-aged disillusionment. Indeed, Helena points out to Alison, in the closing minutes of the play, that he is essentially an old-fashioned figure:

I have discovered what is wrong with Jimmy. It's very simple really. He was born out of his time ... There's no place for people like that any longer – in sex, or politics, or anything. That's why he's so futile. Sometimes, when I listen to him, I feel he thinks he's still in the middle of the French Revolution. And that's where he ought to be ... He'll never do anything, and he'll never amount to anything.

Alison responds: 'I suppose he's what you'd call an Eminent Victorian.'

There is certainly nothing theatrically innovative about Jimmy's rhetoric; it recalls such Shavian loudmouths as Henry Higgins in *Pygmalion* (another misogynist). And arguably the overall model for the play is a good deal older even than Shaw. Mary McCarthy writes that it has 'a great deal in common with *Hamlet*', and goes on:

> Cliff . . . is Jimmy Porter's Horatio, who sticks to him without understanding all the fine points of Jimmy's philosophy; and the scenes Jimmy makes with Alison have the same candid brutality that Hamlet showed to Ophelia . . . [Alison's] brother Nigel is Laertes and [her] mother is cast in the role of Polonius.

McCarthy was unaware that, shortly before writing *Look Back in Anger*, Osborne had played Hamlet, cutting out most of the other characters' lines. *Look Back in Anger* repeats that exercise in modern dress.

11

Wolverhampton Hamlet

As well as accepting *Look Back in Anger*, George Devine hired Osborne as an actor – though not in his own play. Tony Richardson, who was directing *Look Back*, would not allow him to attend rehearsals at first. When permission was eventually granted, Osborne was accosted by Mary Ure, the young Scottish actress playing Alison, who 'carped' at Jimmy Porter's lines about women being noisier than men. 'I tried to point out,' writes Osborne, 'that it was only the opinion of the character in the play, not mine. For once, I was dishonest in this respect.'

Continuing his search for new scripts, Devine became convinced that the country's best novelists should be persuaded to turn playwright. One of his board of management noted that they were hoping for 'plays by someone called Kingsley Amies and John Wayne'. What they got, to open the company's first Royal Court season on 2 April 1956, was *The Mulberry Bush* by the ubiquitous Angus Wilson. Wilson's biographer Margaret Drabble describes it as 'an attack on do-gooding liberalism, and ... not very modern ... The plot dangled family skeletons.' This was followed by the first British production of Arthur Miller's *The Crucible*. Meanwhile Devine's hopes for *Look Back in Anger* were not high; it was initially scheduled for comparatively few performances.

Meanwhile Osborne had run up against the company's part-time press officer, a dyspeptic individual named George Fearon, who had been imported from the Taw and Torridge Festival in Devon.* According to Osborne's recollection, Fearon invited him for a drink

---

* The creation of the English Stage Company had partly come about through some of its founders' participation in this festival.

in a pub, told him how much he disliked the play, and added: 'I suppose you're really – an angry young man.'

Whether or not this conversation took place, Fearon has been widely credited with the invention of this phrase – though it had already been used five years earlier as the title of a volume of memoirs by a middle-aged author named Leslie Paul.* Osborne claims not to have been impressed by Fearon's choice of words, although Fearon was only adding 'young' to one of the play's working titles.

*   *

The first night of *Look Back in Anger*, Tuesday, 8 May 1956, happened to be the anniversary of Osborne's father's birth. Many people have claimed to have been there, but the Royal Court Theatre was far from full, and Osborne found himself sitting in the sparsely populated dress circle. He got 'very drunk' during the two intervals, but remained alert enough to notice the English Stage Company's manager, Oscar Lewenstein, casting nervous glances around him all evening. Sure enough, the all-powerful theatrical impresario Binkie Beaumont was among those who left before the end, while Terence Rattigan was only persuaded to stay by T. C. Worsley, who was covering the play for the *New Statesman*. To another critic, John Barber of the *Daily Express*, Rattigan remarked that Osborne's aim seemed to be: 'Look, Ma, how unlike Terence Rattigan I'm being.' Barber quoted this in his review next morning, and Rattigan wrote to Devine to apologize: '. . . all I meant . . . was that I felt occasionally the author was being a little self-conscious about his "modernism"'.

Osborne woke next morning on his houseboat with a bad hangover, which was made worse by the reviews. 'This first play has passages of good violent writing, but its total gesture is inadequate,' declared *The Times* loftily, explaining: 'The hero regards himself, and clearly is regarded by the author, as the spokesman for the younger postwar generation which looks round at the world and finds nothing right with it.' This point was addressed by virtually all the critics. 'The

* Leslie Paul was a Christian apologist and co-founder of the Woodcraft Folk youth movement. Kenneth Tynan describes *Angry Young Man* as 'the story of a devout Left-Wing agitator who lost his faith in Russia during the 1930s and turned . . . to a vague sort of Christian humanism'.

author and the actors too did not persuade us wholly that they really "spoke for" a lost, maddened generation,' was Philip Hope-Wallace's judgement in the *Manchester Guardian*, while Milton Shulman in the *Evening Standard* asked what Jimmy was so angry about – 'What has turned him into this pugnacious bore other than the fact that he saw his father die?' John Barber answered this in his *Daily Express* review: 'He is young, frustrated, unhappy. In fact, he is like thousands of young Londoners today.' And T. C. Worsley's *New Statesman* review made a link with *Lucky Jim*, describing the play as 'set on the seamy side of the Kingsley Amis world'. Worsley also shrewdly spotted the Shakespearian link: 'The author has written all the soliloquies for his Wolverhampton Hamlet and virtually left out all the other characters and all the action.' But most critics remained puzzled and irritated by Jimmy – though they praised Kenneth Haigh and Mary Ure's performances as Jimmy and Alison, and Tony Richardson's production.

Richardson was at the Royal Court when a gloomy Osborne arrived. 'But what on earth did you *expect*?' he asked Osborne. 'You didn't expect them to *like* it, did you?' Devine was gloomier, but pointed out that there was a good review by Derek Granger in the *Financial Times*, which said that watching the play was almost as uncomfortable as watching one's friends having a row. Moreover Osborne could take heart in that nearly all the critics said that they expected much finer things from his next play. And George Fearon's phrase was catching on; Robert Tee in the *Daily Mirror* described *Look Back in Anger* as 'an angry play by an angry young author'.

Fearon himself was not pleased with the way things were going – he told Osborne there were virtually no bookings at the box-office. Osborne's mother, Nellie Beatrice, came to see the second performance, remarking reproachfully: 'The write-ups weren't very good, were they? I expect you're disappointed, poor kid.' Meanwhile, backstage, Osborne picked up a vague hope that the show might be 'saved by the Sundays'. On the Sunday morning, Osborne bought the two 'posh' papers, and what he read in them sent him scuttling round to Devine's house. 'George was grinning at me over his unlit pipe.'

The review by the middle-aged Harold Hobson, drama critic of the *Sunday Times*, was headed 'A NEW AUTHOR':

Mr John Osborne . . . is a writer who at present does not know what he is doing. He seems to think that he is crashing through the world with deadly right uppercuts, whereas all the time it is his unregarded left that is doing the damage. Though the blinkers still obscure his vision, he is a writer of outstanding promise, and the English Stage Company is to be congratulated on having discovered him.

There are really two plays in *Look Back in Anger*. One of them is ordinary and noisy, and Mr Osborne has written it with some wit but more prolixity; the other is sketched into the margin of the first, and consists of hardly any words at all, but is controlled by a fine and sympathetic imagination, and is superbly played, in long passages of pain and silence, by Miss Mary Ure.

The play that . . . Mr Osborne thinks he has written . . . is yet another of youth's accusations against the world . . . But the inexhaustible outpouring of vicious self-pity comes near to wearying the audience's patience . . . There are episodes of whimsy that might have made Barrie blush . . .

Alison . . . is a subsidiary . . . But it is her endurance, her futile endeavour to escape, and her final breakdown which are the truly moving part of the play . . .

This was not much better than the response of the other critics; but turning to the *Observer*, Osborne found something very different.

Kenneth Tynan, the illegitimate son of a businessman, had been easily the most prominent and flamboyant undergraduate at Oxford in the years immediately after the war. At the age of only twenty-seven, in 1954, he had been appointed the *Observer* drama critic. His review of *Look Back in Anger* was a response not just to the play, but also to what had already been written about it, and to the condition of British drama in general:

'They are scum,' was Mr Maugham's famous verdict on the class of State-aided university students to which Kingsley Amis's Lucky Jim belongs; and since Mr Maugham seldom says anything controversial or uncertain of wide acceptance, his opinion must clearly be that of many. Those who share it had better stay well away from John Osborne's *Look Back in Anger*, which is all scum and a mile wide.

His hero . . . has already been summed up in print as 'a young pup', and it is not hard to see why. What with his flair for introspection, his gift for ribald parody, his excruciating candour, his contempt for 'phoneyness', his weakness for soliloquy and his desperate conviction that the time is out of joint, Jimmy Porter is the completest young pup in our literature since Hamlet . . .

Is Jimmy's anger justified? Why doesn't he *do* something? These questions might be valid if the character had failed to come to life; in the presence of such evident and blazing vitality, I marvel at the pedantry that could ask them. Why don't Chekhov's people *do* something? . . .

There will be time enough to debate Mr Osborne's moral position when he has written a few more plays. In the present one he certainly goes off the deep end, but I cannot regard this as a vice in a theatre that seldom ventures more than a toe into the water.

Look Back in Anger presents postwar youth as it really is, with special emphasis on the non-U intelligentsia who live in bed-sitters* . . . To have done this at all would have been a signal achievement; to have done it in a first play is a minor miracle. All the qualities are there, qualities one had despaired of ever seeing on the stage – the drift towards anarchy, the instinctive leftishness, the automatic rejection of 'official' attitudes, the surrealist sense of humour . . . the casual promiscuity, the sense of lacking a crusade worth fighting . . .

The Porters of our time . . . are classless, and they are also leaderless. Mr Osborne is their first spokesman in the London theatre . . .

That the play needs changes I do not deny: it is twenty minutes too long, and not even Mr Haigh's bravura could blind me to the painful whimsy of the final reconciliation scene. I agree that *Look Back in Anger* is likely to remain a minority taste. What matters, however, is the size of the minority. I estimate it at 6,773,000, which is the number of people in this country between the ages of twenty and thirty. And this figure will doubtless be swelled by refugees from other age-groups who are curious to know precisely what the contemporary young pup is thinking and feeling. I doubt if I could love anyone who did not wish to see *Look Back in Anger*. It is the best young play of its decade.

---

* Tynan expanded on this in a 1958 article: 'The salient thing about Jimmy Porter was that we – the under thirty generation in Britain – recognized him on sight. We had met him; we had pub-crawled with him; we had shared bed-sitting rooms with him. For the first time, the theatre was speaking to us in our own language, on our own terms.'

12

Silly season

Tynan also worked as a script editor for Ealing Studios, and a day or two later he phoned Osborne to invite him to lunch to talk about film projects. He describes his first impressions in a 1958 article:

Osborne is a disconcerting, rather impenetrable person to meet: tall and slim, wearing his shoulders in a defensive bunch around his neck; gentle in manner, yet vocally harsh and cawing; sharp-toothed, yet a convinced vegetarian. He looks wan and driven, and is nervously prone to indulge in sudden, wolfish, silly-ass grins. Sartorially he is something of a peacock, and his sideburns add a sinister touch of the Apache. A dandy, if you like: but a dandy with a machine-gun.

Osborne also went to tea with an American producer at the Dorchester to discuss *Look Back in Anger*'s prospects for Broadway. Magazines interviewed him, and photographed him on the deck of his houseboat. And on 26 May 1956, two weeks after Tynan's review had appeared (and, as it happened, the day before *The Outsider* was reviewed by Connolly and Toynbee), *The Times* ran a rather nervous leader:

WRATH AT THE HELM

People who like to leave the theatre in an argumentative mood will go to the Royal Court Theatre to see Mr John Osborne's play . . . They will remember those reviews in which it has been put forward as an expression of opinion valid for the generation of those in their late twenties. They will see a thoroughly cross young man, caught into an emotional situation where crossness avails nothing. And they may well wonder whether the young men of today are really as embittered, as prompt to offence, as the hero of the play ... Are we ... to think that those who are now in their late twenties are likely to be known above all for their touchiness and their rage?

It does not look so to an older set. The young, in general, seem through the eyes of their parents to have become almost as pleasant to deal with as octogenarians ... Indeed, the young sometimes put on almost too serious a face. There is about the young man a suspicion of a whisker ... The youth of today visits prisons and reads Kierkegaard. Exceptionally, perhaps, the young people of Mr Osborne's play can be found, just as the heroes of Mr Kingsley Amis ring true in a limited setting. But it is likelier that the real tone of our age will be found much closer to that of a century ago. Already our didactic writers are getting back to Samuel Smiles; it is only a matter of time before the evil old men of the day flinch from the stare of some youthful Thomas Arnold.

The play seemed to have become a cause of national concern; yet it was still only doing moderate business at the Royal Court, and came and went for several short runs during late May and June. Osborne, who had begun an affair with Mary Ure (*Look Back*'s Alison), made a couple of appearances as an actor in other plays that Devine was putting on at the Royal Court; Kenneth Tynan was amused to spot him in Nigel Dennis's *Cards of Identity* 'wearing false, sabre teeth and a hairless dome'.

In terms of publicity, *Look Back* was overtaken in early June by *The Outsider*, when a second stream of reviewers hurried to endorse the praise heaped on Colin Wilson by the two Sunday mandarins. Journeyman critics in the *Daily Telegraph* and *New Statesman* hailed it as 'provocative, illuminating, adult', a 'really important' work; the *Listener* declared it to be 'the most remarkable book upon which the reviewer has ever had to pass judgement', and even V. S. Pritchett (in a radio programme) and Elizabeth Bowen (in the *Tatler*) agreed that it was 'brilliant'. In fact almost the only dissenting voice was to be found in the *Spectator*, where it was reviewed by Kingsley Amis.

His first complaint was that Wilson had failed to distinguish between the literary merits of the authors he had cannibalized, so that (for example) an inferior book by H. G. Wells or the diary of mad Nijinsky were placed along writers of the stature of Blake, Nietzsche, Sartre and Camus. Then (continued Amis) the Outsider, as defined by Wilson, 'is always a man'; moreover a certain type of man:

He will have a private income or a patron: the incidence of Outsiderism among builders' foremen or bookies' runners must be low. He is likely to be unmarried and without family ties. He has no strong affections, and his lack of ordinary warmth makes him divide the human race into himself on one side, plus the odd hero-figure or two, and 'the mob' on the other. He tends to amorality, feeling that a spot of murder or child-rape may come in handy as a means of asserting his Will, escaping from the prison of thought, etc., and he is totally devoid of humour. Now it is quite conceivable that chaps like that may really be 'society's spiritual dynamo', but I judge it unlikely.

He suggested that the Outsider would be best cured of his self-centred, adolescent-style *ennui* by turning to a Lucky Jim-style hedonism – 'ordering up another bottle, attending a jam session, or getting introduced to a young lady' – and ended his review: 'Legion of the Lost – DIS-*MISS*!'

Rather surprisingly, shortly after this Amis jibe at Wilson had appeared, both parties agreed to meet over lunch in a Leicester Square pub, at the invitation of Daniel Farson, freelance journalist and photographer, and a denizen of bohemian Soho and Fitzrovia. Farson had already been to Swansea to interview Amis for the *Evening Standard*, and it had proved to be an alcohol-fuelled occasion. 'He greeted me at the station barrier,' Farson wrote in the *Standard*,

and hurried me to the buffet where he had left half a drink (gin and French) and a friend (Dr Bartley), a colleague at the university . . . We lunched at a pub nearby [with] a bottle of red wine. After lunch we had two rounds of port and then walked to Dr Bartley's home with a bottle of whisky. 'Have a potion,' said Dr Bartley, advancing with the bottle.

'Thanks,' I said, 'but I'm not feeling any too well.' I had remembered with alarm that I had not asked Kingsley Amis a single question. 'My train leaves at five-thirty,' I added.

'Nonsense,' said Kingsley Amis, 'stay the night at my place.' Arriving at his home he decided to sleep. He led me to a small room with a sloping roof and pointed to the bed. 'Flannel sheets,' he said, and departed.

I woke with a start. It could have been hours later. Beside me in the dark stood an extremely attractive blonde. We looked at each other in surprise and she left quickly. All I need, I thought, is to set fire to the flannel sheets with a cigarette and I will be the complete Amis hero.

The blonde was Hilly. Farson had some idea that Amis belonged to a group of writers, but at this stage (early May 1956) he seemed very vague about it:

This hero is the pivot of 'The New Movement', the name given to postwar novels by John Wain, Iris Murdoch and Gwyn Thomas,* that all seem to bear the Amis touch.

'What does it feel like to be the founder of a movement?' I asked Amis as we ate under-cooked pork chops and frozen peas in the kitchen. Washing hung above us like bunting.

'I'm a bit resentful of the link,' he said. 'I hate the idea of being thought like John Wain.'

When they met again in London, with Colin Wilson, Amis told Farson he had not seen *Look Back in Anger*, and was surprised and unflattered when Farson told him it had been described as 'an Amis sort of play'. Farson had taken Wilson to a performance, and reported his reaction to Jimmy Porter:

'If I was in the same room with that insufferable young man,' Wilson muttered in the darkness, 'I'd give him a good clout. I'm sick of mixed-up kids.' Afterwards he said: 'He's a pseudo-Outsider; he doesn't possess the strength of mind to create anything. He says "What are we going to do?" and all he does is brew tea and read the papers.'

As to Wilson's attitude to Amis, he claimed not to have read his novels, but dismissed them on the basis of what his girlfriend Joy had said about them. Indeed Farson admitted that the Leicester Square lunch was 'surprisingly gloomy'; but he continued with his plan to

---

* Welsh novelist, short-story writer and playwright (1913–1981), who wrote about working-class life in the mining valleys.

introduce to each other those whom he was convinced were the members of the first generation of significant young British writers to have appeared since the war.

For his next step he invited Osborne and Mary Ure to a wild party at Wilson's Chepstow Villas hang-out in Notting Hill. This was no more of a success than the Wilson–Amis lunch. 'Mary Ure got very drunk,' recalls Wilson, 'and proceeded to tell me that John was the greatest playwright since Sheridan, and that *The Outsider* was merely a ragbag of quotations from other people's books. Being her host – and realizing that it was the brandy that was talking – I made no attempt to defend myself.'

* *

The first person to make public use of George Fearon's felicitous description of Osborne seems to have been a journalist called Thomas Wiseman, in the *Evening Standard*'s 'Show Talk' column on 7 July 1956, two months after the opening of *Look Back*:

ANGRY YOUNG MAN

Success has not made that angry young man, John Osborne, any less angry. Not yet, anyway.

Mr Osborne is the 26-year-old author of London's most controversial play, *Look Back in Anger*, which is a sort of rabbit-punch at present-day society.

It is a brilliant, vital piece of work. It is going to be filmed. And it is going to be produced on Broadway.

Mr Osborne was still lashing out with a sort of polite fury when I met him this week.

He said: 'Laurence Olivier came to see the play and loathed it. Rattigan saw it and detested it. Sir John Gielgud came – he didn't like it either. What can you expect? They live in a different world. But they came, that's the point.'

I sought this outspoken young man's views on the current favourites of the West End.

What did he think of Rattigan? 'About as much as Rattigan thinks of me. Not much. He has no passion, has he?'

And Peter Ustinov? 'Well, he makes me laugh. But it's all so superficial.'

And Noël Coward? 'He doesn't *care*, does he? He never *cared*.'

Was there anyone in the London theatre he admired or respected? 'Not really.'

A number of film companies have been fighting for Mr Osborne's services and this week he paid his first visit to a film studio. What was his verdict?

'Depressing. No wonder they make such bad films in Britain. They want me to clean up a number of scripts. But I won't do it. My time is too precious.'

Why were films so poor? 'I suppose because the industry is in the hands of illiterates.'

What has success meant so far to this young man with the harsh opinion of the world, who in the past has scraped a living from acting and the National Assistance Board?

He has earned £500 from *Look Back in Anger* and is about to be initiated into the mysteries of paying income tax, something he has never had occasion to do before. He is also contemplating buying a suit, which he has done before, once or twice.

I hope he goes on punching, though a good many of his punches go pretty wide of the mark. I hope he goes on punching even when he is swinging in my direction. Oh yes, he indicated that he did not think much of me either.

I, however, think highly of Mr Osborne's talent. I only hope he never stops being angry.

Osborne declares in his memoirs that he thought Fearon's phrase silly and unhelpful, yet he used it himself two days after the *Standard* article, while being interviewed by Malcolm Muggeridge on BBC television's *Panorama*. 'You see,' he told Muggeridge, 'if one recognizes problems and one states them, people say – oh, this is an angry young man.'

Daniel Farson picked up the phrase in a pair of articles he wrote for the *Daily Mail* a few days after Wiseman's piece had appeared in the *Standard*. 'The postwar generation has suddenly arrived,' he told readers of the *Daily Mail* on 12 July 1956. 'A number of remarkable young men have appeared on the scene. I have met them.' First on his list came Amis, whom he described (rather oddly) as 'the only literary movement since the war'; then Osborne, whose 'angry young man Jimmy Porter' typified 'the lack of any real belief' among his generation. Farson made a comparison between Jimmy and the character played by James Dean in *Rebel Without a Cause* – and then introduced a new name to his readers: 'The ultimate in James Deanery has now been achieved by an 18-year-old tailor named Michael Hastings. His first play, *Don't Destroy Me*, published in a magazine earlier this year, will start at the New Lindsey Theatre on July 25.'

Farson was paying the unknown teenage Hastings an enormous compliment by setting him alongside such established names as Amis and Osborne, but his attitude to the young tailor's apprentice was predominantly sneering:

He has not only dedicated his first play to Dean but created a character of such incoherence that delete a few lines and the part could be played by a mute. Sammy, nuzzling the walls in the tenement where his father drinks and his mother carries on an affair with a neighbour, speaks almost entirely in groans and moans.

In fact Hastings's play gives an accurate, unmelodramatic portrayal of the Brixton Jewish community in which he himself had grown up; but Farson, who had gone to the New Lindsey fringe theatre in Notting Hill to watch auditions for the role of Sammy, ended this first *Daily Mail* article with a groan: '"God help us," I thought, "if this is the postwar generation."'

In contrast, the second part of his *Mail* feature, printed the next day, ladled out praise to somebody who had already received plenty of it. 'I have just met my first genius,' the article began. 'His name is Colin Wilson.' Farson had been watching the genius at work: 'When he writes, he types rapidly without correction; at the end it looks as if a professional typist has done it, not a word has to be changed.' He was also charmed by Wilson's lifestyle: 'He lives simply in an untidy room in Bayswater, wears polo-necked sweaters, travels by bicycle, and cooks on a primus that has a tendency to explode.' Whereas Osborne and Hastings (and to some extent Amis) had left Farson depressed about the cultural outlook, he was 'strangely exhilarated' by Wilson, and forecast that the author of *The Outsider* would certainly be 'one of the names of the future'.

Farson's *Daily Mail* articles prompted a copycat feature by John Barber in the *Daily Express* on 26 July 1956, and it was the headline to this that first used Fearon's catch-phrase in the plural: 'TODAY'S ANGRY YOUNG MEN AND HOW THEY DIFFER FROM SHAW'. The centenary of George Bernard Shaw's birth fell on that day, and Barber claimed to find Shavian qualities in the work of 'four new young English writers'. His quartet was the same as Farson's – Amis, Osborne, Wilson and Hastings – and an additional peg for the piece was that Hastings's *Don't Destroy Me* had opened at the New Lindsey the previous evening. Unlike Farson, Barber admired it, describing it as 'a poetic portrait of a slum child's horror when he finds his stepmother is deceiving his father'. Describing Hastings as 'a gangling, beak-faced boy' who said he wanted to be a boxer rather than a writer, Barber summed up the quartet as 'four laughing, urgent, angry young men'.*

* *

Colin Wilson recalls the arrival of the new label: 'For a few weeks the newspapers seemed unable to decide whether to describe myself and Osborne as Outsiders or Angry Young Men, but finally settled on the latter as being more self-explanatory.' He claims to have found it all ridiculous:

We were supposed to be the voice of the younger generation, and since we arrived in midsummer – the 'silly season' when there is a lack of hard news – we found ourselves in the gossip columns every other day. Journalists would ring me up to ask: 'What do you think of the seams in ladies' stockings?' . . . It was all incredibly silly and irrelevant.

Yet he continued to give interviews to anyone who asked, posing in his sleeping bag on Hampstead Heath for a photographer for *Life*, and welcoming *Time* to 24 Chepstow Villas. 'He lives in a two-room London slum flat, overlooking a garden of weeds,' wrote *Time*'s reporter,

feeds on sausages, beer and chocolate biscuits, and sleeps on an inflatable green rubber mattress. Wilson is tall and thin, favors black-and-white turtle-neck sweaters, beaver-colored corduroy pants and brown leather sandals. His pale blue eyes stare through horn-rimmed glasses at neat rows of worn, secondhand books and a door covered with hieroglyphics and an Einstein formula.

---

* Hastings, who after this disappeared from journalists' lists of the Angry Young Men, has enjoyed a sporadically successful career as a playwright, his biggest achievement being *Tom and Viv*, about the marriage of T. S. Eliot and Vivienne Haigh-Wood, which was staged at the Royal Court in 1984 and afterwards filmed.

Harry Ritchie has pointed out that, until the press discovered Colin Wilson, 'there was no fixed image of young arty types, although they were beginning to be associated with the new espresso [coffee] bars'. A feature on youth fashions published two weeks before *The Outsider* claimed that a 'Bohemian' style of dressing was becoming popular among the young, but seemed very vague about it:

Francis was a Teddy boy. Now quite common people are Teddy boys, and Francis has become a pioneer of the Bohemian.

There are smart Bohemians and scruffy Bohemians. Scruffy Bohemians wear expensive sandals, tight green Harris tweed trousers, black roll-neck sweater and red shirt, casual jacket . . .

Francis spends his working life in a fantasy world. 'I think I'm the world's greatest jazz trumpeter . . .'

It would be interesting to trace the spread [of this image] from Sartre and existentialism, through drainpipe slacks in Saint-Germain-des-Prés cellar clubs, Humphrey Lyttelton and espresso bars to Francis and his kind.

Wilson provided a more defined image, as Ritchie explains:

Cecil Beaton photographed Wilson for his 1957 collection *The Face of the World*, and parodists and cartoonists latched on to the distinctive look with glee. Soon the horn-rimmed glasses, lank hair and inevitable polo-neck sweater were adorning caricatures of the celebrity philosopher. Wilson provided the essential components for a new literary type, as the cover illustration for the November 1957 issue of *Twentieth Century* demonstrates; three generations of writers are represented, the youngest by an author wearing the mandatory costume of Wilsonian spectacles and sweater and holding an (Amis-inspired) glass of beer.

He was offering a new literary image at a time when one was badly needed.

Writing in February 1956, before the appearance of *The Outsider*, the *Evening Standard*'s fashion correspondent Amanda Marshall complained that 'poets (who have all abandoned opium and debauchery) have a tendency to look like bank officials, and sometimes actually are,*

---

* T. S. Eliot had worked in a bank.

and women novelists are more likely to be university dons than figures of intrinsic glamour'. A year later, Marshall was complaining about the excessive sartorial influence of Colin Wilson:* 'The current beau ideal is distinctly ungroomed, either singing the blues to a very untender guitar or chattering about being an angry young outsider.' The *Sunday Times* columnist 'Atticus' summed up 1956 as the year of 'Rock'n'Roll. Pizza. Cigarillos – cigarette-sized cheroots. Tortoiseshell-tinted hair. *The Outsider.* Records of *My Fair Lady.* Angry young men . . . Skiffle groups.'

By October 1956, 20,000 copies of *The Outsider* had been bought in hardback, translation rights were already sold to five countries, and the American edition had been selected as a Book of the Month. Wilson's earnings were considerable, yet Stuart Holroyd recalls that, while he 'spent lavishly on expensive wines, malt whiskies and long-playing records', he 'cared little what he wore or ate or what his surroundings were like', and went on slumming it in Chepstow Villas. 'If I hadn't been settled with Joy,' Wilson himself writes, 'the greatest bonus would probably have been the sexual possibilities; but since I had no intention of getting rid of her, I had to put that temptation behind me. I admit that this was my keenest regret.'

John Osborne and Mary Ure moved into a tiny house she had bought in Woodfall Street, off the King's Road. He recalls that George Devine and Tony Richardson showed little enthusiasm for the 'Angry Young Man' label. However (he writes),

I can't pretend that, for me, the absurd spotlight and the feigned friendliness . . . of what would now be deadeningly described as the 'media' . . . were not invigorating . . . I gave interviews and wrote articles on crass subjects ('What's Wrong with Women Today'); I was offered ten times my weekly salary for 700 words which even I had the facility to turn out in an hour or so.

Nevertheless *Look Back in Anger* did not become a sell-out until a twenty-five-minute excerpt, introduced by Lord Harewood, was broadcast on BBC television on 16 October 1956. 'The response at

* Not just sartorial; Harry Ritchie records that an advertisement appeared in the *New Statesman* in which an 'Outsider, 24' offered other Outsiders a share of his caravan.

the box-office was immediate,' writes Osborne, and this is confirmed by Michael Halifax, stage director at the Royal Court:

The houses were appalling. Then, after the TV extract, all these people started arriving. People you never see in theatres. Young people gazing around wondering where to go and what the rules were. A completely new audience: just what we were trying to find.

The success of *Look Back* was finally assured when the entire play was screened by Granada on the ITV network, at peak viewing time, on 28 November. Denis Forman of Granada made an introductory speech to camera in which he warned that it was 'a play for adults and ... you can send the children to bed ... If you are over forty-five, I think I should tell you that some critics think it is not very suitable for you either.'

Shortly afterwards *Look Back* moved from the Royal Court to the Lyric, Hammersmith, to make way for fresh Devine–Richardson productions.* Meanwhile Jimmy Porter's assertion that 'there aren't any good, brave causes left' was being put dramatically to the test in the international political arena.

---

* Despite the play's success, the only West End manager to take an interest in it was Donald Albery, who demanded cuts (particularly the 'squirrels and bears' ending) which Osborne found unacceptable. Consequently, '*Look Back* waited nine years for its first West End presentation,' he writes.

13

Good, brave causes

One day in early November 1956, Kingsley Amis took part in another demonstration on the streets of Swansea. 'University students and staff formed up in a column, all quite light-hearted,' he recalled,

and marched to the Cricketers – a pub needless to say – for the lunch-time session. There we all put on placards – mine said EDEN ABIDE BY U.N. DECISION – and a student R S M type said 'Right, get into line and remember the rules. No interference with the police. Twenty yards apart. Same as we did with Capital Punishment. Mr Amis, we'd like you to go to the head of the column: we're anticipating some trouble from the Engineering students.'

But it wasn't any of the Engineering students who troubled me: it was a little, heavy-set housewife in Princess Street who darted out and tried to snatch my placard.

What to do? I mean, one can't clobber little housewives, even if they are heavy-set. So I broke into a run – and she chased me – until I outstripped her – outside Sidney Heath & Co. it was – and the engineers started shouting 'Bugger off home to Moscow, you commies.'

Just over three months earlier, President Nasser of Egypt had announced that his country was 'nationalizing' the Suez Canal – in other words, seizing it from the other owners, including Great Britain, the majority shareholder in this crucial trade route for oil and means of naval access to the Far East.

Sir Anthony Eden, who had succeeded Churchill as prime minister and Conservative Party leader the previous year, announced that the country would take 'a firm stand' against the Egyptians. Initially, almost the entire British press supported him. Even the pro-Labour

Daily Herald carried the front-page headline 'NO MORE ADOLF HITLERS!'. Harold Macmillan, then Chancellor of the Exchequer, declared that 'This is Munich all over again', adding that if England did not accept 'Egypt's challenge' she 'would become another Netherlands'.

Supported openly by France and secretly by Israel, Britain bombed Egypt and landed troops at Port Said. Meanwhile Nasser blocked the canal by sinking concrete-filled ships; the full scale of American opposition to the British offensive became clear; and the British press and public began to come rather belatedly to their senses.

'THIS IS FOLLY,' declared the *Daily Herald*, and there were big protest rallies against the government's Suez policy, in Trafalgar Square and the Albert Hall, with students chanting 'Eden must go'. Even the *Daily Telegraph* admitted to 'deep anxiety' about the military offensive, while *The Times* observed that there were 'very great risks'. Some ex-National Serviceman who received recall papers for the Suez campaign sent them back with 'bollocks' scrawled across them.

Nevertheless the landing of allied troops at Port Said began, but the USSR sent a threatening note to Eden, reminding him that Soviet nuclear rockets were far superior in power to the British forces being deployed in Egypt. The United Nations voted in support of an American resolution for a ceasefire, and it was now that Amis and his Swansea students took to the streets.

Afterwards, Amis said he had been reacting against 'what I took to be an imperialist aggression' which seemed to him very un-British. 'Also,' he continued,

to demonstrate was fun. It was righteous. It was fraternally enlightened. There was a pleasing atmosphere of solidarity (a Russian virtue), togetherness (an American virtue), esprit de corps (a French virtue) and companionability (a student virtue). The more so since there were no grim little men in mackintoshes and – so far as I could detect – no subversives. It was quite simply a genuine protest against something we all took to be a mistake or even a crime.

Amis's essentially light-hearted reminiscence catches the spirit of that Suez autumn, when schoolboys went around chanting 'Nasser has only got one ball', and there was a muddle of political feeling rather than a strong sense of anti-Eden protest.

Dennis Potter, who became an Oxford student just as the crisis was beginning, wrote in the *New Statesman* two years later: 'Suez . . . was a shock . . . For the first time many undergraduates realized that politics was much too important a thing to be left to the government.' Yet for every student whose politics turned leftwards as a result, there was at least one household cancelling its order for the newspapers which opposed Eden.

On 7 November the *Daily Herald* headline was 'EDEN CALLS IT OFF'. The paper's leader-writer commented: 'A squalid episode ends in a pitiable climb-down . . . Our moral authority in the world has been destroyed.' Yet most people's feelings were not of shame but of irritation that, because the Canal was shut, Britain had had to reintroduce petrol rationing.

Colin Wilson recalls that initially he supported Eden: 'I was interested to observe in myself a certain feeling of anger with the Egyptians, and a hope that the invasion would teach them a lesson, then disappointment that it hadn't come off, and a feeling that perhaps we ought to have ignored threats – as the Russians would have done – and taken our rights.' But once Eden withdrew the troops, Wilson felt it served the country right: 'The Suez defeat was for the best. The English have overrated themselves for too long. Maybe we shall now begin to concentrate on more meaningful forms of top-doggery – for example, in intellect and imagination.'

Having fled from the Swansea housewife, Amis handed back his placard to the organizers of the demonstration, and made no mention of Suez in his letters to Larkin. 'Actually I have been a bit of an old fool,' he confessed in one of them, 'getting tied up with a young woman here, not to say really tied up, just started fucking her what.' Besides this Swansea entanglement, he was borrowing Robert Conquest's London flat 'to entertain a young lady'.

Hilly, well aware of her husband's misdemeanours, was now indulging in a relationship of her own. This was with Henry Fairlie, the *Spectator* journalist who had coined the phrase 'the Establishment', and who supported Eden's Suez policy. The affair turned serious enough for her to threaten to leave Kingsley. His response was to write

Fairlie an eloquently moralistic letter, in which he declared that his family was 'the most valuable thing I own', and that Fairlie was inflicting selfish cruelty by threatening to remove Hilly and the children (who would presumably go with her). Moreover (he continued) there were the feelings of Fairlie's own wife and children to be considered. Yet when Hilly agreed to give up Fairlie for a trial period of six months, Kingsley immediately resumed his own covert infidelities.

Not surprisingly, this way of life began to be reflected in his fiction. The novel he was writing in the autumn of 1956, *I Like It Here*, was based on a trip the Amises had made to Portugal, financed by Kingsley's Somerset Maugham Award. Adultery played virtually no part in it. But it was to prove the exception. 'Adulterous husbands are prominent in Amis's novels from his second, *That Uncertain Feeling*,' writes his biographer Eric Jacobs, 'and it is possible to see Amis examining his own concerns about his own behaviour in many of them.'

* *

In the early hours of Sunday, 4 November 1956, at the height of the Suez crisis, Soviet troops launched a massive dawn attack on Budapest, crushing the twelve-day-old Hungarian uprising. Amis afterwards claimed that this had a far more profound effect on him than Suez: 'Russia's war of intervention in Hungary ... put paid for ever to my hopes that Communism might not be as bad as more and more voluminous and unignorable evidence kept suggesting to me it was – hopes that had flickered up momentarily at and after the death of Stalin.'

Yet this was written some while after the events of 1956. Immediately following the twin crises of Suez and Hungary, he had sent to the press a pamphlet for the Fabian Society (a 're-hash' of a talk given to one of their weekend schools) which displayed a remarkable apathy about the world issues of that autumn. Describing himself as 'an elderly young intellectual with left-wing sympathies', he stated that he had always voted Labour, but felt no inclination to join the party. Suez and Hungary earned only the briefest of mentions; he remarked that only a fanatical British Communist could continue to admire Russia after the Hungarian invasion, but he felt that, compared with the Spanish Civil War and the rise of Fascism in the Thirties, Hungary was unlikely to become a left-wing cause in Britain – or at least, 'I should not like to venture a prediction'.

Colin Wilson has suggested that 'it may well have been the concatenation of Suez and Hungary [which] liberated [Britain] from a culture that had become high Tory', but there is little evidence that any such major political shift actually took place. As with Suez, the political and intellectual consequences of the events in Hungary were confused. Some 7,000 people (about a fifth of the membership) resigned from the British Communist Party in protest at the Soviet aggression. Some defected to Labour (or further right), while others formed what became known as the New Left, a loose group of radical intellectuals (including the historian E. P. Thompson) who tried to revitalize British left-wing thinking through the pages of such journals as the *Universities and Left Review*. Yet, as Kingsley Amis remarked, the political fall-out from Hungary was not as great as might have been expected. 'A curious feature of the Hungary episode,' he wrote eleven years after it,

in its effect on British opinion at least, is the speed with which its memory has been revised or effaced. What at the time was almost everywhere taken as a mortal blow to the far Left, has mellowed here, if not elsewhere, into an unfortunate error that would certainly not be made today ... To ... the young Left, Hungary is at most something that happened to middle-aged people.

* *

John Osborne accurately describes the mood of Britain in late 1956 as a 'muddle of feeling about Suez and Hungary', and says that this was 'implicit' in his next play, *The Entertainer*, to the extent that casting Sir Laurence Olivier in the leading role 'seemed as dangerous as exposing the Royal Family to politics'.*

The Entertainer – which takes its title from Scott Joplin's ragtime† tune – takes on the considerable challenge of following, and not

---

* But he emphasizes that Olivier was an afterthought, proposed by George Devine: 'People ... persuaded themselves that I wrote the play for Olivier, which I didn't.'
† But played in a jazz style. Osborne recalled: 'I'd heard it ... played by this old man, Bunk Johnson, who was an old trumpet player ... It seemed such a touching ... and a very lonely and solitary and sweet tune.'

seeming inferior to, *Look Back in Anger*. Osborne's success had made him not just the darling of Fleet Street but also the target of its envy. Picking Osborne as 'the most CONTROVERSIAL personality of the year' in his Top Ten of 1956, *Evening Standard* journalist Thomas Wiseman went on: 'The danger is that having reputedly made about £30,000* out of this one play [*Look Back in Anger*] he may find in 1957 that life doesn't stink quite so much, and so have nothing more to say.' Moreover his divorce from Pamela Lane and his relationship with Mary Ure (whom he married in the summer of 1957) were making front-page news. To come up with a second highly original play in these circumstances was certainly an achievement.

The Entertainer is built around the somewhat Brechtian device of presenting the story of a family of music-hall entertainers as if it were itself a series of music-hall turns.† On the surface, nothing could seem further from the ultra-realism of *Look Back in Anger* than Archie Rice's stand-up comedy routines, delivered direct to the audience with a microphone (this is the role taken by Olivier). Yet in a sense Archie is simply the ranting Jimmy Porter grown old, and the play is just as autobiographical as its predecessor. The Rices will be familiar to any reader of Osborne's memoirs, because in them he is portraying not a real comedian and his family, but his own mother's play-acting relatives, 'the Grove Family Repertory':

BILLY: I used to have half a bottle of three star brandy for breakfast–
ARCHIE: And a pound of steak and a couple of chorus girls. He'll tell you the whole story at the drop of a hat.

This, of course, is Osborne's publican grandfather, recalling his days of glory.

The references in *The Entertainer* to the political events of 1956 have nothing to do with this, and therefore seem uncalled for and superficial:

* Grossly exaggerated. Samuel French paid Osborne a mere £25 for the amateur rights, and Osborne describes the £300 he received for the German rights as an 'amazing windfall'.
† Osborne had been appearing in the Royal Court production of Brecht's *The Good Woman of Sezuan*.

JEAN: I went to the Rally in Trafalgar Square last Sunday ... Because, Grandad, somehow – with a whole lot of other people, strange as it may seem – I managed to get steamed up about the way things were going.

But what those 'things' are, Osborne never specifies.

In his brief introduction to the play, he suggests that the death of music-hall, as symbolized by Archie, represents the decline of post-imperialist (and post-Suez) Britain. Archie sings: 'Those bits of red still on the map / We won't give up without a scrap.' But this is not the heart of the play. The pivotal moment is Archie's big speech to (and about) his family:

We're dead beat and down and outs. We're drunks, maniacs, we're crazy, we're bonkers, the whole flaming bunch of us. Why, we have problems that nobody's ever heard of, we're characters out of something that nobody believes in ... We don't get on with anything. We don't ever succeed in anything. We're a nuisance, we do nothing but make a God almighty fuss about anything we do.

Harold Hobson described the 'theatrical effect' of this and Archie's other monologues as 'enormous', and told his *Sunday Times* readers: 'You will not see more magnificent acting than this anywhere in the world.' But there is something equally histrionic about the Rices' expectation of the return home, from the Suez campaign, of their National Serviceman son Mick. It is predictable from the outset that he will not come back, that his Egyptian captors will murder him, because *The Entertainer* belongs in the world of melodrama, where such things always happen. Actually the Rice family is tragic enough without such a corny device. Its tragedy lies in its members' total inability to pay attention to anyone other than themselves.

Kenneth Tynan greatly enjoyed the play, but was acutely aware of its self-contradictions. He agreed that Archie was 'one of the great acting parts of our age', but was disappointed by the limp portrayal of Jean and her tepid politics, and felt that Osborne had lost his touch for portraying the concerns of the young.

Osborne himself says that at one point the English Stage Company decided not to go ahead with the play, implying that this was for political reasons. But Oscar Lewenstein, the Royal Court's manager, has recorded that he and others felt 'disappointment' with it, compared with *Look Back in Anger*, 'plus thinking that George [Devine], by giving it to Larry [Olivier], had by-passed the Artistic Committee', who were 'determined that it should not be a theatre for stars'. Devine agreed that the play was not as 'stunning' as *Look Back*; but it went ahead, and 'we made a pile'.

The Entertainer opened at the Royal Court in April 1957 and transferred in the autumn to the Palace Theatre in the West End. Its first night at the Palace was a glittering occasion, with Osborne and Mary Ure photographed by the press alongside Olivier and his film-star wife, Vivien Leigh. 'Miss Leigh,' reported the *Evening Standard*, 'swept from dressing-room to dressing-room with a rustle of pink silk.' The reports of the play made no mention of its references to Suez, which were already causing it to seem rather dated.

14

Two naked women . . . covered
in jewels

A few weeks before *The Entertainer* opened at the Royal Court, on 14 March 1957, a thirty-four-year-old Yorkshire librarian was on his way to work at a branch library in a mining village near Barnsley. He had overslept (his wife was recovering in hospital after the birth of their first child) and had hastily downed a cup of tea and a slice of bread before catching the bus. Now, as it took him through a grim landscape of pit-heads and slag-heaps, he opened the *Yorkshire Post*, in the hope that there might be some mention of his first novel, which was published that morning.

He was not disappointed. 'Mr Braine,' wrote the *Post*'s chief book critic, Kenneth Young, 'is certainly one of the year's finds.' The review had nothing but praise for the novel, *Room at the Top*.

Reading it, John Braine felt as if the grim Yorkshire mining landscape had melted away – 'as if I were riding on the Golden Arrow past mimosa and violets and palm trees. The praise in the very long review was as nourishing as steak and Burgundy . . . That morning . . . I did not work at all, but read and re-read the review until my eyes ached.'

The London papers were equally full of praise, and they immediately identified Braine as a new recruit to the Angry Young Men. John Davenport in the *Observer* described *Room at the Top*'s Joe Lampton as

a callous, ambitious, sexy L-cky J-m . . . Joe inhabits the same sort of world . . . as Mr Amis's hero. L-cky J-m [is] saved by [his] amiability: Joe Lampton reveals the obverse side of the medal; he is a beast, and his story is the autobiography of a cad . . . He is a ruthless rather than an angry young man: any anger he has is the driving force of his ambition.

'R.G.' in *Punch* made a comparison with Osborne's Jimmy Porter – 'Joe Lampton looks back more in sorrow than in anger' – and David Holloway wrote in the *News Chronicle*: 'If I were given to movement-hailing, I would welcome Mr John Braine as the leader of a new school, "The Lecherous Young Men". But ... the love-making is handled with directness that is totally void of offence and the book crackles with life.' The *Daily Express*, announcing that it had bought the serial rights of *Room at the Top* (a very rare accolade for a first novel), described Braine as one of 'three youngish men' who had 'geysered into the writing world', the other two being Amis and Osborne (there was no mention of Colin Wilson). 'To my mind,' wrote the *Express*'s Anthony Hern, 'he [Braine] is the best of the three.'

Many years later, Braine was asked how he had felt about being identified – the instant that *Room at the Top* was published – with the Angry Young Men. He said he 'wasn't bothered', and had been glad of the publicity. And a few months after publication, in an interview with Kenneth Allsop, he became the first 'AYM' to accept that there was some validity in the label. 'Looking at British writing generally, from about 1949 to now,' he told Allsop, 'I sensed a certain deadness of feeling among writers. Now things seem to be moving. Angry Young Man is a misused and over-used label, but it does have some significance if only that it means that the young writer is rejecting literary formulas.' He even suggested that, now he had given up his library job (because he was making so much money from *Room at the Top*), he might make a public display of anger:

I personally haven't recently espoused any causes, simply because of lack of time, but now that conditions have changed for me and I have the time I shall throw my weight in for anything in which I believe. I shan't achieve much by so doing but if I don't protest – I who, as far as anyone ever can be, am a free man – who will?

Unlike his fellow AYM, he seemed to conform to the popular stereotype of being working-class and left-wing. He even appeared to be concerned about the effects of Suez:

I've been a member of the Labour Party and will be again. I'm not starry-eyed about it, but certain things in which I believe can only be achieved by the Labour Party. Put it this way – although I'd like to be in the proper sense of the word an idiot and not bother about Suez and the rest of it, it is my duty to be concerned to do what little I can – let's be really old-fashioned – to make the world a better place. Or, more important, to make sure that there is a habitable world, not a radio-active desert.

* *

In fact, from the outset, John Gerard Braine was neither working-class nor left-wing. He had been born in Bradford on 13 April 1922, and liked to describe his birthplace as a terraced street in a 'smoky valley', and to emphasize that his maternal grandparents (*émigrés* from Catholic Ireland) had both 'worked at the mills'. In fact his upbringing was lower-middle-class. 'I'm the son of a supervisor of a sewage works and a lady librarian,' he said in a comparatively rare moment of honesty about this. Moreover Fred Braine – a foreman with the Bradford Corporation sewage department – was a highly literate individual. 'My father has to date made more money out of his writings than I have,' John Braine said in early 1957, just before his windfall from *Room at the Top*. 'He has the knack of winning literary competitions in newspapers and magazines. He once won £300 . . .'

John's education was thoroughly middle-class, too, or would have been if he had pursued it to the end. At the age of eleven he won a scholarship to the local grammar school, St Bede's; but (like Colin Wilson) he left at sixteen, without taking his School Certificate examinations (the equivalent of present-day GCSEs). He said that at school he had spent most of the time 'in a mental fog – not the school's fault but mine'.

Like Wilson, he took a job as a laboratory assistant, at Bradford Technical College, and hated the work:

There may have been a laboratory assistant who was more idle, who broke more expensive glassware and equipment, one who was less fitted for the world of science, but I have yet to hear of him. My wage was 11s 6d, which even in those days didn't permit one to lead a rich and full life. And I knew that the job was the blindest of blind alleys.

He attended evening classes in shorthand and typing, but gave up halfway through the course, 'the mental fog . . . having not yet been disturbed'.

However, 'I read a great deal – Huxley, Lawrence, and all the left-wing poets of the Thirties – and tried to write.' Looking back from the vantage point of literary success, he felt that his juvenile essays and poems were best forgotten:

They were failures from the beginning because of my choice of subject. I had never met a racing driver, an artist, an actor, a novelist, or a bullfighter, and I had never been to Spain, Italy, the Riviera, or even London. But that was what I wrote about.

He gave up being a lab assistant, and – again like Wilson – took a variety of dead-end jobs, selling furniture and second-hand books, and working as a progress-chaser in a piston-ring factory, before settling at last, at the age of eighteen, for a job that promised some sort of career: an assistant in the public library service in the town of Bingley, a few miles north of Bradford.

The work scarcely excited him; but this was 1940, and he had hopes of the conflict against Hitler: 'War promised change, foreign countries, money in my pocket to take girls out, and aeroplanes and tanks for toys. At last my life would have some purpose.' However, he had to wait two years for his call-up, and when it came, he found himself being trained as a naval telegraphist in 'a melancholy and hideous collection of huts in the sad, flat Hampshire countryside'. He never went to sea, because the X-ray check given to all cadets had shown up a tubercular patch on one of his lungs, and he passed his twenty-second birthday in an isolation hospital at Grassington in the Yorkshire Dales.

He was there for five months, wrote a poem every day, and eventually had one published in an obscure literary magazine. 'I wasn't paid a penny for it but I didn't care. I was a writer; that was what mattered.' By the end of 1943 he was well enough to resume his Bingley library job, and he now belatedly took his School Certificate, studying by correspondence course. Next came a course at Leeds School of Librarianship, which he passed at the fourth attempt. Meanwhile, like Joe Lampton in *Room at the Top*, he was discovering the hothouse world of amateur theatricals. He joined the Little Theatre at Bingley, and wrote a verse drama – a modern-day *Faust* – which was produced there.

It was a flop; and at this point Fred Braine stepped in. In 1949, when John was twenty-seven,

my father gave me the first push along the path which led to *Room at the Top*. 'Why on earth,' he asked me, 'don't you write an article on something you know about?' I knew something about Little Theatres and I knew something about pubs so I wrote an article about the kind of pub patronized by members of the Little Theatres. It was fictional in approach but was based solidly on fact; it was accepted by *Tribune* immediately.

Tribune (the Labour Party weekly) published other articles by him, and this led to the more glamorous platform of the *New Statesman*. In its pages, under the name 'J. G. Braine', he was soon publishing colourful pieces about aspects of contemporary Yorkshire life. One such describes a typical day in a provincial town hall, where the smell of cabbage and onion from the Municipal Restaurant* drifts into the murder trial in the courtroom. Another is a portrait of his Irish grandmother and her working-class Irish Catholic community in 'Blackersford' (Bradford); and a piece called 'Nowhere' describes a typical provincial 'roadhouse' – the generic name for the big flashy pubs that had grown up to serve the motoring trade during the Thirties, and were flourishing again in the Fifties:

Here . . . in the Lounge . . . is the unmistakable smell of money: cigars, whisky, and the kind of perfume which friends like to give to a girl. The talk is of money, when I went over in the Skymaster, money, what I said to the man from Whitehall, money, I got ninety out of her on the Great North Road, money, old Harry's slipping and money – deals, arrangements, contracts, bonds, stocks and shares, you can't trust these bloody Jews – a paper jungle with whisky at the drinking-holes.

---

* Municipal Restaurants, run by local councils, offered cheap but reasonably nourishing meals during the years of postwar austerity.

The quality of Braine's writing in such pieces caught the eye of the future novelist Paul Scott, then a fledgling London literary agent. He invited Braine to call on him in the autumn of 1951, and Braine arrived with his verse play, some more articles about north country life – and an idea for a novel, to be called either *Born Favourite*, or *Joe for King*. This, at any rate, is how Scott remembered it; but Braine gave the credit for suggesting the novel to Scott: 'I had a talk with Paul at his office, and he said he thought I had the makings of a novelist. I didn't really before then think of writing a novel, but I went away and started writing a novel.'

The project aroused the interest of the *New Statesman*'s book imprint, Turnstile Press, who said they would commission it if Braine could produce a satisfactory synopsis and specimen chapter. On the strength of this and Paul Scott's enthusiasm, Braine resigned his library job. 'I left Yorkshire to become a freelance writer in London.' His parents thought he was mad, and in retrospect so did he.

* *

'I had £150 saved up and I took a room in Kensington,' Braine recalled. 'In [that] land of the bedsitter and the old men and women who wander up and down the High Street muttering to themselves . . . I learned . . . what it was like to be lonely, to come home to a solitary meal of a boiled egg and a cup of coffee made over a gas ring.'

On previous visits he had found London 'a wonderful and bewitching city . . . I'd just sat in pubs, certain that any moment something marvellous would happen that would change my whole life.' Now, 'It was very frightening when I closed the door and realized that there was nothing I wanted to write about.'

Nevertheless he completed the specimen chapter and synopsis, and sent them to Turnstile Press. Meanwhile Paul Scott 'obtained for me a BBC audition which to my surprise resulted in my being asked to make two broadcasts'. The first was as a reader of a short story written by somebody else, and in the second he read a comic piece of his own about amateur dramatics. The BBC liked his Yorkshire accent, and more work seemed likely to be offered. However, Braine now received a telegram with the news that his mother had been knocked down by a car and was dead.

Returning to London after the funeral, he struggled on, but soon developed acute laryngitis, which made broadcasting impossible. 'I had lost my voice and hadn't any money. Then the Turnstile Press rejected the chapter and synopsis.' He went back to Bradford, where he was again diagnosed as tubercular. 'In January 1952 [I] found myself at Grassington Sanatorium again.'

From hospital, he wrote to one of the BBC producers who had employed him:

I heard you'd phoned me, so I thought I'd let you know I shan't be in London again for some time. I'll be as good as new in six months, and then, I think, will live a quiet life in Hampstead.

The rest is exactly what I'm needing, and I've time to work on my novel. Films are the main deprivation (though in another two months I'll be allowed to visit the hospital cinema) and I spend a great deal of my time unreeling ones I've seen – in my mind, that is.

In fact he had to stay there for eighteen months. 'I was ill, I hadn't any money, I hadn't got a job, and the only thing I really could do when I went into the hospital was to begin the novel again . . . I just had to start from scratch.' He felt that 'it wouldn't really matter if I died after it had been finished; what was important was that it should be known that I had been alive.

'By the time I'd left the sanatorium in 1953 I'd finished the first draft – a shapeless, shambling mastodon of a narrative some 160,000 words in length – and by September 1954 had half-finished the final draft.' Asked many years later if the novel had been written in anger, he answered: 'Oh no. You can't write in anger, any more than you can make love in anger . . . What you write from is . . . love . . . a love of the world, and all the human beings in it . . . all the complexity of it . . . You want to glorify all this. Anger's got nothing to do with it.'

In the autumn of 1953, 'I returned to librarianship and the comfort of the monthly salary cheque. I went to work for the Northumberland County Library.' It was there that he met a schoolteacher called Pat Wood, and they were married the following year. Completing *Room at the Top* – as it was now called – Braine dedicated the novel to her.

Paul Scott began to submit it to London publishers. The first four rejected it. Then came an enthusiastic response from Maurice Temple-Smith, managing director of Eyre & Spottiswoode, who accepted it despite the grave doubts of some of his colleagues.

Braine claimed that the novel's hero, Joe Lampton, was in no respect a self-portrait, on the grounds that, in his own mid-twenties, he was

very far from being a precocious Don Juan. I simply wanted to meet girls, to take them out, not with a view to marriage, but not with a view to seduction, either. And meeting girls was rather difficult as I was cut off from the working classes by my grammar-school education and cut off from the middle classes by the fact that I'd made no use of that education, that I was in a menial position.

He certainly bore no physical resemblance to the conventionally handsome Joe. Kingsley Amis, who first met him soon after the publication of *Room at the Top*, describes him as 'pale, bespectacled, chubby, with a perpetual look of being out of condition', and an interviewer in *Books and Bookmen* in 1957 wrote:

I half expected him to be a Colin Wilson type . . . A bulky figure, coddled in several layers of heavy clothing, he looks like many of the other inhabitants of our northern industrial towns. He wears a trilby hat with the brim turned up all the way round, over a head of hair which has a faint reddish tinge. When he speaks, it is with a ripe, round Yorkshire accent, and he sounds and looks neither young nor angry.

Stan Barstow has written that 'Braine [was] a nicer man than most of his characters', but Kingsley Amis is less sure: 'How like Joe Lampton . . . was he really? Not ruthless and cruel, certainly, but how much of what Joe wanted did John really want?' During the explosion of publicity following the novel's overnight success, Braine told one reporter: 'What I want to do is to drive through Bradford in a Rolls-Royce with two naked women on either side of me covered in jewels.'

The blurb of a recent paperback edition of *Room at the Top* describes Joe as 'the original "angry young man" of the Fifties'. In fact the novel is set in 1946. Braine told Kenneth Allsop: 'Joe Lampton isn't meant . . . to be of this period . . .' (i.e. the Fifties). To some extent

Joe's ambitions to further himself socially are a reaction to the extreme austerity of the immediately postwar years, long before prosperity began to return to Britain in the mid-Fifties. The book virtually salivates as it describes material goods and upmarket lifestyles which would have been inaccessible to most of the population immediately after the war. 'It's already difficult to remember the days of rationing,' says Joe, describing a party at the home of a well-off family (and recalling his own experiences as a prisoner-of-war),

but I am sure of one thing: [in 1946] one was always hungry. Not hungry in the way I'd been at Stalag 1000, but hungry for profusion, hungry for more than enough, hungry for cream and pineapples and roast pork and chocolate. The Carstairs were in the business, of course; but the meal laid out in the dining-room would have been considered sumptuous even today [the mid-1950s]. There was lobster, mushroom patties, anchovy rolls, chicken sandwiches, ham sandwiches, turkey sandwiches, smoked roe on ryebread, real fruit salad flavoured with sherry, meringues, apple pie, Danish Blue and Cheshire and Gorgonzola and a dozen different kinds of cake loaded with cream and chocolate and fruit and marzipan. Susan watched me eat with a pleased maternal expression. 'Where does it all go?'

'No difficulty,' I said with my mouth full.

Arguably, Joe's determination to achieve affluence in a time of severe austerity is a metaphor for Britain's greed in the postwar years, demonstrated by the country's repeated rejection of Labour (which had created the Welfare State) in favour of the Tories at the general elections of 1951, 1955 and 1959. Four months after the publication of *Room at the Top*, in a speech at Bedford on 20 July 1957, the Conservative prime minister Harold Macmillan complacently told his supporters: 'Let's be frank about it; most of our people have never had it so good. Go around the country, go to the industrial towns, go to the farms, and you will see a state of prosperity such as we have never had in my lifetime – nor indeed in the history of this country.'

Room at the Top begins, like several Fifties novels (including Wain's *Hurry On Down* and Amis's *Take a Girl Like You*), with the main character arriving in a town that is new to him or her, and moving into a rented bedsitter – just as Braine himself had done in London.

(Philip Larkin's 1955 poem 'Mr Bleaney' epitomizes the potential loneliness of this situation.) Joe, aged twenty-five and (unlike Braine) from a solidly working-class background, has recently been demobilized from wartime service in the RAF. He is now bettering himself by resigning from a town hall clerkship in the nearby mill town of Dufton (based on Thackley, where Braine's father now lived) to a better municipal job in the much more prosperous Warley (based on Bingley). His bedsitter is in the home of a comfortably-off married couple in an upmarket hillside area of Warley known as The Top (pronounced 'T'Top'), and Joe wallows in his new lifestyle:

The bathroom was the sort you'd expect to find in any middle-class home – green tiles, green enamel, chromium towel-rails, a big mirror with toothmug and toothbrush holders, a steel cabinet, a flush-sided bath with a shower attachment, and a light operated by a cord instead of a switch. It was immaculately clean, smelling faintly of scented soap and freshly laundered towels: it was nothing except a bathroom, it had been designed as a bathroom.

The bathroom I'd used the night before I came to Warley had been adapted from a bedroom. At the time the houses in Oak Crescent [in Dufton] were built it wasn't considered that the working classes needed baths.

The book is filled with this sort of finely observed social detail. As *The Times Literary Supplement* reviewer put it, 'Mr Braine's . . . eye both for the girl and the bathroom could not be more clear.'

As to the girls, Joe spends the novel pursuing two women he has met through the local dramatic society, nineteen-year-old Susan Brown, pretty daughter of a local business magnate, and thirty-four-year-old Alice Aisgill, a married woman who quickly takes him as her lover.* The story's structure is not unlike *Lucky Jim* – there is even a Bertrand figure, Susan's boyfriend Jack Wales, 'Bags of money, about seven foot tall and a beautiful RAF moustache' – except that this time it is the glamorous young female, rather than the older woman, who makes the reader squirm with her appalling whimsical turns of speech:

* Braine portrays a pre-feminist world where men can chat up women openly at their first meeting, and also vice versa: ' "He's smashing," said Beryl. She stared at me impudently.'

'Darling Joekins,' she burbles when Joe begins his romantic advances, 'Susan tingle. Susan tingle up and down.' The reader longs for Joe to abandon her for the mature-minded Alice. But the opposite happens. This is for two reasons, one of them consciously planned by Braine, the other probably not.

Joe portrays himself as a social climber, or rather a go-getter for the good things in life – sports cars, pretty girls from well-off homes, and above all money and power:

As I watched the tail-end of the Aston-Martin with its shiny new G.B. plate go out of sight . . . I made my choice there and then: I was going to enjoy all the luxuries which that young man enjoyed. I was going to collect that legacy.

According to Joe (and Braine), this is why he eventually abandons Alice for the awful Susan.

Writing in the *New Statesman* a few weeks after the publication of *Room at the Top*, Geoffrey Gorer asserted that the sexual aspirations of Joe Lampton, Jimmy Porter in *Look Back in Anger*, and Jim Dixon in *Lucky Jim* were all 'hypergamous' – they all desired to attach themselves to women of higher social standing. This is certainly true of Osborne's hero, but more doubtful with Amis's, since Christine is not of significantly higher status than Jim; rather, she represents the lure of metropolitan as opposed to provincial life. Joe Lampton does indeed seem to be hypergamous in his determination to win Susan; yet there is another layer to *Room at the Top* which suggests a different kind of reason for the novel to conclude as it does.

For all his declarations of ambition, Joe is not really an unscrupulous rogue. Such anger as he experiences is usually directed at himself, for making the wrong emotional decisions. He is far less resentful of the social establishment of Warley than Jim Dixon is of his university. True, there are brief glimpses of satirical anger in Joe's memories of conversations with Charles, his friend back in Dufton town hall – 'Anyone we didn't approve of [we] called zombies', and they nickname it 'Dead Dufton'. Yet if Joe really wants single-mindedly to advance his career, why should he ignore his town hall boss's advice and take Susan out behind her parents' back, thereby risking disaster – *and* continue his affair with Alice, which most of Warley knows about?

The real *Room at the Top* is not a portrait of ruthless social and financial ambition, but a Lawrentian novel about different kinds of sex – the mature, deeply physical relationship between Joe and Alice, contrasted with the conventional suburban sexless transactions with the immature Susan: 'She [Alice] pressed my hand deep into her breast. "I want you to hurt me there. Oh God, you're so beautiful. You've lovely eyes, like Christ's . . ."'

Joe, far from being a moral mould-breaker, is deeply conventional in sexual matters. At one point he walks out on Alice because he learns she once modelled in the nude:

'Oh God,' I said miserably, 'what did you do it for? You didn't have to, there's millions of women have been as poor as you were and they'd rather have died than expose themselves like that for a few lousy shillings. Damn you to hell, I'd like to beat you black and blue.'

This is sheer Victorian melodrama, and the novel's plot becomes tritely theatrical at the end. As John Bayley put it in his *Spectator* review of *Room at the Top*, Braine 'has to make [Joe's] business success dependent on sexual success, and invents a wholly fantastic hardheaded Yorkshire businessman who, because the hero has seduced his daughter, sets him up in a partnership after "testing" him, in the old comedy convention, by offering him job and money if he never sees his daughter again'. *The Times Literary Supplement* reviewer judged that the death of Alice was unnecessarily melodramatic too: 'One feels that it was added to make the hero feel more bitter and more cut off from the world which he succeeds in conquering . . .'

Room at the Top is essentially a novel of finely tuned social observation grafted on to a creaky plot. But whatever the book's shortcomings, Braine's writing is always full of energy – 'An extraordinary vitality', as the *TLS* critic put it – while the setting and subject-matter (sex amid the slagheaps) was a breakthrough for the period. Stan Barstow writes of this:

It is hard now to convey the importance of . . . *Room at the Top* . . . for a generation of writers from the North of England; not because it in any way showed the best of [Braine's] contemporaries how or what to write, but because its huge success in the discouraging literary climate of the 1950s confirmed each in his determination to use as the basis of his art the regional working-class life he knew from the inside, which at the time was far from being the fashionable mine of material it later became.

* *

John and Pat Braine used the advance on the novel to put down a deposit on a small semi-detached house in Wakefield, where he had taken a new post with the West Riding County Library. Then came the *Daily Express* serialization deal. The first episode, on 22 April 1957, promised readers a tale of 'Ambition and women ... explosive stuff !', but in fact the sex scenes were heavily cut, and most of Braine's best writing disappeared too.

Bookshop sales were excellent (some 35,000 copies in the first year), and in the summer of 1957 Braine left the library service for the last time. 'He has already made £10,000,' reported *Books and Bookmen* in September, 'but he has no intention of coming down to London.' He and Pat moved to a larger home on the edge of the moors. 'Mr Braine['s] first book is a bestseller,' stated the *Daily Express*. 'He has just had his first baby ... He would like it made known that he couldn't be less angry.'

15

The game is up, Wilson!

Though he did not move his family south, John Braine started to pay frequent visits to London, where he rented a *pied-à-terre* in the Notting Hill house used by the Colin Wilson gang (Wilson greatly admired *Room at the Top*, and was amused by Braine's bluff Yorkshire persona). 'The fact is, the whole Angry Young Men business is nonsense,' Braine remarked some years later. 'There never was a group, and all the people who have been labelled Angry Young Men are all very different.' But he went on: 'In fact, England being a small country, I know most of them [the A Y M].'

He was commissioned to write a magazine profile of Kingsley Amis, who invited him down to Swansea. As with Daniel Farson's visit, Amis plied his visitor with enormous amounts of alcohol, to which Braine eventually succumbed. 'He was put to bed in an attic room,' writes Amis,

there being no question of his returning to London that night as he had planned. The next morning he was found there with the electric fire full on and near enough to the bed to have caused it to burst into flames had he not rendered the sheets non-inflammable. He retains the prize – a closely fought distinction – for producing the most thoroughly maltreated bedroom I have ever set eyes on.

This may explain Amis's report to Larkin of an encounter at a *Spectator* party: '. . . looking over my shoulder, man says "Oh, here's John Wain." Self: "AaaaAAAGHGH." Man: "Sorry, I mean John Braine." Self: "Aaaa*AAGHGH*."'

Wain had now gone freelance and was living by his pen. One of

Amis's letters to Larkin, disparaging a short story Wain had published in *Harper's Bazaar*, refers to him as 'ole John Whine'. In January 1957, Wain sent Larkin the typescript of his third novel, *The Contenders*, asking if he might dedicate it to him. 'Thank you,' replied Larkin, whose fourth collection of poems, *The Less Deceived*, had appeared just over a year earlier, 'I'd be delighted to accept the dedication of *The Contenders*, but heaven knows when I'll be able to return it – Sunday writers like myself do about a book a decade . . .' Sure enough, the next Larkin collection, *The Whitsun Weddings*, did not appear until 1964.

Larkin was asked by Wain to comment on the novel, and his reply was not very enthusiastic: 'My own feeling is that it could stand a great deal more complexity in the three main characters . . . I think that certain parts should be shortened, and others re-written.' The book is the story of three men from the Potteries, two of whom, an artist and a businessman, are both close friends and deadly rivals; the third is a corpulent journalist who narrates their adventures. *The Contenders* (published in 1958) is undemandingly readable, but Wain does not seem to have followed Larkin's advice, since the central characters remain two-dimensional.

Wain's name now rarely featured in journalists' lists of the Angry Young Men, but the AYM craze continued as frenetically as ever in the press. When a ground-breaking study of contemporary mass culture and its social effects, *The Uses of Literacy*, was published in February 1957, the book's thirty-seven-year-old author had the label stuck on to him by the *Daily Herald*: 'An angry young man named Richard Hoggart, bawling above the din of mass-made entertainment, flings an angry question at us: Are we becoming a nation of robots?'

Wain did get mentioned in an article by Colin Wilson on his fellow Angries, published in the popular Sunday paper *Reynolds News*, under the headline 'What are the ANGRY young men ANGRY ABOUT?':

Mr Amis and Mr Wain seem to lack any sense of there being something wrong with our civilization. Their 'comic' novels produce an unutterably sinister effect on me – like an insane clown wandering over a bloody battlefield, muttering corny jokes . . . It may be possible that Mr Osborne will turn out to have dramatic genius. But it is not constructive.

By February 1957, when this was printed, Wilson was often coming under attack himself. He says he 'became aware of a change in the atmosphere, an unmistakable sense of hostility' a mere few weeks after the publication of *The Outsider*. 'The *Sunday Times* asked me if I would like to become a regular reviewer. But although my first review appeared promptly, they took several months to print my second one and thereafter sent me no more books for review.' He became aware of 'a rumour that most sales of *The Outsider* were "furniture sales" – that is, people bought it to leave around on their coffee tables to show they were intellectuals, but seldom actually read it'. Worst of all, 'It was reported to me that Cyril Connolly had been assuring his friends that he had not actually read *The Outsider*, but had simply glanced at it and decided it deserved a good review.' At Christmas 1956, in the *Sunday Times* 'Books of the Year' column, Arthur Koestler wrote sardonically: 'Bubble of the year: *The Outsider*, in which a young man discovers that men of genius suffer from *weltschmerz*.'

People were also discovering how easy it was to mock Wilson. He recalls that 'strangers who claimed to be Outsiders wrote me long letters explaining their symptoms and asking for advice, until I began to suspect parody'. *Punch* ran a spoof on the book, in which Lewis Carroll's Alice is 'oppressed by the *angst* of being an Outsider', and there was a *New Statesman* competition in which readers were invited to submit 'an excerpt... from a new masterpiece entitled *The Offsider* ...written in collaboration by Messrs Angus, Sandy and Colin Wilson'. (Nobody managed to rise very successfully to this challenge.)

Early in 1957, Wilson's girlfriend Joy Stewart developed tonsillitis, and went into hospital near her family home in Bedford. While visiting her, Wilson left at her parents' house a bag containing his journals. Joy's eighteen-year-old sister Fay read them. A week or two later, on 19 February 1957, Wilson and Joy were back in London, at Chepstow Villas, 'giving dinner,' recalls Wilson,

to an old poof called Gerald Hamilton, who was Mr Norris in Christopher Isherwood's novel *Mr Norris Changes Trains*,* when suddenly the door burst

---

* Published in America as *The Last of Mr Norris*.

open and in came Joy's family. Her mother, father, brother Neil, sister Fay, and her father shouted: 'The game is up, Wilson!'

It seems that Fay had told them from reading my journals that I was a homosexual and that I had six mistresses. I laughed and said, 'Here's the journal, take it yourself,' and he [Joy's father] raised a horsewhip and tried to hit me with it. I gave him a push in the chest and he fell down; the mother shouted 'How dare you hit an old man?' and began hitting me with her umbrella. I thought this was so funny I literally doubled up roaring with laughter and fell on the floor, whereupon Joy's mother proceeded to kick me!

I managed to get to the phone and rang the police. They turned up in five minutes and said to Joy's parents: 'How old is she?' They said, 'She's twenty-four.' The police said, 'Well, if she's twenty-four she can do what she likes. You'll have to leave this gentleman's flat because, you know, you're not allowed on other people's premises without their permission.' Joy's family went off, and then I noticed that Gerald Hamilton had also disappeared.

In about ten minutes there was a ring at the doorbell; I went down and it was a reporter and a photographer – obviously Gerald had rushed straight to the telephone and rung up all Fleet Street.

I let them in, told them what had happened – thinking that this would be a kind of insurance from Joy's parents ever trying it again. But no sooner had we got rid of them than there were more [journalists] below. So we decided to sneak out the back door and spend the night at a friend's.

The next day's popular press had plenty of fun with the incident. The *Daily Mail* went for the AYM angle:

HORSEWHIP THREAT TO 'OUTSIDER' WILSON

Angry Young Man Colin Wilson ... was even angrier last night when the peace of his Notting Hill Gate flat was shattered. But he was not so angry as the middle-aged father who ... confronted him with a horsewhip.

The story ran for several days, with Mr Stewart brandishing Wilson's journal at reporters – 'Read it! Read it for yourself ... Ravings! ... Thinks he is God, talks of sadism and murder and Jack the Ripper' – and Wilson apparently sanctioning publication of excerpts from the journal in the *Mail*. 'The day must come when I'm hailed as a major prophet,' read one passage. 'I *am* the major literary genius of our century . . . the most serious man of our age.' Readers were kept agog as Wilson and Joy fled dramatically to Daniel Farson's parents' house in the West Country: 'COLIN AND JOY: "WE'LL GO ABROAD." RUN-AWAYS TURN UP IN DEVON'. The news-hounds also dug up Wilson's estranged wife Betty, who told them she had 'felt like horsewhipping Colin myself sometimes'.

Just as readers might have been wondering whether the whole thing was a conspiracy between the Stewarts and Wilson to gain him publicity, the story faded away – and was immediately taken up by George Melly and Wally Fawkes (writing and drawing under the joint pseudonym 'Trog') in their 'Flook' satirical cartoon strip in the *Daily Mail*. The two heroes – the teddy bear Flook and its owner Rufus – spent the next month trying to be Angry Young Men, or, as Flook himself phrased it, Displeased Non-Elderly Males. They lodged in a house like 24 Chepstow Villas, alongside a Jimmy Porter lookalike called Len, who was trying to make his name in the world of skiffle, while his upper-class wife Amanda presided at the ironing board. A month after the Wilson–Stewart horsewhip incident, Amanda's tweedy mother burst in on the ménage and beat Len over the head with her umbrella – 'You've been mistreating my daughter again, you cad!' But the best joke to come out of the affair was made by the American magazine *Time*. Reporting the horsewhip incident, it captioned a photograph of Wilson: 'Egghead, scrambled.'

* *

Despite the wobbling reputation of *The Outsider*, Victor Gollancz had signed a contract with Wilson for a sequel. Wilson wanted to call it *The Rebel*, but Gollancz persuaded him to go for the more portentous title *Religion and the Rebel*. Pre-publication publicity included an interview which Wilson had given to Daniel Farson for a short-lived Beaverbrook magazine called *Books and Art*. Once again he described himself as a genius, and this time he also applied the label to his friend Bill Hopkins, telling Farson: 'Before the year is out his name will be known all over England.'

Sure enough, readers of *Books and Art* only had to wait a month before learning more about Hopkins, whose novel *The Divine and the Decay* had just been published. The reviewer, Anthony Hern, summarized what he called the 'preposterous' plot – 'Peter Plowart arranges to have his Party chief murdered while . . . he lodges with an impotent cripple whose wife has taken a local giant as her lover' – before labelling Hopkins's style 'second-rate Victoriana', and judging that he would have been wiser not to have written the novel at all, but to have simply let Wilson go on telling the world he was a genius. *The Times Literary Supplement* reviewer was equally scornful of the style ('a remarkable book . . . in the badness of its writing'), but did allow that there was 'a kind of power behind Mr Hopkins's absurdities . . . a sense of urgency [in his] statement of neo-Fascist nihilism'.

The Divine and the Decay is actually very entertaining in a weird way. Hopkins's hero Plowart has a Wilsonian view of himself – 'I'm the greatest man of our time,' he assures the inhabitants of Vachau, the mysterious Channel island where he has come to establish an alibi – and Hopkins makes no secret of Plowart's political orientation; his list of those 'men who had changed the world' whom he particularly admires begins with Hitler. Plowart's Mosley-style New Britain League is busily 'recruiting thousands of young, ardent men and women to bring a new epoch to life and a new name of fire to the scroll of history'. The book includes what Kenneth Allsop describes as 'the dullest rape scene in literature', but for most of the time its Gothic plot whizzes happily along with absolutely no concessions to plausibility. Nevertheless Malcolm Bradbury, writing on Hopkins in 1960, took *The Divine and the Decay* seriously, confessing to a feeling of 'deep disturbance' at Hopkins's implicitly fascist message.

Speaking today, Hopkins vehemently denies that either he or his novel is fascist:

Of course the book has a political structure; that's what gives it its tension. And when I was asked by Kenneth Allsop who was the most important man of the century, I said: 'Undoubtedly Adolf Hitler. He was the greatest man.' And Allsop said, 'How can you say that?' And I said, 'I'm not talking in moral terms, Kenneth, I'm talking in historical terms. Hitler changed a totally exhausted and moribund Europe into a revolution – absolutely unaided, like a dynamo; and that makes him absolutely superior, in terms of energy, to any other man of modern times. He ranks with Napoleon, and his name will live till eternity.' This was turned by Allsop into the allegation that I was a Hitlerite. It was done deliberately and with malice.

Hopkins also claims that he was made to suffer personally on account of the book. He had given up his Fleet Street job (which by this time was night editor at the London bureau of the *New York Times*) in order to complete *The Divine and the Decay*; but his publishers, MacGibbon & Kee, lost their nerve when the book was described by reviewers as fascist. 'They pulped the remainder of the edition,' says Hopkins,

so that people couldn't find it in the bookshops. And they said they wouldn't publish anything else by me – but wouldn't release me from my contract. So my writing career was brought abruptly to a halt, and I was soon penniless. Fortunately Colin gave me a helping hand.

The year 1957 also saw the emergence of the first book by Colin Wilson's other satellite, Stuart Holroyd. Gollancz published his *Emergence from Chaos* during the summer, wrapped in a dust-jacket which promised another *Outsider*, while simultaneously claiming that Holroyd was 'in no way influenced by Mr Wilson'. The book earned a few puzzled reviews; Philip Toynbee said that it was 'better written and better organized than *The Outsider*', but he could not see the point of Holroyd's arid quest for religious meaning in the works of various twentieth-century poets. And a year after the publication of *Emergence from Chaos*, in an article on the A Y M for an American magazine, Ken Tynan put Holroyd in a rather more sinister spotlight:

Emergence from Chaos . . . more or less followed the Wilson line. According to Holroyd, democracy was 'a myth' and government was best left to 'an expert minority'; but by now it was beginning to dawn on many people that such ideas, if not consciously fascist, were certainly the soil in which fascism grew.

In the same article, Tynan claimed that 'the Wilson cultists' excused Hitler on the grounds that he, too, was an Outsider. Bill Hopkins says of this: 'All Tynan thought of was spanking people. He was a total degenerate, a totally despicable, nauseating person. I'm very proud to have been insulted by him!' Meanwhile Wilson himself – when not featuring in the horsewhip saga – maintained an Olympian political position. In the *London Magazine* during the spring of 1957, he brushed aside the two major recent international turmoils with a Wildean nonchalance: 'I would hardly count the Hungarian oppression or the Suez crisis matters of supreme importance.'

Even Victor Gollancz seems to have sensed that Wilson's star was fading, judging by the low-key send-off he gave his new book in October 1957. *Religion and the Rebel* played naively into the hands of those (and there were now many of them) who were waiting to ambush Wilson. It began with a lengthy 'Autobiographical Introduction', in which he admitted that it had been a struggle to write the book. He concluded this opening chapter with what seemed to be a sinister promise that he would soon emerge as a new Oswald Mosley: 'I am not necessarily a writer. The moment writing ceases to be a convenient discipline for subduing my stupidity and laziness, I shall give it up and turn to some more practical form.' (Wilson says he did not mean this to be taken as a political threat – quite the opposite, since he was actually toying with the idea of becoming a monk.)

Not every review of *Religion and the Rebel* was a hundred per cent dismissive. Iris Murdoch, Oxford philosopher as well as burgeoning novelist, was a surprise supporter, declaring that Wilson's 'rashness' was 'welcome at a time when philosophy is being increasingly reserved for specialists'. But even she had found the book 'disappointing and unconvincing'; and most of the other reviewers did not bother to dilute their contempt.* 'Wilson's second book is really his first all over again,' complained the *Evening Standard*, suggesting that his real talent was for 'personal publicity' on the level of rock 'n' roll stars.

In the *New Statesman*, Janet Adam Smith was relieved that a protracted hoax had come to an end:

Now that we have *Religion and the Rebel* it is difficult to see that anyone can be a sucker any longer for Mr Wilson's kind of mystery. Again he whirls us off on a lightning tour of Great Outsiders, laying such clumsy paws on them

---

* Wilson says that Murdoch encouraged him to go to university, but he could not see the point.

that we have to keep reminding ourselves that it's not Rimbaud's or Rilke's fault if they feature in Mr Wilson's circus. There is no coherent argument, only a machine-gun of explosive assertions.

She was also dismayed by the Autobiographical Introduction:

No one counts but Colin Wilson; none of the other characters – family, friends, enemies, mistress, wife – for a minute comes to life. All he seems to ask of other people is that they shall add in some way to the image of himself ... John Osborne, his rival in the attention of the popular press, may be equally weak in logical reasoning, but he knows that other people exist.

The *Sunday Times* review was not by Connolly, but Raymond Mortimer. Headed 'NOT ANGRY ENOUGH', it began: 'Anyone who attacks a writer for being an angry young man displays his own vulgarity or ignorance. Young men with brains and hearts are right to be angry, and usually have been.' But after this rather vague piece of AYM bandwaggoning, Mortimer went on:

I cannot enjoy Mr Wilson's writings ... He distrusts reason, which I venerate, and he loathes human beings, whom on the whole I like ... He is never enlightening and sometimes inaccurate ... He ... is ... indifferent to human suffering and injustice, except when the victims are his fellow Outsiders ... He has never thought of himself as primarily a writer, he tells us: he feels merely that he is a man of genius: 'I may be the only man to bring things back to consciousness in this present age.' An English Luther or Hitler? Should we be shivering in our shoes?

In *Books and Art*, Anthony Hartley – former co-inventor and publicist of the Movement – not only savaged *Religion and the Rebel* as a 'mixture of banality and incomprehensibility', but cackled gleefully at the spectacle of Wilson's original promoters retreating swiftly: 'This is rather unpleasant; I hope they run a long way and, this time, uphill.'

Philip Toynbee, in his *Observer* review, did indeed seem to be covered with embarrassment. Under the heading 'UNHAPPY SEQUEL', he tried to wriggle off the hook he had made for himself eighteen months earlier:

The Outsider was an interesting and praiseworthy book for a number of quite different reasons . . . It was clumsily written and still more clumsily composed, but these faults were largely atoned for by the prevailing note of genuine passion . . . But if one was, and remains, a well-wisher of Mr Wilson's it is best to say as clearly as possible that his second book is a deplorable piece of work . . . He writes now as if he were a famous and established thinker with a rightful place in the most exalted company . . . The *naïveté* and monotony . . . are deeply depressing . . . No quotation can do justice to the flaccid banality of Mr Wilson's writing style, or . . . to . . . the grandiloquence of his claims . . . He has, I believe, a talent for something . . . But if he publishes another vulgarizing rubbish-bin of this kind it is hard to see how he will ever recover from it.

* *

Wilson was now trying his hand at the theatre. He had told Daniel Farson, after they had watched *Look Back in Anger* together, 'I can hardly wait to write my own play.' George Devine duly invited him to have a go, and he came up with a script called *The Death of God*. Meanwhile he caused a mild sensation at a Royal Court symposium by declaring that Shakespeare was a second-rate quote-monger.

Most authors in Wilson's situation would have kept thoroughly quiet upon receiving a rejection slip, but when Devine and his associates turned down *The Death of God* in the autumn of 1957, Wilson scurried off to his favourite sanctuary, Fleet Street. 'OUTSIDER'S PLAY IS THROWN OUT', proclaimed his old friend the *Daily Mail*. Wilson had given the paper a copy of his indignant reply to Devine – 'I am a busy writer with a great deal to do and you know that I regarded the play as practically commissioned by you' – but had presumably not reckoned on the *Mail* digging up another of the English Stage Company's progenitors, Ronald Duncan, who gave a very candid explanation of the rejection:

The play was bad. It was all argument and no drama . . . [It] is set in the year 2000. Atomic war is raging. There is a demented dictator being subjected to religious brainwashing. You can detect the influence of *Arms and the Man*, but the main inspiration seems to be a TV children's serial. It is dreary science fiction full of long arguments . . .

Mr Wilson cannot understand why we have not accepted him as the new Bernard Shaw he regards himself to be. What he should really be is a publicity man for a detergent firm.

As a final sting, the *Mail* asserted that Wilson had 'already cast Sir Laurence Olivier'.

Not only had Wilson fallen into disfavour with those who had virtually conjured his success out of nowhere; the AYM cult itself was now beginning to be rubbished by its own prophets. The issue of *Books and Bookmen* looking back on 1957 included a column headed 'CREDITS AND DISCREDITS':

> Surprise Success of the Year: *Room at the Top* by John Braine
> Flop of the Year: *Religion and the Rebel* by Colin Wilson
> Most Publicized Author of the Year: Colin Wilson
> We are tired of: Angry Young Men . . .

Similarly the books editor of the *News Chronicle* accompanied a scathing review of *Religion and the Rebel* with this little paragraph: 'STOP PRESS: From now on, the phrase "Angry Young Man" will not be used, on this page, in any context whatsoever.' But to be fair, this was caused not just by *Religion and the Rebel*, but also by the appearance (at the same time as Wilson's book) of what was meant to be an AYM symposium. It turned out to be disastrous in its own right.

16

The death of the 'angry epoch'

Declaration was the brainchild of Tom Maschler, future inventor of the Booker Prize, who in 1957 was an editor at MacGibbon & Kee, the firm that was publishing Bill Hopkins's *The Divine and the Decay*. He invited all the AYM to take part except John Braine, 'because I thought *Room at the Top* indifferent – it didn't interest or attract me'.

Only Kingsley Amis turned down Maschler's invitation, telling him: 'I hate all this pharisaical twittering about the "state of our civilization" and I suspect anyone who wants to buttonhole me about my "role in society"' – these being the main issues that Maschler wanted his contributors to raise. Maschler told the press: 'It takes a lot of guts to declare yourself to the world at such an early stage in your career. I won't say Amis hasn't got guts. But he has suffered a lot from being "grouped" with the others.' Amis was amused that John Wain had agreed to take part. 'He's not an angry young man,' Amis wrote to Larkin, 'so he gets together with them all to say he isn't.'

Curiously, the blurb did not mention the AYM at all (Maschler says he thought the label was 'demeaning to the kind of book we were trying to do'); but without Amis the whole thing looked rather slender, and Maschler had padded it out by enrolling Kenneth Tynan and the left-wing film-maker Lindsay Anderson.* Nor could the opening essay be described as the work of an Angry Young Man, since its author was by the thirty-eight-year-old Doris Lessing.

---

* Tynan described Anderson in a 1958 magazine article: 'A formidable film critic, director and polemicist, he has done more than anyone else to bring the idea of "committed art" into public controversy. Many Continental critics today speak of Anderson as if he were the dominant force in British cinema . . . He won an Academy

In her memoirs, Lessing (who by this time had published three novels) recalls how Maschler, 'very young – twenty-three – handsome, and ambitious' – arrived in her flat

with the demand that I write a piece for a book he planned, called *Declaration*. I said I hated writing think pieces. He said reproachfully that his whole future depended on this book. I later discovered that this was how we all agreed [to contribute essays]: we could not withstand Tom's need. Besides, he had approached Iris Murdoch – he said – and she had said no, and he had to have a woman in it: I could not let him down. This is how I became an angry young man.

The blurb claimed that these were writers who 'together . . . will help to mould our tomorrow'; yet it admitted that they did not 'form part of a united movement'. Similarly, in his brief introduction, Maschler dismissed the AYM label as a piece of low journalism, and complained that 'the writers who have set themselves the task of waking us up have been rendered harmless in the AYM cage'. He continued: 'It is important to note that although most of the contributors to this volume have at some time or other been labelled Angry Young Men they do *not* belong to a united movement . . . *Declaration* is a collection of separate positions.'

Similarly in his *Declaration* essay John Wain called the AYM label fatuous, 'a journalistic stunt', and John Osborne emphasized the non-existence of the group: 'I have only met Mr Amis once briefly, and I have never met Mr Wain, nor any of the rest of these poor successful freaks.' Yet Lessing seemed inclined to believe that there *was* such a group. Referring to 'the emergence of the Angry Young Men', she continued: 'I use the phrase, not because I think it is in any way an adequate description, but because it is immediately recognizable.' Moreover, she declared that 'the work of the angry young men [*sic*] was like an injection of vitality into the withered arm of British literature'. She continued:

Award in 1955 for *Thursday's Child*, a documentary about the education of deaf mutes, and a Venice Grand Prix two years later for a forty-minute exploration of life in Covent Garden; and though he has yet to make a feature film, his position as a critical moralist and spokesman for life-embracing cinema is unique in Britain.'

It seems to me that the work of all the new younger writers is essentially a protest against the pettiness and narrowness of what is offered them. From Jimmy Porter to Lucky Jim they are saying: 'I am too good for what I am offered.' And so they are. British life is at the moment petty and frustrating.

She also emphasized the limitations of the AYM: '... they are extremely provincial ... I do not mean ... that they come from or write about the provinces. I mean that their horizons are bounded by their immediate experience of British life and standards.' (She referred to Amis as 'a Welshman'.) She took John Braine as an example of what she meant, comparing *Room at the Top* with Stendhal: '... the hero of *Room at the Top*, whose values are similar to Stendhal's heroes ... does not see himself in relation to any larger vision. Therefore he remains petty.'

Though she revealed that she was a former Communist, and said she still believed that 'literature should be committed', Lessing came to no strong political conclusion in her essay. She deplored the latest hydrogen bomb tests which the British government had been conducting in the Pacific, but she did not propose that there should be any sort of organized protest. Similarly John Osborne expressed himself outraged, not so much by the tests themselves but by the jingoistic attitude taken by the popular press. Osborne quoted the *Daily Express* headline 'It's Our H-Bomb!', and went on:

The copywriters even managed to make it sound like cricket. As the *Daily Mail* put it ... 'The argument about whether or not Britain should explode her H-Bomb is ended. It has vanished in a mushroom over the Central Pacific.' The following day it printed a chatty piece about the wives of men who had made that mushroom. 'The H-Bomb Wives' it called them ... One of them was shown holding her baby. No one knows ... whether one day some Japanese housewife may hold up a baby that is not quite so well-formed or healthy because of a few British husbands and their game of nuclear cricket.

If Colin Wilson was aware of the nuclear arms race, he gave no sign of it in his *Declaration* essay. He declared that he could no longer call himself an Outsider, thanks to the success of that book; but this did not stop him devoting the essay to a redefinition of Outsiderism ('He is the "rebel without a cause"'). He also forecast 'the evolution of a higher type of man ... hardly less than superman'; but then, rather oddly, so did Doris Lessing: 'I am convinced,' she wrote, 'that there is a new man about to be born ...' She did not say whether he might resemble Colin Wilson.

John Osborne did not complain about the inclusion of Wilson in *Declaration*, but he was disgusted that Maschler's invitation had also been extended to Bill Hopkins and Stuart Holroyd, whom he described as Wilson's 'two altar boys'; he felt that their inclusion marred the book's 'literary clout'. (Peter Green, writing a mocking piece about *Declaration* in *Time and Tide*, labelled the Wilson–Hopkins–Holroyd trio 'the Spotty Nietzscheans'.)

Hopkins's *Declaration* piece forecast 'the end of pure rationalism as the foundation of our thinking', and declared that this would require 'a new leadership'. Similarly Holroyd brushed aside what he called 'the myths of democracy and representative government'. Reviewing *Declaration* in the *Observer*, Angus Wilson remarked that the Nazi party had been founded on this very mixture of ideas – 'the mystique of power' blended with 'vague, unsystematized radical discontent'. In *Declaration* itself, Kenneth Tynan described Wilson and his followers as 'young *Führers* of the soul ... who declare that Hitler, for all his faults, was after all an outsider'.

Tynan and Lindsay Anderson took a conventional left-wing stance in their essays (Lessing describes them as the book's 'real left-wing', and says that in comparison John Wain 'was a young Tory if there ever was one'). 'I want drama to be vocal in protest,' wrote Tynan, 'and I frankly do not see whence the voices will come if not from the Left.' Anderson rebuked Kingsley Amis for the political feebleness of his Fabian Society pamphlet: 'Socialism as a positive ideal ... apparently means nothing to him ... One can only wonder why he continues to vote Left ...' But this was mild stuff compared with John Osborne's essay.

He recalls that it was 'written hastily over a weekend punctuated by Maschler's deadline calls'. Working against the clock, he turned out a magnificent rant more than worthy of Jimmy Porter or Archie Rice. 'I want to make people feel,' he roared, 'to give them lessons in feeling. They can think afterwards.'

He launched what in 1957 was still certain to shock many readers –

an attack on the nation's worshipful attitude to the Royal Family. 'Royalty religion' was his term for it, and he compared it to pig-swill: 'The leader-writers and the bribed gossip-mongers only have to rattle their sticks in the royalty bucket for most of their readers to put their heads down in this trough of Queen-worship . . .' Royalty itself was like a 'gold filling in a mouthful of decay', and he was distressed that 'there should be so many empty minds, so many empty lives in Britain to sustain this fatuous [royalty] industry; that no one should have had the wit to laugh it into extinction, or the honesty to resist it'.

He then turned to the Church of England, which he claimed had 'repeatedly ducked' any burning moral issue – 'poverty, unemployment, fascism, war, South Africa, the H-Bomb . . . Its bishops have sounded like bewigged old perverts at Assizes.' And he proudly flaunted (indeed, somewhat exaggerated) the lowness of his own low social origins, describing his Grove grandmother as 'a tough, sly old Cockney'.

Yet he fought shy of taking up an altogether clear political position: 'I am not going to define my own socialism. Socialism is an experimental idea, not a dogma; an attitude to truth and liberty, the way people should live and treat each other.' And he recalled the sole occasion on which he had assumed a public political stance: 'During the Suez crisis I . . . collected signatures to a letter to *The Times* . . . It was a very militant letter, possibly seditious even, which may have been the reason why it was not published. This time [the nuclear tests] I didn't even send a letter to *The Times*.'

* *

Declaration was due to be launched in October 1957 with a party at the Royal Court, but George Devine's board of directors wished to dissociate themselves from Osborne's 'criticism of royalty', as the *Daily Herald* put it; though he had carefully refrained from attacking the Royal Family as such.* The party was relocated to what Osborne calls 'a crumbling, recherché bohemian retreat' – a basement club near

---

* In his book on George Devine, Irving Wardle suggests another reason – that the Royal Court 'had got wind of a plot to tip a bucket of whitewash over Colin Wilson (who had lately been kicking up a fuss because the Court had rejected one of his plays)'.

the theatre, called the Pheasantry. The magazine *Books and Bookmen* printed a whole page of photos of the evening – John Wain chatting to Doris Lessing, Ken Tynan with Lindsay Anderson – but admitted that it had been something of a disappointment for A Y M-watchers: 'Everybody was waiting for Colin Wilson, who, it was announced, was on the train from Cornwall' – where Wilson was now making his home, with Joy Stewart, in a rented cottage. 'Neither the train nor Colin Wilson arrived. John Osborne was in America, Stuart Holroyd was otherwise engaged. This left only the rump of the group represented in the book, and Bill Hopkins appeared to be camera-shy.'

On the opposite page, *Books and Bookmen* carried a scathing review of *Declaration* by Daniel Farson. 'The really heartening thing,' he began,

is its complete failure. Not its commercial failure, for I believe the first edition has sold out, but its failure as a statement of any real significance or permanence. It would have been too awful if this conceited and remote little document had been acclaimed as the voice of a generation, but the opposite has happened. For the first time we see the 'angry young men' in their proper perspective. They not only disagree, they actively dislike each other and they are not nearly angry enough; there is instead a note of sullen petulance. *Declaration* marks the death of the 'angry epoch' . . .

The only attempt at a movement comes from Colin Wilson who is trailed by Stuart Holroyd and, inevitably, by his literary dog, Mr Bill Hopkins, whose inclusion in the book is one of its mysteries.

Other reviewers included Henry Fairlie. Writing in *Tribune*, which had just printed extracts from *Declaration*, he wondered 'why should a Socialist newspaper present these writers as either desirable or representative contemporary figures? For let there be no doubt what their protest is about. They resent the fact that Britain is no longer a Great Power. They don't like being Little Englanders . . .'

But the most pertinent review came from Angus Wilson in the *Observer*. Like Doris Lessing, he felt that there really had been a literary movement called the Angry Young Men. One of their characteristics had been their recognition that 'the Press is the most powerful organ of propaganda in the modern world and that serious writers should not hesitate to use it. The misrepresentation they complain of is perhaps the price they pay.' This acceptance of media publicity explained 'the strange atmosphere of group advertisement which they have allowed to grow round them . . . No one who is anyone . . . can afford to be seen without *Declaration* . . .'

Turning to what the AYM had actually said and done, he went on:

. . . nobody under fifty . . . can sincerely feel content with the present state of the arts. We are all waiting for someone great to turn up. And in our discontent we are often led to speculate whether England's artistic death does not reflect a wider sterility in the social and political structure of the country. To have voiced this gnawing fear . . . is surely the real achievement of the Angry Young Men as a group. Much of their picture is pure myth but it responds to our present discontents . . .

However, he felt that *Declaration* was a total failure as an AYM manifesto: 'these contributions . . . are simply not serious enough for the important protest they claim to be voicing . . . the total content is trivial . . .'

Tom Maschler recalls that, despite the reviews, *Declaration* sold extremely well – 'about 20,000 copies in the UK alone, and there were five or six translations. It far exceeded my wildest hopes and dreams.'

* *

Angus Wilson's observation that the AYM loved publicity was borne out in the month of *Declaration*'s launch, when Colin Wilson even used the terrible reviews he had been getting for *Religion and the Rebel* as an opportunity for a gossip-column story. 'He declared himself well pleased,' claimed the *News Chronicle* on 23 October 1957.

From Old Walls, his tiny, blue-painted, galvanized-roofed cottage near Mevagissey, in Cornwall, he declared: 'The opinions expressed by the critics have been mostly fair, and some very good. It is very encouraging for a young man like myself to find various book critics running over themselves to get in a "first line" – good, bad or indifferent – about what I write.'

Wilson – who had been advised by Victor Gollancz to give up trying to write for a living and get himself a job – has claimed elsewhere that the failure of *Religion and the Rebel* was something of a relief to him:

I got so sick of having that spotlight beating on me for eighteen months that to suddenly be once again in a dark corner brought a marvellous feeling of relaxation. I'd said in *The Outsider* that the whole point about an Outsider is that he goes his own way; he plods along, and refuses to be diverted by the insiders. So I thought it was incumbent upon me to do precisely that. But I must confess it was pretty hard work.

The press had not altogether lost interest in Wilson. The *News Chronicle* reported in September 1958 that he, Hopkins and Holroyd were going to live under the same roof 'for a marathon writing stint. They intend to work on a new three-part study of the heroic mentality. Each man's share: 50,000 words.' This came to nothing, as did Wilson's attempt to get his second play, *The Metal Flower Blossom*, put on by a theatrical group in Plymouth, with himself in the cast. Again, the *News Chronicle* picked up the story: 'Mr Wilson will be on the stage for five or ten minutes. The character he plays will make a very long speech as a sort of spokesman for existentialist philosophy.'

Surprisingly, Fleet Street took little interest in Hopkins's announcement that he was forming a new political party, the Spartacans. Word also got round that Wilson and Hopkins had paid a visit to Sir Oswald Mosley. Holroyd says it was 'merely a social call', and Kenneth Allsop reports that Wilson, who described Mosley as 'rather a decent chap', had 'no knowledge *whatever* of the history of Mosley and the British Union of Fascists'. Allsop remarks on the 'vast virgin forests of naïveté' which occupied much of Wilson's mind.

Now that Wilson had settled in Cornwall, the community in Notting Hill began to break up. Bill Hopkins commissioned a home-made blue plaque to be fixed to the house,* which stated that a community of geniuses had lived there; but it soon disappeared. Meanwhile Holroyd managed to get a play accepted by the Royal Court, for a single Sunday

---

* They had already left 24 Chepstow Villas for a house in nearby Chepstow Road. Wilson says he never actually lived there, but had the use of a room when he came up from Cornwall.

performance. It was called *The Tenth Chance*, and John Osborne was in the audience. 'How anyone,' he writes, 'could have countenanced this farrago . . . even as a bad joke on a Sunday night was mystifying.' The poet Christopher Logue recalls being there too, sitting with Ken Tynan:

The play concerned a man finding God under torture by the Nazis . . . The hero, tied to a chair, was beaten by officials of the Gestapo, while other members of the cast paced the stage, intoning: 'Receive him into the kingdom of light!' . . . At which point, rather to my own surprise, I shouted out: 'Rubbish!'

Someone – according to Holroyd it was Colin Wilson – called out to Logue to shut up or get out, whereupon Logue made a noisy exit. Osborne says that when the curtain came down, 'custard-pie anarchy broke out in the audience', and Holroyd says there were faction fights which continued in the pub next door – an 'Angry Young Brawl', as the newspapers inevitably reported it – though Holroyd claims he arrived too late to witness it himself:

Colin, Bill [Hopkins] and Michael Hastings were involved in a scene with Logue and Tynan. Colin was reported to have said, 'We'll get you. We'll stamp you out, Tynan,' and 'Tell your friend to keep his filthy mouth closed in future.' To which Tynan replied, 'Stay out of my life, Wilson,' and said to onlookers: 'There's your supposed leader, your younger generation. He's a dictator.' Then there was a scuffle in the course of which Logue landed on the floor. One report had it that he had been dragged down by the hair by Colin, and another that Michael had pulled away his chair from under him. When I went into the pub I was steered away from the corner where all the action was . . . Sandy Wilson . . . led me to the bar where John Osborne . . . said, 'Terrific! It looks as though the English theatre's waking up at last.'

17

John knocked down the door

By the summer of 1957, Kenneth Allsop was sufficiently convinced that the whole AYM episode had run its course that he began to write a book about it, called *The Angry Decade: a survey of the cultural revolt of the nineteen fifties*. Although the decade still had two years to run, the book was published the following spring.

Tackling the usual question of whether the AYM actually existed as a group, Allsop came up with a compromise answer:

Is the Angry Young Man label wildly off the mark? Certainly all who have been herded together under the banner, while perhaps finding the advertisement not without value and the accompanying fame not unpleasant, individually hotly denies that that has any connection with *him*. But it does ring a response in most people today. The names Kingsley Amis, Colin Wilson and John Osborne peal out like a treble bob, cracked with discord to those with more sophisticated ears, but there they are, the Three Musketeers of the revolutionary army ... Amis, flippant and facetious ... Osborne, whirling words like a meat cleaver; and Wilson, a sort of philosophical steeplejack scaling sickening heights with untested equipment.

More dramatically, Allsop felt able to declare that 'a generation [has] suddenly made up its mind. Not so much to rebel against the old order of authority and standards, but to refuse to vote for it.' Yet the substance of his book was merely a predictable plod through the writings of the AYM (and a number of other writers whose work he considered to have affinities with them), with no attempt to survey the feelings of their audience or to prove his claim that a 'cultural revolt' had really been taking place on a wide scale.

In his chapter on Colin Wilson and his followers, Allsop observed that there was 'more than a sniff of fascism' about them; yet he declared that Wilson was 'obligatory reading' because 'he has . . . fumbled his way through to a *European* attitude that is almost unique among our postwar rebels'.

Towards the end of the book, Allsop turned to America, mentioning the imminent publication in Britain of 'an outlandish novel' called *On the Road*, by 'Jack Kerouac, the self-nominated spokesman for what he has named the "beat" (short for beatific) generation'. Allsop continued: 'The beats appear to be a minority of separatists . . . a rootless gang of jukebox hobos . . . who hurl around the American continent in stolen or borrowed cars . . . They shout "Yes!" to every experience . . .' He felt that they had few things in common with the AYM.

In 1959 two Americans, Gene Feldman and Max Gartenberg, published an anthology titled *The Beat Generation and the Angry Young Men*, in which they set out to prove that the two 'movements' were similar searches for freedom and self-identity. 'In the United States of America,' they wrote,

those 'new barbarians' . . . are the Beat Generation. In England, with certain differences, they are the Angry Young Men. Both . . . are social phenomena which have found increasing literary expression . . . In the long run, they may well be the advance column of a vast moral revolution.

But the extracts they chose for the anthology made it clear that the Beats had not the slightest resemblance to the AYM. Passages from Kerouac and Allen Ginsberg, dwelling on drugs and sex, made the AYM excerpts – which included Jim Dixon giving his Merrie England lecture, Joe Lampton confronting his future father-in-law, and the opening chapter of *The Outsider* – look by comparison like a storm in a tea-shop.

In November 1958, while he was on a visiting lectureship to Princeton, Amis shared a platform in New York with Kerouac. According to Amis, Kerouac talked 'incoherently' and for far too long, while Ginsberg, who was in the audience, contributed nothing audible. Writing in *Punch* the following month, Malcolm Bradbury invented the 'Beet Generation', a group of would-be intellectuals in the English

Midlands, so named 'because the only work they did was to work in the sugar beet factory at harvest time'. Influenced by Colin Wilson, they 'kept diaries about their phallic selves and every entry began: "The agony continues – unabated." '*

* *

The AYM were still newsworthy. Colin Wilson noted in the autumn of 1959 that '*Woman's Hour* has just rung Bill Hopkins to ask his opinion of seams in ladies' stockings', and 'last night the *Evening Standard* woke me up to tell me the Russian rocket had landed on the moon and had I any comment?'

The film industry was helping to keep the AYM in the public eye. 'Mr John Braine,' wrote Thomas Wiseman of the *Evening Standard*, who had been to watch the filming of *Room at the Top* in Yorkshire in June 1958,

allowed his eyes to linger on Mr Laurence Harvey and Miss Heather Sears. Then he said: 'You are all just figments of my imagination' . . . *Room at the Top* has now sold 200,000 copies throughout the world . . . Mr Braine . . . has even gone so far as to be an extra in his own story . . . 'Of course I want it to be a good film,' he said, 'because the more successful it is the more copies of my book will be sold . . . I got £5,000 for [the film rights]' . . . If Mr Braine's preoccupation with hard cash is at all typical, pretty soon all that the angry young angries will have left to be angry about will be income tax.

A film of *Lucky Jim* had been released during 1957, produced and directed by the Boulting Brothers, with the British light-comedy actor Ian Carmichael in the title role. Amis told Larkin he was 'all smiles' about it in public, but his private feelings were 'a very different kettle of fish'. Kenneth Allsop describes it as 'a skimming of the slapstick, with the book's mild acidity drained off or watered down. When the picture came out the London *Evening Standard* also further dissemi-

---

* Something like the Beet Generation is portrayed in a 1960 novel by Noel Woodin, *Room at the Bottom*, a first-person narrative by a young would-be poet, Julian Starke, who supports himself by taking various jobs, including agricultural labouring. Despite its title, the book is picaresque rather than parody.

nated the adventures of Jim Dixon by serializing "the story of the film".' The film of *Look Back in Anger*, released in 1959, ought to have been closer in spirit to the original, since Osborne was closely involved with the production; it was the first to be made by Woodfall Films, a company (named after the Chelsea street where Osborne had shared a house with Mary Ure) set up by Osborne himself and Tony Richardson, initially to film *Look Back* and *The Entertainer*. Richard Burton, though at thirty-four rather old for the part, turned in a creditable performance as Jimmy Porter, and Richardson's direction was faithful to the spirit of his stage production; but Osborne says the film was 'politely' rather than enthusiastically received, and was 'described as "beautifully made", a certain euphemism for dull and arty'. It was chosen for the 1959 royal film première 'in the gracious presence of HRH Princess Margaret'.

Jimmy Porter had become a member of the Establishment; but by 1959 his assertion that 'there aren't any good, brave causes left' was seeming a little premature. The Campaign for Nuclear Disarmament had been formally constituted at the beginning of the previous year, and the first protest march took place at Easter 1958 – from London to the government's Atomic Weapons Research Establishment at Aldermaston, rather than the other way round, as was subsequently the case. 'Not many marchers left London that day,' writes Doris Lessing, a founder member of CND. 'But there was something about this march, and people kept joining all along the route.'

Lessing emphasizes the width of the marchers' political spectrum: '. . . the banners were a map of socialist Britain. There were even Tory groups.' But one group – if it existed – was notably absent. Lessing recalls that 'John Wain, who didn't approve of the march at all, stood on a bridge that crossed the route, looking down, and, while friends waved up to him, shouting, "Come and join us", tragically shook his head.' Kingsley Amis, though he had demonstrated over Suez, was nowhere to be seen.* John Osborne later attended the inaugural meeting of another nuclear protest group, the Committee of 100, but never

---

* The nearest Amis got to supporting CND was to complain, in a 1961 letter to Karl Miller, then literary editor of the *New Statesman*, of a leader in that magazine which criticized CND for dividing the Labour Party over the issue of unilateral disarmament.

joined the march. Indeed Kenneth Allsop, writing a few months after it, seems to be right in his statement that 'not a single' Angry Young Man was there.

However, the marchers did include a young man whose plays were about to continue the theatrical revolution begun by *Look Back in Anger*.

* *

Arnold Wesker was three years younger than Osborne. Born in 1932 into the working-class Jewish community in the Stepney district of east London, he left school at sixteen, undertook odd jobs, and then (at eighteen) was signed up for two years' National Service in the RAF, which later inspired his play *Chips with Everything*. Next he moved to Norfolk, did farm labouring, and worked as a kitchen porter in Norwich. Returning to London, he became a trainee chef in a West End restaurant, then went with his girlfriend 'Dusty' Bicker to Paris, again working in a restaurant. Meanwhile he saved enough to study at London School of Film Technique (1955–6). There, he met Lindsay Anderson, who encouraged him to write. He was very excited by Anderson's trenchant left-wing essay in *Declaration*: 'I believe [it] to be one of the latchkeys that unlocked my first successful writing.'

Wesker's first completed play, *The Kitchen*, was entered in an *Observer* play competition in 1956, without success, and was rejected by several managements. However, two years later Wesker's *Chicken Soup with Barley* opened at the Belgrade in Coventry in July 1958 and transferred (in the same month) to the Royal Court for a week. *Roots* opened at Coventry in May 1959, transferred to the Royal Court in June, and had a short West End run. *I'm Talking about Jerusalem* opened in Coventry in April 1960, and the entire 'Wesker Trilogy' (these three plays) was presented at the Royal Court in the summer of 1960. (Devine had meanwhile put on *The Kitchen* at the Court in September 1959.)

A. Alvarez, reviewing *The Kitchen* in the *New Statesman*, observed that 'a great deal of second-rate work has got by because its authors were Clever Young Men, Angry Young Men, or simply Young Men ... *The Kitchen* needs no excuses; it is a first-rate dramatic achievement in its own right and by any standards.' But another cliché was being coined: the 'kitchen-sink' drama.

The Kitchen follows life in a restaurant kitchen from dawn till late at night. Kenneth Tynan said that it 'achieves something that few playwrights have ever attempted; it dramatizes work, the daily collision of man with economic necessity, the repetitive toil that consumes that large portion of human life which is not devoted to living'. The Trilogy covers the period 1936–1959, as seen through the life of the Kahns, a Jewish East End family like Wesker's.

The playwright David Hare has remarked how Osborne led the way for Wesker and many others: 'John knocked down the door and a whole generation of playwrights came piling through, many of them not even acknowledging him as they came . . .' Wesker says he was 'oblivious' of *Look Back in Anger* when it was first staged in 1956, but when he saw it the following year the impact on him was enormous:

I remember . . . the energy of the dialogue and the way it fused to the personality of Jimmy Porter . . . the image of those dead Sunday [church] bells ringing as they had rung emptily for me in Norwich . . . and an exhilarated feeling that not only was theatre an activity where important things were happening but one where I could add to what was happening. Six months later . . . I began to write *Chicken Soup with Barley*.

The Royal Court, as well as staging Wesker, made other discoveries of new writing talent. In February 1958 Devine co-directed, with its thirty-year-old author Ann Jellicoe, an experimental play (which had won an *Observer* prize) about a London street gang, *The Sport of My Mad Mother*. A play by twenty-seven-year-old former architecture student John Arden, *The Waters of Babylon*, was given a Sunday night performance by Devine in October 1957, and Arden's *Live Like Pigs*, about social conflict in a housing estate, had a run on the main stage in September the following year (and caused much controversy). Harold Pinter, whose *The Birthday Party* had flopped in the West End in 1958, fared better when the Court staged two of his one-act plays, *The Room* and *The Dumb Waiter*, in March 1960. Meanwhile in May 1958 Joan Littlewood's Theatre Workshop in east London had staged *A Taste of Honey* by Salford-born Shelagh Delaney, who had failed the eleven-plus, left school at sixteen, and had begun writing the play – a portrait of the relationship between a 'semi-whore' and her worldly-wise schoolgirl daughter – when she was only seventeen. (It transferred to the West End and was filmed by Tony Richardson for his and Osborne's company Woodfall in 1962.) Littlewood also gave the first productions outside Ireland of *The Quare Fellow* (1956) and *The Hostage* (1958) by Brendan Behan, while *The Hamlet of Stepney Green*, a portrait of East End Jewish life by thirty-two-year-old Bernard Kops, was first staged by Frank Hauser at the Oxford Playhouse in 1958. Arnold Wesker makes the point that these mould-breaking playwrights had not reached theatrical success via the usual route: 'Look, the mirror showed, you don't need a university education to be an artist – Osborne . . . Pinter . . . Behan, Delaney, Kops . . .'

In his 1962 book *Anger and After*, a study of these 'kitchen-sink' playwrights, critic John Russell Taylor made the same point, emphasizing 'their predominantly working-class origins'. Generally speaking their politics were left-wing; Wesker, for example, not only marched to Aldermaston but was (along with Bertrand Russell) among the handful of Committee of 100 anti-nuclear protesters jailed for civil disobedience. But Wesker stresses that, while he and his fellow young playwrights were politically motivated, they felt no anger against the society that had thrust them to sudden fame:

There never was an Angry Young Man . . . Neither John Osborne nor we, his peers, were angry. On the contrary, we were very happy. Our work was being performed and we were earning more money in a year than in our entire lives till then. Ill-informed interviewers still ask, as though it were the most perceptive question ever, '*Are you still angry?*' It is a miracle they escape being murdered on the spot.

18

Angry Old Men

Looked at superficially, Kingsley Amis's life from *Lucky Jim* onwards seems to have been a continuous series of successes. By the time he died in 1995, at the age of seventy-three, he had won the Booker Prize (for his 1986 novel *The Old Devils*) and had been knighted (in 1990). Moreover he had managed to remain iconoclastic to the end: for example his novels *Jake's Thing* (1978) and *Stanley and the Women* (1984) were a misogynistic counterblast to the fashionable feminism of the Seventies and Eighties. On the personal level, however, it was a life with a considerable amount of unhappiness, or at least discontent. The novels he wrote after *Lucky Jim* – almost two dozen of them – chart the decline and eventual collapse of his marriage to Hilly, the happy beginning of his relationship with Elizabeth Jane Howard (whom he married in 1965), but then the downhill slide of this second marriage. Following his second divorce, in 1983, he caused a certain amount of public amusement by choosing to share his house with Hilly and her third husband, chiefly so that he could be looked after as his heavy drinking fuelled the decline of his health. Having metamorphosed from Angry Young Man to Old Devil, he ended up pathetically dependent on the woman he had chosen to reject.

Philip Larkin's later life, when examined cursorily, seems to have been narrow and disappointing. He never married, remained a university librarian until the end of his days, and wrote fewer and fewer poems as time passed. After *The Less Deceived* (1955) and *The Whitsun Weddings* (1964) came *High Windows* (1974), and then virtually silence, until his death from cancer in 1985, at the age of sixty-three. 'I haven't given poetry up,' he said in the last year of his life, 'but I rather think that poetry has given me up, which is a great sorrow to me.' However, he went on: 'I would sooner not write any poems than write bad poems'; and *High Windows* contains few poems that are not faultless. Moreover by the 1980s he had achieved a level of fame and popularity only equalled by John Betjeman. Shortly before his death he was made a Companion of Honour; a little while earlier he had been offered, and had declined, the Poet Laureateship.

Asked in 1984 what he felt about the enormous popularity of his poetry, he replied:

It does surprise me rather . . . You write down things that you think are absolutely peculiar to yourself . . . Then you suddenly find people writing in from all over the place, saying, 'That's what I felt' . . . I find this very, very gratifying indeed.

John Wain struggled on as a freelance, through the late Fifties and the Sixties, producing a novel every two or three years, usually to mixed reviews. *A Travelling Woman* (1959), which dealt with adultery, was criticized for the shallowness of its characters. *Strike the Father Dead* (1962) is based on a much more original idea: the teenage son of a pedantic classics professor drops out to become a jazz pianist in seedy nightclubs. This book recaptures something of the dreamlike oddity and charm of *Hurry On Down*. The other Wain novel from this period that leaves a permanent impression on the mind is *The Smaller Sky* (1967), about a scientist experiencing a mid-life crisis that drives him to make his home in Paddington Station – with eventually fatal results.

Wain enjoyed a modest renewal of fame in 1973, when he was elected to Oxford's five-year Professorship of Poetry. He frequently published collections of his verse, as well as critical essays, an autobiography (*Sprightly Running*, 1962), and a biography of Samuel Johnson (1974). His final work of fiction was a nostalgic trilogy set in Oxford, *Where the Rivers Meet* (1988–94). He married again twice, was gradually hampered by failing eyesight and diabetes, and died, aged sixty-eight, just before the final volume of the trilogy was published.

One of his sons by his second marriage, Will Wain, denies that his father was a disappointed man, envious of the much greater success enjoyed by his former protégés, Amis and Larkin: 'He remained very loyal to Philip, and never said a bad word about him or his poetry.

With Amis there had been a bust-up, but my father regretted this, and always felt they could have mended the friendship if they had run into each other in a pub – he wasn't a vindictive type.' Amis describes this rift with Wain in his memoirs:

Several times after moving to Swansea I had asked him to come and stay. He never came, so, as one does, I stopped asking him. Later, perhaps years later, some third party, whose own views on proper behaviour could themselves have done with a lick of paint, told me John had confided to him that the reason for the declined invitations was his fear that Hilly would 'break down his bedroom door' to get her hands on him. The reader must take it from me that that had never been her way, and even if it had been, she had assured me with repeated emphasis that many and many a door would have had to fall before she got to John's. Too angry to have the sense to keep my mouth shut, I faced him with the story. Instead of denying it, he remarked that it showed a grave deficiency in my informant's sense of humour. From that moment I considered myself released from any duty to keep to myself what I thought of his books . . .

Amis's later letters are indeed peppered with sneers at Wain and his writings. In 1973 Amis told Anthony Thwaite he was abstaining from voting for the Oxford poetry chair, 'feeling it wouldn't be enough of a disaster if [Stephen] Spender got in to justify voting for Wain. Because if W. gets in, he won't be amazed, overjoyed, grateful, etc. Oh no, he'll *think it's his due*, do you see . . . ?' And when he heard about Wain's failing eyesight, he joked to Larkin it was the 'result of meths-drinking to save on drink bills'. (Wain was indeed seriously short of money towards the end of his life, and had to rely heavily on handouts from the Society of Authors and a Civil List pension.) These and many other such jibes by Amis remained unpublished until after Wain's death, but he was still alive when Thwaite's edition of Larkin's letters appeared in 1992, and Will Wain says he was 'very hurt' by some of the references to him.

* *

Ritual in the Dark, the Jack the Ripper novel that Colin Wilson had begun before writing *The Outsider*, was finally published in 1960. 'The

Outsider was hastily written and I have no very high opinion of it,' Wilson told one of the Sunday papers. 'The novel which I have been writing for the past five years is far more important.' Reviewing *Ritual in the Dark*, *The Times Literary Supplement* judged Wilson to be

no prose stylist. He is not witty. His ear for dialogue is rudimentary . . . Much of the page-acreage is devoted to . . . making and drinking tea . . . going to the lavatory and so on. The corresponding negative virtue of the writing is that it is clear, unornate and thus unpretentious.

Other reviews were more hostile (Frank Kermode wrote that the book displayed 'an immature arrogance'), but Wilson says that the novel was 'fairly successful – it didn't sell as well as *The Outsider* but it did sell quite well'. Over the next ten years he published nine further novels, several with 'outsider' heroes and themes, though by the end of the Sixties he was moving into science fiction. Alongside the novels he continued to write *Outsider*-type non-fiction, including *Origins of the Sexual Impulse* (1963), *Beyond the Outsider: the Philosophy of the Future* (1965), and *Introduction to the New Existentialism* (1967) – books which he recalls were either 'ignored' or 'slammed' by the critics.

Wilson also says that his literary prolixity was due to a chronic shortage of cash:

The Outsider made a fair amount of money; it had been translated into sixteen languages, but then it only brought in about a shilling a copy . . . So we were and always have been permanently broke, which explains to a large extent why I've written so many books.

He also made some money from lecture tours of America: 'I usually returned to England with just enough money to pay all the outstanding bills, and start again from square one.'

In the 1970s his work took a new turn, when he was invited by an American publisher to write a book about the occult:

I accepted it simply as a commission, as a way of making some money, without any real belief in the subject at all. To my astonishment, when I began to study the subject I found that I got more and more absorbed; before long, I realized that the paranormal has as secure a foundation as physics or chemistry.

The commercial success of *The Occult* (1971) led to a stream of further Wilson books on the paranormal; meanwhile he also diversified into 'true crime', with titles such as *A Casebook of Murder* (1969). Other ventures in more recent years have included books on the Atlantis myth, and a 'Spider World' series of Tolkienesque fantasy novels. By the end of the twentieth century he had published about a hundred books.

In a 1986 letter, Kingsley Amis claimed that Wilson was still making fantastic claims about his literary stature, telling a BBC reporter: 'It's Dante, Shakespeare, Shaw and me, okay? Otherwise no interview.' Certainly an interview with him that same year included the remark: 'I suspect that I am probably the greatest writer of the twentieth century.' Asked about this, Wilson says there was 'a tongue-in-cheek' element about his claims for himself – but then makes them all over again:

Obviously I'm pretty talented, pretty clever – I'd be stupid if I didn't recognize that. And it strikes me that in five hundred years' time they'll say 'Wilson was a genius', because I'm a turning-point in intellectual history. The problem of pessimism is lying across our contemporary culture like some giant log, and somebody had to come along and shift it. And I think that's what I've done, and one day that achievement will be recognized.

In his 1958 book on the Angry Young Men, Kenneth Allsop reported that Bill Hopkins was working on a second novel, called *Time of Totality*, while Stuart Holroyd was writing *The Despair of Europe*, 'which he intends as a survey of the collapse of the moral order in Europe'. Neither book came to pass, though Holroyd completed an autobiography, *Flight and Pursuit*, which was published in 1959. The *TLS* review of it began scathingly:

There is something pathetic in his sublime disregard of his own pretentiousness ... When it comes to the business of getting into bed with a girl there is surely no excuse for saying that he has 'contracted a sexual relationship with [his] mistress' as though he had contracted smallpox . . . Yet . . . there are insights . . . and large stretches of reasoned argument which are notably absent from the writings of . . . Mr Colin Wilson and Mr Bill Hopkins . . . [The book has] if not a permanent value, at least an element of promise.

1959 was also the year in which Sir Oswald Mosley tried to enlist the support of Wilson, Holroyd and Hopkins for his candidacy in the 1959 General Election. Wilson liked Mosley, describing him as 'sincere' and blaming his notoriety on his followers rather than his fascist policies. Bill Hopkins agrees: 'He was an enormously cultured and enlightened man, but he did have this silly admiration for Hitler.' Hopkins had been half-seriously attempting, in 1958, to form his Spartacan political party, named after the anti-Rome rebel Spartacus. 'It was on the lines of World Government,' he explains, 'but it didn't get very far, because I was totally penniless.' The alliance between Mosley and the Wilsonites never happened, and Mosley failed to win a parliamentary seat.

Holroyd writes that he 'left London and the literary scene in 1959 and went to live in St Leonards-on-Sea'. There he opened a language school, followed by others in Hastings and Eastbourne, but later he returned to full-time writing, producing (like Wilson) books on the paranormal and related subjects, as well as a sex manual.

The 'sexual revolution' of the Sixties brought the Wilson–Hopkins–Holroyd trio together again briefly in 1965, when Hopkins played a part in founding the magazine *Penthouse*. This is how he recalls it:

Bob Guccione phoned me one day, and said: 'I'm told you're the only man in Fleet Street who can start a magazine without any money. And I've got an idea, because I'm the greatest photographer of nudes in the world.' So of course my satanic sense of humour was aroused. And I was the first editor and founder of it.

The first issue of *Penthouse: The Magazine for Men*, published in March 1965, actually names Guccione as 'Editor and Publisher', Hopkins as 'Editorial Director', and Colin Wilson as 'Contributing Editor'. Hopkins explains that the editorial policy was to mix Guccione's nudes with 'the big names of literature', a number of whom agreed to take part – though most of them changed their minds when flyers for the magazine were destroyed by the Post Office on grounds of obscenity, and questions began to be asked in Parliament.

The first *Penthouse* included a symposium on whether the 'changing moral climate' of Britain amounted to a true 'sexual revolution'; among the participants were Hopkins, Wilson, Holroyd and Alan Sillitoe. Hopkins recalls that John Braine agreed to contribute, but then backed out. The text accompanying the nude photos and the men's fashion advertisements had faint echoes of Braine's first novel: 'Young Man Hits The Top! Plenty of room for anything up there . . .'

Hopkins's name disappeared from *Penthouse* after the first issue (he describes Guccione as a 'scorpion'); Wilson's lingered until the second. After this episode, Hopkins began to dabble in the antiques trade, and eventually became the owner of several shops in the Portobello Road, a few blocks away from Chepstow Villas. He continued to write in his spare time, and (at the time of writing) is still doing so, in his seventies:

I've written and destroyed at least half a dozen novels. They didn't fulfil what I wanted. You see, basically my life has been dedicated to one idea: that English literature can never be anything until we formulate new heroes and heroines. Under liberal, democratic thinking, we've removed the apparatus for people to occupy heroic positions and suffer classic downfalls. And that is the major flaw that has stopped English literature from being great. So my life has been dedicated to trying to create such heroes and heroines, and it's very difficult.

* *

John Braine's second novel, *The Vodi*, was published in 1959, the year after *Room at the Top*. The *TLS* reviewer generously gave away the plot:

. . . the . . . subject [is] Failure. The hero, Dick Corvey, is a patient in a tuberculosis sanatorium, allergic to antibiotics, likely – and even willing – to die. His will to live is restored by an affair with a pretty nurse; meanwhile, his unsuccessful career until early middle age is related in a series of flashbacks. He has been haunted throughout his life by a childhood fantasy of Evil: a race of malevolent beings known as the Vodi, ruled by a hideous ogress called Nelly. He recovers from his illness, and the Vodi seem to be exorcised; then the nurse, who has half-reciprocated his affection, decides to marry her rich careerist lover after all. A tragic ending seems inevitable: the loss of Dick's regained will to live, his relapse and death. He decides, however, to compound with his destiny (or the Vodi), and to accept a second-best solution: an affair with a less attractive nurse and, when he is discharged as cured, a job as a male nurse in the sanatorium. Here it might have been better to leave him; but Mr Braine, having decided to write a novel about failure, cannot bear that the failure shall be complete, and the bitch-goddess beckons once again . . .

The book has not the drive and confidence of its predecessor, but is in some respects a more interesting novel . . .

Braine himself said that the Vodi represented 'the essential unfairness of life'. The book sold poorly, and Braine then returned to the adventures of Joe Lampton, with a sequel called *Life at the Top* (1962). Asked whether this was 'an easy way out', Braine replied: 'I wanted to go on and see what those characters grew into.' In Joe's case, he had grown into a husband impatient with his sterile married state, but lacking the conviction to abandon family responsibilities for personal fulfilment.

If Braine was marking time here and in his next book, *The Jealous God* (1964) – the study of a man whose sexual awakening is inhibited by his repressive Catholic mother – he then made an abrupt move; but not in a direction that his readers might have expected. In *The Crying Game* (1968), a novel about the shallowness of the 'permissive society', he began his metamorphosis into an unashamed Conservative, and an extreme right-wing one at that. Kingsley Amis remarks that, when they had first become acquainted, Braine was 'a full-dress, Aldermaston-marching nuclear disarmer', but during the mid-Sixties he converted to 'an extreme right-winger it was embarrassing to be allied with' – strong language, considering that Amis himself had undergone a similar conversion.

As early as 1956, a perceptive individual (A. Watkin Jones) in the BBC's Welsh Region, when asked whether Amis would be a suitable panellist for a radio current affairs discussion programme called *Any Questions*, gave this answer:

He has no politics that you could easily catalogue under any of the accepted headings. At times he appears extremely right-wing, but at other times he shows a great sympathy with leftists' point of view . . . Possibly, he could be described as 'anarchist' . . . I would hesitate to use him in *Any Questions* unless I were definitely in an experimental mood.

By 1967 the left-wing element in this idiosyncratic mixture had mostly evaporated, as Amis himself explained in an article headlined 'Why Lucky Jim Turned Right':

In 1964 I voted Labour for the last time, chickened out the following year by voting for the Anti-Common Market character who put up in my constituency, and voted Conservative for the first time at the G[reater] L[ondon] C[ouncil] elections this spring . . .

Growing older, I have lost the need to be political, which means in this country, the need to be Left. I am driven into grudging toleration of the Conservative Party because it is the party of nonpolitics, of resistance to politics. I have seen how many of the evils of life – failure, loneliness, fear, boredom, inability to communicate – are ineradicable by political means, and that attempts to eradicate them are disastrous.

During the remainder of his life, Amis (as his biographer Eric Jacobs puts it) continued this metamorphosis, steadily becoming a 'clubman, curmudgeon, anti-trendy, Tory, misogynist, blimp – with only a fondness for drink connecting him to the old image'. Yet even so, he protests in his memoirs at the vehemence of Braine's right-wing convictions, or rather, the tedious and repetitive manner in which they were expressed:

Seeing his moon face at the table aroused mixed feelings, of pleasure at seeing a warm-hearted friend, of resignation to hearing a good deal of preaching to the converted. Nobody at those gatherings had much time for, say, the Soviet political system, but John made certain its demerits were never to be overlooked. Taking the chair next to his was liable to bring the familiar mild discomfort of being with someone you like but find it oddly difficult to think of anything to say to.

The table in question was in London, at Bertorelli's restaurant in Charlotte Street. Braine's conversion to the right had coincided with his moving with his wife and family from Yorkshire southwards to the stockbroker-belt. Thereafter, for several years, he would take the train up to town for a weekly lunchtime gathering at Bertorelli's. Besides Amis, others around the table might include Anthony Burgess, Bernard Levin and Anthony Powell. Asked by an interviewer, some years later, if the participants had had any shared ideology, Braine answered: 'The only thing we had in common was that we weren't left-wing. We just refused to accept the liberal package deal.' He went on:

Around 1967 we sent a letter to *The Times*. Ten or fifteen of us signed it and supported the American position in Vietnam. We didn't say we approved of everything; indeed, we didn't. Although Vietnam is a hell of a long way from us, if they [the Communists] take over Vietnam, they're that much nearer, and that can't be good for us. Very simple reasoning.

All hell popped. There were indignant letters to *The Times*. We got lots of absolutely lunatic letters. A group of academics took out a full page in *The Times* condemning us. We did give the group a name after that. We called it the Fascist Beast Luncheon Group.

Braine himself determinedly lived up to this name, calling for the restoration of both corporal and capital punishment, pledging his support for apartheid in South Africa, and chanting 'Down with Oxfam!' Asked by Amis what had driven him from left to right, Braine replied that it had begun when he read that some such woolly-liberal figure as Lord Longford had declared that 'society' was the guilty party in the Moors murders. More plausible was Braine's explanation that he had changed sides because of having to pay a vast amount of income tax.

But really there had been no changing of sides. The young John Braine may have given lip-service to socialism, but Joe Lampton in *Room at the Top* is the embodiment of capitalist greed – just as Amis's Jim Dixon is an expert practitioner of selfishness. However, while Amis spun a successful later literary career out of his unfashionable and politically incorrect view of the world – for the simple reason that his books were usually very funny – Braine's later novels suffered badly from his rigid political views, as Amis concedes: 'Even [their] reactionary tendency was not enough to attract me to them.' He guesses that Braine's readers were 'largely of the comparatively lowly sort that enjoy stories about well-off powerful people – verbal soap-opera, in fact'.* And he points out that *Room at the Top* literally became a soap-opera in the early 1970s, when Thames Television made two series (written by Braine) called *Man at the Top*. These featured further sexual adventures of Joe Lampton, played by Kenneth Haigh – the original Jimmy Porter. 'Joe,' writes Amis, 'had taken on an independent existence on the small screen, sneering and seducing his way through the middle reaches of the London smart set.'

Braine's last two novels, *One and Last Love* (1981) and *These Golden Days*, published in 1985, the year before his death at the age of sixty-four, were virtually autobiographical narratives about a northern writer who had shifted to Surrey, embarked on an adulterous love-affair, and moved in with his mistress – all of which had happened to Braine. Amis felt that these books were 'a further step down' in Braine's literary deterioration – especially in the wish-fulfilling portrayal of the middle-aged hero Tim Harnforth, Braine's *alter ego*, who is described by his mistress as 'like a boy . . . so young, your skin's so smooth'. Amis's conclusion to this portrait of Braine in his memoirs is that ultimately Braine was 'like Joe Lampton. There was more than a joke in John's declaration that his dream of real success was of a triumphal procession through Bradford with himself at the head, flanked by a pair of naked beauties draped with jewels.'

* *

Given the media's determination, once the label Angry Young Man had been invented, to attach it to anyone whose work might remotely justify it, there is no clear explanation why Alan Sillitoe missed the AYM bus. Perhaps it was simply a matter of timing.

Unlike *Lucky Jim*, *Room at the Top*, and *Look Back in Anger*, Sillitoe's *Saturday Night and Sunday Morning* portrays a milieu that is exclusively working-class, while the brutality of his hero, the boozing and womanizing Arthur Seaton, makes Jim Dixon, Joe Lampton and Jimmy Porter seem prim and timid by comparison. The book opens with Arthur spewing up thirteen pints of beer and seven small gins

---

* There were plenty of such readers. By the end of his life, Braine was among the twenty authors whose books were borrowed from public libraries in such quantities that they qualified for the maximum annual payment (then £5,000) for Public Lending Right.

over a group of customers in a working-men's club, and ends with him determined to go on 'fighting every day until I die . . . Fighting with mothers and wives, landlords and gaffers, coppers, army, government . . . There's bound to be trouble in store for me every day of my life, because trouble it's always been and always will be.' Nor was there any doubt that Sillitoe knew what he was writing about. He had left school at fourteen and worked as a lathe-operator (Arthur Seaton's job) in a local factory. Like Braine, he had taught himself to write while confined to hospital with tuberculosis. And he was still young – just thirty – when *Saturday Night and Sunday Morning* was published in October 1958.

But by that time, the height of the AYM craze was over. The book earned reviews that were respectful rather than ecstatic – John Wain praised it as 'solid and accurate' – and it was not until the novel was adapted for the screen (by Sillitoe himself) and released in the autumn of 1960 that it became a bestseller.

Albert Finney played Arthur Seaton; he also took the title role in the stage adaptation of another novel about working-class life written by an insider, Keith Waterhouse's *Billy Liar*.* Waterhouse, who was a year younger than Sillitoe and had scraped a living (like Billy) as a teenager in Leeds (before becoming a journalist), might have qualified as an AYM if he had published the book a little earlier. But he did not turn to fiction until a newspaper strike left him idle during 1956, and *Billy Liar* did not reach the shops until 1959, by which time the AYM craze was definitely old hat.

* *

After playing Arthur Seaton and Billy Liar, Albert Finney took the title role in *Luther* (1961), John Osborne's next success after *The Entertainer*. But not his next play: that had been a disastrous musical, *The World of Paul Slickey*, considered so awful by its first-night audience in the summer of 1959 that, when Osborne injudiciously left the theatre via the front of house, 'they chased me down Charing Cross Road, and I had to fight . . . It was quite ugly . . . Fortunately I got a taxi . . . I don't think that's happened to many playwrights . . . I think it probably should.'

* Billy was portrayed on screen by Tom Courtenay.

There was no fracas after *Luther* – indeed the play became an A-level set text; and *Inadmissible Evidence* (1964), a brilliant portrayal of a failed lawyer, Bill Maitland, arguably equals *Look Back in Anger* and *The Entertainer*. But, looking back, Osborne describes his relationship with his audience for the greater part of his theatrical career as one of mutual hatred:

Most of my work in the theatre has, at some time, lurched head on into the milling tattoo of clanging seats and often quite beefy booing . . . Once, during a performance of *A Sense of Detachment* [1972], a lady got up and threw her boots on the stage . . . I had a special enjoyment out of that.

The most successful creation of his later years was not a play, but a pair of books – the two volumes of his memoirs, *A Better Class of Person* (1981) and *Almost a Gentleman* (1991). These give the impression that, after *The Entertainer*, the sexual and romantic dramas of his private life excited him far more than writing plays. As his marriage to Mary Ure broke down, he became involved with a string of impressive women: the Australian-born painter and designer Jocelyn Rickards (whose other lovers included Graham Greene and A. J. Ayer); film critic Penelope Gilliatt, whom Osborne effortlessly prised away from her neurologist husband, and eventually married; and his fourth wife, actress Jill Bennett. According to Jocelyn Rickards, Osborne was 'sexually obsessed' with Bennett 'before and during their marriage'; but in *Almost a Gentleman* he writes about Bennett with undiluted hatred, describing her suicide in 1990 in an unforgettable but very strange phrase – 'the coarse posturing of an overheated housemaid' – and declaring that he wished he had been able to 'drop a good, large mess in her eye' as she lay in an open coffin.

This, of course, is what Jimmy Porter would have said; and with hindsight, *Look Back in Anger* seems more than ever to have been a self-portrait. Osborne married again after Bennett's suicide, but survived her by only four years, dying of diabetes and other complications at the age of sixty-five. His former mistress Jocelyn Rickards sums him up harshly: 'I see him now as a flawed and disappointed man, who just occasionally wrote like an angel.'

Flawed, maybe; but there is little evidence of disappointment in his two superb volumes of autobiography. He recalls with relish not merely the Feydeauesque complications of his private life, but even the popular press's relentless pursuit of him and his latest mistress whenever he was attempting to consummate a new affair. There is a particularly splendid moment in the story in 1961, after he has annoyed conservative-minded Britons with a letter (published in *Tribune*) which includes the phrase 'Damn you England'. Still technically married to Mary Ure, he has just whisked his latest woman down to a country retreat at Hillingly in Sussex, where they are besieged not just by the press, but also by several elderly local residents, who arrive at the front gate with three placards:

DAMN YOU OSBORNE

HELLINGLY WANTS MARY URE

ENGLAND'S ANGRY OLD MEN OBJECT

* *

In 1960, Victor Gollancz attempted to launch a new Angry Young Man, publishing a critique of contemporary British politics and society by a twenty-four-year-old Oxford graduate who was a miner's son from the Forest of Dean. 'Maybe the big emotional orgies have disappeared, as Jimmy Porter raves,' wrote Dennis Potter,

but a great greyness has blanketed all the rest – admass,* a diluted Welfare State, a sense of shame and disillusion, contempt for authority, a widespread desire to emigrate or cheat ... a feeling of the flatness and bleakness of everyday England ... Doesn't it all make you sick? Or does it make you certain of the need to be awake and articulate, pompous perhaps, but *alive*?

Potter's *The Glittering Coffin* earned some enthusiastic reviews – Kenneth Allsop in the *Daily Mail* called it 'superbly honest' – but Potter afterwards admitted that the book had been the work of 'a young man on the make'; and this was no longer the way to do it. By the time *The Glittering Coffin* was published, Potter was working for

---

* The fashionable term of disapproval for advertising-led consumerism.

BBC television, and in the autumn of 1962 he was one of a number of young writers who began to contribute sketches to the BBC's daring new late-night Saturday show, *That Was The Week That Was* (known for short as *TW3*).

The BBC had woken up quite late to the fact that, from the spring of 1961, Anger had been replaced by Satire. The revue *Beyond the Fringe*, written and performed by Alan Bennett, Peter Cook, Jonathan Miller and Dudley Moore, arrived in the West End (from the Edinburgh Festival, via Cambridge and Brighton) in May that year, and was immediately hailed by Kenneth Tynan with the same degree of passion as his reaction to *Look Back in Anger*, four years earlier:

. . . the funniest revue that London has seen since the Allies dropped the bomb on Hiroshima. Future historians may well thank me for providing them with a full account of the moment when English comedy took its first decisive step into the second half of the twentieth century.

A few months later, in the autumn of 1961, Peter Cook opened a satirical nightclub, The Establishment, in Soho, and simultaneously (but coincidentally) a home-made-looking yellow pamphlet called *Private Eye* began to go on sale in the capital's coffee-bars. Suddenly, everyone wanted to be a satirist.

Maybe the Angry Young Men had paved the way; there are certainly affinities between *Lucky Jim* and the methodical mockery of British culture and institutions in *Beyond the Fringe*. But the Angries themselves soon became the target of the satirists – *Private Eye* re-named Osborne as 'John Osbore', and a sketch in *TW3* mocked (in a poem modelled on Rupert Brooke's 'Grantchester') the fashion for north-country working-class novels:

> Ah God, to see the branches stir
> Across the moon, at Manchester . . .
> Those Yorkshire moors, that pelting rain,
> Those daily tea-cakes with John Braine.

The poem was by Malcolm Bradbury, who has recalled the 'enormous euphoria' caused by the TV satire show, as if the great British log jam was being broken at last. All my age group was carried away by it, week on week, and it did have an important effect in changing views of – and deference towards – politicians and institutions generally.

Keith Waterhouse, who had very nearly been an AYM, and now teamed up with Willis Hall to write more material for *TW3* than any other contributors, recalls the Tory politician Edward Heath blaming *TW3* for what he called 'the death of deference'.

So the satirists who followed the AYM managed effortlessly to effect a change in British society that the Angries had failed to bring about, despite all the huffing and puffing. But in truth that huffing and puffing had been done not by the AYM themselves, but by the media, who had willed them into existence. And it had only been a fragile sort of existence; or maybe even none at all. Harry Ritchie, at the end of his exhaustive study of the invention and publicizing of the AYM, comes to the stark conclusion that 'not only the label but the entire notion of the grouping was completely unjustified'.

And yet people *believed* they had existed; or at least there was a concept which seemed to have been in the air for a few years, and then vanished with the arrival of the new decade. 'Me used to be Angry Young Man,' runs the lyric of a 1967 Beatles song by Lennon and McCartney,

> Me hiding me head in the sand
> You gave me the word
> I finally heard
> I'm doing the best that I can . . .
>
> I admit it's getting better
> A little better all the time
> Yes I admit it's getting better
> It's getting better since you've been mine.

If we are talking about a standard of living, it had been 'getting better' in Britain since the economic upturn of the late Fifties, but not until the Sixties did the British learn to enjoy themselves. So, at least, runs the legend which seems to be implied by the song; and Arnold Wesker has compared the Beatles with the AYM: 'I think the Beatles and so on are the consequence of another but parallel development. *They* stemmed from the skiffle groups, which preceded the working-class school of writers and actors, but was an essentially working-class thing.'

Typically, Philip Larkin, who had helped to set off the AYM movement (if there really had been such a movement), greeted the arrival of the new decade with gloom. On 8 January 1960 he wrote to John Wain: 'It seems funny to be writing "1960" – the ageing of the century gets into one's mind, depressingly. Better to be born in the '60s, & be writing '01, '02 just when the inescapable old guy with the scythe is falling in alongside you.'

But Al Alvarez, who had been involved in the AYM's predecessor, the Movement, recalls that he was full of enthusiasm for the decade that was just dawning: 'The Sixties may have been mindless and muddled and awash with false sentiment, but at least they were full of possibilities. I was thirty when they began and I had crammed my twenties with toil . . . I couldn't wait to have some fun.'

Bibliography

The abbreviations in the left-hand column are those used in the Source Notes.

A Bit Off the Map	Angus Wilson, *A Bit Off the Map and Other Stories* (Secker & Warburg, 1957)
Allsop	Kenneth Allsop, *The Angry Decade: a Survey of the Cultural Revolt of the Nineteen-fifties* (John Goodchild, 1985; first published 1958)
Alvarez, *Where*	A. Alvarez, *Where Did It All Go Right?* (Richard Cohen Books, 1999)
Amis, *Frame*	Kingsley Amis, *A Frame of Mind: Eighteen Poems* (University of Reading, 1953)
Amis, *LJ*	Kingsley Amis, *Lucky Jim* (Penguin Books, 1961; first published 1954)
Amis, *Memoirs*	Kingsley Amis, *Memoirs* (Hutchinson, 1991)
Amis, *WBJA*	Kingsley Amis, *What Became of Jane Austen? and Other Questions* (Jonathan Cape, 1970)
Beat Generation	Gene Feldman and Max Gartenberg, *Protest: the Beat Generation and the Angry Young Men* (Souvenir Press, 1959)
Braddon	Russell Braddon, *Suez: Splitting of a Nation* (Collins, 1973)
Braine, *RATT*	John Braine, *Room at the Top* (Mandarin, 1989; first published 1957)
Braine, *WTTT*	John Braine, 'Way to the Top', three articles in *Reynolds News*, 10, 17 and 24 November 1957
Declaration	Tom Maschler (ed.), *Declaration* (MacGibbon & Kee, 1957)
DLB	*The Dictionary of Literary Biography* (Gale Research Company, various dates: identified in the Source Notes by volume number)

DLB Yearbook 1986	*The Dictionary of Literary Biography Yearbook 1986* (Gale Research Company, 1987)
Dossor	Howard F. Dossor, *Colin Wilson: the Man and His Mind* (Element Books, 1990)
Drabble	Margaret Drabble, *Angus Wilson: a Biography* (Secker & Warburg, 1995)
Edwards	Ruth Dudley Edwards, *Victor Gollancz: a Biography* (Gollancz, 1987)
Experience	Martin Amis, *Experience* (Jonathan Cape, 2000)
Farson	Daniel Farson, *Never a Normal Man: an Autobiography* (HarperCollins, 1997)
Hatziolou	Elizabeth Hatziolou, *John Wain: a Man of Letters* (Pisces Press, 1997)
Hewison	Robert Hewison, *In Anger: Culture in the Cold War 1945–60* (Weidenfeld & Nicolson, 1981)
Hodges	Sheila Hodges, *Gollancz: the Story of a Publishing House* (Gollancz, 1978)
Holroyd, *Contraries*	Stuart Holroyd, *Contraries: a Personal Progression* (Bodley Head, 1975)
Hopkins interview	Interview with Bill Hopkins, London, 25 October 2001
Jacobs	Eric Jacobs, *Kingsley Amis: a Biography* (paperback (revised) edition, Sceptre, 1996)
KA/PL	The originals of Amis's letters to Larkin, Bodleian Library, Oxford, MSS Eng. c. 6044–54
Larkin, *Collected Poems*	Philip Larkin, *Collected Poems* (Faber & Faber, 1988)
Larkin, *Jill*	Philip Larkin, *Jill* (Faber Library edition, 1996)
Larkin, *Required Writing*	Philip Larkin, *Required Writing: Miscellaneous Pieces 1955–1982* (Faber & Faber, 1983)
Leader	Zachary Leader (ed.), *The Letters of Kingsley Amis* (HarperCollins, 2000)
Lessing	Doris Lessing, *Walking in the Shade: Volume Two of My Autobiography, 1949–1962* (HarperCollins, 1997)
Logue	Christopher Logue, *Prince Charming: a Memoir* (Faber & Faber, 1999)
Maschler	Interview with Tom Maschler, by telephone, 7 December 2001
Motion	Andrew Motion, *Philip Larkin: a Writer's Life* (Faber & Faber, 1993)

ODID | John Osborne interviewed by Roy Plomley in *Desert Island Discs*, BBC Radio 4, 27 February 1982

Osborne, *Entertainer* | John Osborne, *The Entertainer* (Faber & Faber, 1957)

Osborne, *LB* | John Osborne, *Looking Back: Never Explain, Never Apologise* (one-volume paperback of *A Better Class of Person* (1981) and *Almost a Gentleman* (1991), Faber & Faber, 1999)

Osborne, *LBIA* | John Osborne, *Look Back in Anger* (Faber & Faber, 1996 edition)

Rain Taxi | Undated interview with Colin Wilson from *Rain Taxi*, on website www.raintaxi.com/wilson.htm

Ritchie | Harry Ritchie, *Success Stories: Literature and the Media in England, 1950–1959* (Faber & Faber, 1988)

Roberts | Philip Roberts, *The Royal Court Theatre and the Modern Stage* (Cambridge University Press, 1999)

Salwak, *Interviews* | Dale Salwak, *Interviews with Britain's Angry Young Men* (Borgo Press, 1984)

Salwak, *KALL* | Dale Salwak, *Kingsley Amis in Life and Letters* (Macmillan, 1990)

Salwak, *KAMN* | Dale Salwak, *Kingsley Amis: Modern Novelist* (Harvester Wheatsheaf, 1992)

Taylor, *Casebook* | John Russell Taylor (ed.), *John Osborne: Look Back in Anger: a Casebook* (Macmillan, 1968)

Thwaite | Anthony Thwaite (ed.), *Selected Letters of Philip Larkin 1940–1985* (Faber & Faber, 1992)

Tynan, *Holiday* | Kenneth Tynan, 'The Men of Anger', *Holiday*, April 1958

WAC | Material held at the BBC Written Archives Centre, Caversham Park, Reading

Wain, *Hurry* | John Wain, *Hurry On Down* (Penguin Books, 1960; first published 1953)

Wain, *Mixed Feelings* | John Wain, *Mixed Feelings: Nineteen Poems* (University of Reading, 1951)

Wain papers | Photostats lent by William Wain of letters to his father from Philip Larkin

Wain, *SR* | John Wain, *Sprightly Running: Part of an Autobiography* (Macmillan, 1965; first published 1962)

Wesker, *AMAID*	Arnold Wesker, *As Much as I Dare: an Autobiography (1932–1959)* (Century, 1994)
Will Wain interview	Interview with William Wain, Oxford, 23 October 2001
Wilson, *Adrift*	Colin Wilson, *Adrift in Soho* (Gollancz, 1961)
Wilson, *AR*	Colin Wilson, *Autobiographical Reflections* (Paupers' Press, 1988)
Wilson interview	Interview with Colin Wilson, Cornwall, 23 November 2001
Wilson, *Outsider*	Colin Wilson, *The Outsider* (Indigo, 1997; first published 1956)
Wilson, *RATR*	Colin Wilson, *Religion and the Rebel* (Gollancz, 1957)
Wilson, *Voyage*	Colin Wilson, *Voyage to a Beginning: a Preliminary Autobiography* (Cecil and Amelia Woolf, 1969)

Source Notes

Quotations are identified by the first words. When two or more quotations from the same source follow each other with little intervening narrative, I have used only the first quotation for identification. Abbreviations can be found in the Bibliography.

PROLOGUE

All quotes from Colin Wilson:
  Wilson interview, and e-mail to
  the author, 20.2.02
'Between ourselves', Leader 1046
'the Angry Young Man
  "movement"', ibid. 704
'The "Angry Young Men" cult',
  News Chronicle, 27.2.57
'I sometimes feel', *Encounter*,
  November 1959

CHAPTER I

'They fuck you up', Larkin,
  Required Writing 48
'dull . . . and slightly mad', Motion
  14
'desolate', ibid. 175
'My father was a', Larkin, *Required
  Writing* 48
'a forgotten boredom', Larkin,
  Collected Poems 33

'Actually, I like to think', Larkin,
  Required Writing 47
'I was an unsuccessful schoolboy',
  ibid. 48
'I had friends', ibid. 47
'Oxford must have been', Amis,
  Memoirs 37
'the Oxford of . . . Charles Ryder',
  Larkin, *Required Writing* 18
'hailed the mention', ibid. 19–21
'one of a pair of twins', Jacobs 19
'Of the lower classes', *Experience* 15
'there was no trace', Salwak,
  KAMN 2
'took about three minutes', Leader
  255
'the most English human being',
  Amis, *WBJA* 192
'He got no further', Amis, *Memoirs*
  18
'He was never bitter', Amis, *WBJA*
  197
'Norbury, SW 16', Amis, *Memoirs* 16
'semi-detached, morning coffee',
  ibid. 21

'my mother and father', ibid. 10

'no belief in', Salwak, *KAMN* 12

'I only suspect this', Amis, *WBJA* 193f.

'He liked and collected books', Amis, *Memoirs* 5

'a talent for physical clowning', ibid. 18

'My father loved his mother', *Experience* 164

'we quarrelled violently', Amis, *WBJA* 195, 197

'who refused to drive', *Experience* 4

'We were divided', Amis, *WBJA* 195

'not a word or a concept', Amis, *Memoirs* 15

'the damned wireless', Amis, *WBJA* 196f.

'suggesting on rainy afternoons', Amis, *Memoirs* 22

'gambling successfully', ibid. 18

'much less dramatically satisfying', ibid. 51f.

'It was not a BBC Variety Hour', Larkin, *Required Writing* 21f.

'I had also joined', Amis, *Memoirs* 37

'so that we need not', Larkin, *Required Writing* 22

'A lot of people', ODID

'with some proficiency', Amis, *Memoirs* 53, 55

'like a sun', Motion 44

'The army claimed me', Amis, *Memoirs* 40, 80

'Betty . . . came to see me off ', Leader 6, 10

[Footnote:] 'no casual dalliance', *Experience* 164n.

'It's true', Leader 12

'all women are stupid beings', Thwaite 63, 61f., 64

'soft porn fairy stories', Motion 86

'a few messy encounters', ibid. 65

'without overmuch repulsion', Thwaite 40, 42, 45f.

'Did you know *Golding*', Leader 25

'I am told', ibid. 9

'I am beginning to wonder', ibid. 17

'Darling Brunette', ibid. 55f.

'It was love', *Experience* 238

'Cunt and bugger', Thwaite 15; Motion 62

'Hilary was stupider', Leader 49, 62

'Her breasts are concave on top', KA/PL 7.3.46

'He had a grand piano', Larkin, *Required Writing* xiv–xv

'This man', Amis, *Memoirs* 71

'Whatever made you think', KA/PL 13.2.46

'Wheres Bruce gone', ibid. 21.12.45

'Don't breathe a word', ibid. 29.11.46

CHAPTER 2

'The library is', Thwaite 85f.

'lustfully and playfully savage', Larkin, *Jill* 37

'A little twerp', Thwaite 83

'Kemp the Warner-fearer', Leader 194

'the school captain', Thwaite 102, 104f.

'Do something about it', Leader 55, 124

'I was very glad', KA/PL 25.1.47

'enthralled', Thwaite 44

[Footnote:] 'He died owning 91

houses', Timothy d'Arch Smith, *R. A. Caton and the Fortune Press* (Bertram Rota, 1983), 12

'submit a volume', Motion 128

'aroused no public comment', Larkin, *Jill* xv

'seen any Jills', Leader 101, 127

'Your ability to write', ibid. 26, 81

'Won't Bruce not like me', ibid. 76

'the last and most charming', Julian Symons, *Bloody Murder: from the Detective Story to the Crime Novel: a History* (Viking, revised ed. 1985), 142

'I don't like all those silly', Leader 41

'which is CORNY', ibid. 131, 125

'the ex-schoolboy', Larkin, *Required Writing* 28

'shimmer . . . continually', ibid. 129

'Thank you . . . for your review', KA/PL 15.3.48

'Someone has told us', Kingsley Amis, *Bright November* (Fortune Press, 1947), 26

'went wide and far', Larkin, *Collected Poems* 302

'It is a deathly book', Thwaite 109f.

'The book is a study', *Mandrake*, vol. 1, no. 5 (1947), 85f.

'Now I am thinking', Thwaite 109f.

'I'm very sorry you've stopped', KA/PL 28.3.49

'The double sorwe', Leader 143

'the Cuntherbelly', ibid. 66f., 96

'I started on Lerlyrical Berballads', KA/PL 31.5.47

'A man called Mister C. Day Lewis', ibid. 30.9.46

'Turd Pro-gram', Leader 120

'I was unable to decide', ibid. 95

'*I must say*', KA/PL 27.2.47

'Do you think he is right?', ibid. 8.7.46

[Footnote:] 'I knew him to be incapable', *Experience* 24, 335

[Footnote:] 'They thought I hadn't', Leader 251

'Tell Monica', KA/PL 20.5.48

'that POSTURING QUACK', Leader 186

'Laze – laze and gentlemen', Amis, *Memoirs* 101

'Did you know', Leader 97

'John Wain was in', KA/PL 31.10.46

'I found him most attractive', Amis, *Memoirs* 41f.

'wasn't a musician', Will Wain interview

'The legacy is swimming', KA/PL 29.7.48

'caught the virus', Wain, *SR* 204

'To-morrow I am going', KA/PL 15.5.47

'I am working', ibid. 31.5.47

'I have already had', ibid. 22.6.47

'a comic eighteenth-century story', ibid. 22.2.48

'Hilly and I', Leader 145

'As regards the impending', ibid. 154f.

'the father', ibid. 79

'Welch Home Service', KA/PL 20.5.48

'I looked round', Amis, *Memoirs* 56

'I laffed like bogray', KA/PL 2.11.48

'You know, when I've finished', ibid. 20.8.48

'The way you hang', ibid. 11.8.46

'I have jotted down', Leader 195

'He was . . . an amateur musician',
  Experience 131
[Footnote:] 'Boredom, I am sorry',
  Amis, *WBJA* 198

CHAPTER 3

'a melodrama', Osborne, *LB* 167f.,
  172
'Retired, rotten', ibid. 23
'a childhood', ibid. xiv–xv
'I spent years', ibid. 7
'blundering misalliance', ibid. 108
'My father', ibid. 25
'Fulham in the 1930s', ibid. 8
'an eager', ibid. 15
'the Grove Repertory Company',
  ibid. 21
[Footnote:] 'Not only were',
  Declaration 82
'half a bottle', Osborne, *LB* 15
'the only recorded', ibid. 13
'He told me', ibid. 16
[Footnote:] 'frowned upon', ibid. 74
'I was probably', ODID
'I grew up', Osborne, *LB* 20
'Bankclerk's Tudor', ibid. 31
'where we would be safer', ibid. 87
'I was sitting', ibid. 93
'For ten months', ibid. 112
'I listened all day', ibid. 78
'I thought I'd be', ODID
'more like a Borstal', Osborne, *LB*
  114
'the lower depths', ibid. 121
'the merest, timid', ibid. 123
'and I looked forward', ibid. 127
'I don't think', ODID
'loveless clinch', Osborne, *LB* 114
'cream cakes', ibid. 28

'I have seen none', ibid. 108
'With its short', ibid. 168
'Renee Shippard', ibid. 161
'Sheila, a twenty-two-year-old', ibid.
  171
'the forty-eight', ibid. 172
'We seldom progressed', ibid. 194
'I had to rely', ibid. 176
'I began . . . in the dressing-room',
  ibid. 179
'neurotically frigid', ibid. 180
'Stella was about', ibid. 186
'unprepossessing', ibid. 195
'Speeches were too long', ibid. 190
'began making love', ibid. 196
'Christ, I was only', ibid. 196
'it was to take place', ibid. 204
'seemed to have', ibid. 214f.
'watching the world', ibid. 216f.

CHAPTER 4

'too poor', Wain, *SR* 212
'I can't make', ibid. 214, 91
'bursting', ibid. 4
'had had her own', ibid. 58
'Mine was a lonely', ibid. 37
'the perpetual sense', ibid. 4
'Now we're coming', ibid. 7
'dangerous, uncouth', ibid. 13
'simple-lifers', ibid. 32
'underweight, pale', ibid. 28f.
'The main danger', ibid. 53
'My hero tried', ibid. 62f.
'by journalists', ibid. 96
'Nobody suggested', ibid. 94–6
'expanded', ibid. 63
'whose attitude', ibid. 102
'a miniature Lewis', ibid. 138
'My parents', ibid. 67

'sexual fulfilment', ibid. 82

'Philip . . . was just', ibid. 187f.

'a man called Wain', Larkin,
   Required Writing 23

'we urchins', Wain, *SR* 188

'He . . . seemed', Amis, *Memoirs* 42

'employing odds and ends', Wain,
   SR 165

'Kingsley . . . spoke', ibid. 204

'encouraged me', Amis, *Memoirs* 42

'lay for long spells', Wain, *SR* 165

[Footnote:] 'a sort of spider',
   Spectator, 7.10.55

'hurled into the midst', Wain, *SR*
   167–9

CHAPTER 5

'I . . . have re-started', KA/PL 2.8.49

'probably another', Leader 205

'the greater part', ibid. 196

'I hate him', ibid. 208f.

'Martin is really', ibid. 210

'cunt-only place', ibid. 206

'Welch life', ibid. 215

'stew dunce', KA/PL 9.3.50

'I've had to work hard', KA/PL
   27.1.50

'the bathroom', Leader 221

'I wish I could', ibid. 223

'to keep on shutting', ibid. 228f.

'I don't think it's', ibid. 243

'lest they shd.', ibid. 268

'I'm too frightened', ibid. 271

'a pang', ibid. 286

'When I read', Larkin, *Required
   Writing* 59

'I wanted to tell', Leader 288

[Footnote:] 'wrong make-up', KA/
   PL 17.9.50

[Footnote:] 'her make-up', ibid.
   11.10.50

[Footnote:] 'Am working', ibid.
   8.2.50

'so many threads', Leader 297

'What a stupid', ibid. 265

'I know the miracles', KA/PL
   10.10.51

'as funny as', ibid. 14.9.51

'the most inconclusive', Leader 256

'We've settled it', KA/PL 10.8.50

'evidence . . . of declining
   civilization', Salwak, *KAMN* 79

'it takes a serious', *Spectator*,
   20.11.53

'I got hold of ', KA/PL 11.10.50

'Re *Scenes*', ibid. 28.10.50

'. . . this afternoon I have',
   ibid. 6.2.50

'On Friday', ibid. 6.2.50

'I am getting', ibid. 28.10.50

'The lady student', ibid. 27.11.50

'boyfriend', Leader 315

'No, my wife's', ibid. 322

'That old winged', ibid. 271

'I've started sending', KA/PL
   6.2.50

'The lissner', ibid. 18.2.50

'currently engaged', Salwak,
   KAMN 58

'Yes, of course', Leader 299f.

'It wouldn't be any use', ibid. 310

[Footnote:] 'Don't worry', KA/PL
   30.3.53

'sweating now', Leader 312f.

'As you'll see', ibid. 314

'that they're going to broadcast',
   ibid. 315

'Wain Division', ibid. 316

'use these programmes', script of
   First Reading No. 1, WAC

'I think it is', Jacobs 155
'I was overjoyed', Leader 318
'Not a proper', ibid. 318

CHAPTER 6

'deplorable', *New Statesman*,
  18.7.53
'very flattered', Alvarez, *Where* 13
'the mess', Hatziolou 70
'was an inspiring', Alvarez, *Where*
  136
'Having got as far', quoted *New
  Statesman*, 18.7.53
'Mr Wain['s] implication', ibid.
'Did you see', Leader 328
'JBW . . . *is* portentous', KA/PL
  13.8.53
'amateurish', *New Statesman*,
  25.7.53
'If I drew up', Wain, *SR* 168
'Sorry about the drabness', Leader
  240
'a very good example', ibid. 123f.
[Footnote:] 'I was Bowen Thomas',
  Kingsley Amis, *That Uncertain
  Feeling* (Gollancz, 1955), 112
'the suspicion that', John Wain,
  Preliminary Essays (Macmillan,
  1957), 182
'trying to treat', Leader 233
'I . . . read the cocktale farty', KA/
  PL 17.5.50
'grim and impoverished', Alvarez,
  Where 111, 121–3
'her personal fantasies', *Essays in
  Criticism*, July 1952, 345
'inattentive', ibid., October 1953,
  473
'Yes, you told me', KA/PL 3.8.53

'. . . did you see those poems',
  Leader 286, 312
'Silence? no hint', Wain, *Mixed
  Feelings* 11
'Dr Ramsden', John Betjeman,
  Collected Poems (John Murray,
  1987 ed.), 208
'taking us from', Amis, *Memoirs*
  263
'I hope to feel', Wain, *Mixed
  Feelings* 14
'John Wain read me', KA/PL
  19.8.52
'a mediocre degree in History',
  Wain, *Hurry* 7
'a dingy huddle', ibid. 11
'Speech would never', ibid. 18
'I was just wondering', ibid. 19
'the ivory', ibid. 21
'mushroom-shaped cloud', ibid. 29
'He thought', ibid. 37f.
'With one bound', ibid. 32
'A king ringed', ibid. 65
'letting the side down', ibid. 174
'chipped mug[s]', ibid. 190
'Dense blue smoke', ibid. 45
'takin' the bread', ibid. 62
'This was Rosa's father's', ibid. 183,
  186f.
'milk-bars within', ibid. 199
'to make them look', ibid. 179
'the way the working-class',
  ibid. 149
'the Oak Lounge', Amis, *LJ* 21
'Technicolor landscape', ibid. 223
'squeezing you', ibid. 93
'had his pipe', ibid. 203
'the sounds', ibid. 109f.
'for some of the top', ibid. 241
'The runaway fight', ibid. 250
'does succeed', Leader 341

'all *right*', KA/PL 6.10.53

'come to nearly', Leader 335

'inventive, impulsive', Hatziolou 88f.

'the power of sustaining', Wain, *SR*
162

'I [was] improvising', Hatziolou 87

'any social statement', Leader 745

'the boredom-detector', Amis, *LJ*
215

'his Chinese', ibid. 69, 97, 102, 220

'such a queer', ibid. 138

'Do you hate', ibid. 156

'Throw her', ibid. 121

[Footnote:] 'D[ixon] has more',
Leader 289

'Dixon . . . asked', Amis, *LJ* 9

'the green Paisley', ibid. 11, 20, 163

'Dixon looked again', ibid. 47

'the ringing', ibid. 13

'Kingsley's masterpiece', Larkin, *Jill*
xii

[Footnote:] 'He'd have to be',
Leader 291

'if you'll pardon', Amis, *LJ* 48

'. . . And I happen', ibid. 51

'in certain quarters', Salwak, *KALL* 8

'He wants to test', Amis, *LJ* 24

'Culture's good', Salwak, *KAMN*
63

'recognizable to Dixon', Amis, *LJ*
63

[Footnote:] 'I'm sorry', Leader 226,
263

'One wants to', Salwak, *KAMN* 72

'For a moment', Amis, *LJ* 50

'Having a relationship', ibid. 141

'The stuff coming', ibid. 60f.

'sometimes wished', ibid. 140

'If one man's', ibid. 51

'Those who professed', ibid. 87

'advocacy of ', ibid. 176

'leave the provinces', ibid. 26

'. . . he pronounced', ibid. 250

[Footnote:] 'Human life', Kingsley
Amis, *One Fat Englishman*
(Gollancz, 1963), 47

[Footnote:] 'Jeremy smiled',
Kingsley Amis, *You Can't Do
Both* (Flamingo, 1995), 35

'nice things are', Amis, *LJ* 140

'The phrase', Leader 746

'two great classes', Amis, *LJ* 143

'Doing what you', ibid. 146

'The bloody old', ibid. 209

CHAPTER 7

'the *naïf* who', *New Statesman*,
30.1.54

'Dixon . . . has no chip', *Times*,
27.1.54

'Mr Amis['s] hero', *Observer*,
24.1.54

'a new funny book', *Daily
Telegraph*, 5.2.54

'Much better', Salwak, *KAMN* 74

'an ignoble buffoon', *Sunday Times*,
24.1.54

'a relief ', *News Chronicle*, 11.2.54

'A new hero', *New Statesman*,
30.1.54

'Mr Amis is', *Punch*, 3.2.54

'more than a few', KA/PL 15.9.55

'Just pipe-dreaming', Leader 346

'mean, malicious', Ritchie 72

[Footnote:] 'white-collar
proletariat', ibid. 72

'especially Auden', *Spectator*, 8.1.54

'flanked by you', Leader 375

'Give me a thrill', Larkin, *Collected
Poems* 34

'Between the GARDENING', Amis, *Frame*

'a well-made essay', Alvarez, *Where* 124

'I don't give', Leader 375

'"dissenting" and non-conformist', *Spectator*, 27.8.54

'a level conversational', G. S. Fraser and Iain Fletcher (eds.), *Springtime* (Peter Owen, 1973), 7

'The circulation', *Spectator*, 16.4.77

'The bus service', ibid. 1.10.54

'the lone Existentialist', Alvarez, *Where* 115

'All seems very *unreal*', Leader 467

'It is bored', *Spectator*, 1.10.54

'It struck a nerve', ibid. 16.4.77

'I have read', ibid. 8.10.54

'Ames', Salwak, *KALL* 9

'Well, what a lot', Leader 405

'old gag', ibid. 342

'Oxford's young', Alvarez, *Where* 115

'we . . . have in common', Leader 525

'he once came', Salwak, *KAMN* 28

'The first few', Alvarez, *Where* 123f., 188

'Larkin is easily', Leader 525

'exasperate only', *Manchester Guardian*, 30.11.56

'Speech fails', Amis, *Frame*

'I spent a weekend', Alvarez, *Where* 186f.

CHAPTER 8

'blousy waitresses', John Wain, *Living in the Present* (Secker & Warburg, 1955), 11f.

'the deadly boredom', Elizabeth David, *A Book of Mediterranean Food* (Penguin Books, 1991 ed.), 1

'So startlingly different', ibid. 3

'The atmosphere', Tom Hiney and Frank McShane (eds.), *The Raymond Chandler Papers* (Hamish Hamilton, 2000), 101

'the fascinating native life', *Spectator*, 28.1.55

'the *chic* attitude', ibid. 7.10.55

'a small passing twinge', ibid. 2.12.55

'. . . what I call the "Establishment"', ibid. 23.9.55

'appalled by the lack', ibid. 7.1.55

'I've really been doing', Leader 397

'I tried hard to work up some emotion as positive as boredom', *Spectator*, 17.9.54

'A great deal', ibid. 8.7.55

'He explained', Leader 395f.

'If *Living in the Present*', *Spectator*, 29.7.55

'It isn't so much', Leader 434

'There are two classes', *New Statesman*, 20.8.55

'One of the prime', *Spectator*, 15.6.56

'Had an incredible', Leader 470

CHAPTER 9

'I recall', Wilson, *Outsider* 1

'The sensible thing', Wilson, *AR* 22

'It seemed', Wilson, *Outsider* 1f.

'My background', Wilson, *AR* 1–3

'I . . . had this desire', *Rain Taxi*

'I experienced', Wilson, *AR* 4, 6f.

'I wanted to become', *Rain Taxi*

'At the age', Wilson, *AR* 8f.

'came bottom', Allsop 151, 153

'vaguely intending', Wilson, *AR*
9–11

'I bought a huge', *Rain Taxi*;
Wilson, *AR* 12

'Again, it was', Wilson, *AR* 13–18

'These were the days', Drabble 214

'Finally, in January', Wilson, *AR* 18

'I was working', Wilson, *Adrift*
111f., 31, 96

'wishy-washy', Holroyd, *Contraries*
38, 19, 21, 32, 13

'declared that he', Wilson, *Voyage*
91f.

'My father', Hopkins interview

'You are a man', Dossor 23

'a shared conception', Holroyd,
Contraries 16

'It seemed to me', Wilson, *Adrift*
25f.

'I decided', Wilson, *AR* 20

'That's right, Col', Dossor 26

'I usually woke', Wilson, *AR* 21–3

'Huggett's a genius', *A Bit Off the
Map*, *passim*

'We wandered', *Rain Taxi*

'I decided', Wilson, *AR* 23f.

'astonishing', Ritchie 144

'Women get in', Holroyd,
Contraries 65

'I'd already had', *Rain Taxi*; Wilson,
Outsider 5

'A Major Writer', Ritchie 144

[Footnote:] 'I shall christen', Cyril
Connolly, *Enemies of Promise*
(Penguin Books, 1961), 24f.

'got up at about', *Rain Taxi*

'I feel a quickening', *Sunday Times*,
27.5.56

[Footnote:] 'Mersault . . . is sensual',

Albert Camus, *The Outsider*
(Penguin Books, 1961), 8

'It is an exhaustive', *Observer*,
27.5.56

'the links between', Wilson,
Outsider 5, 21, 31, 37f.

'puerile pontification', Ritchie 163,
161, 160

'As one ploughed', Tynan, *Holiday*

'I have no capacity', *London
Magazine*, January 1957

'Abstract thought', Jeremy Lewis,
Cyril Connolly: a Life (Jonathan
Cape, 1997), 486

'the phone was ringing', *Rain Taxi*

'after a hard week', *Observer*, 3.6.56

'pleasant, unassuming', ibid.

'I went to see', Wilson, *AR* 26

CHAPTER 10

'Anthony . . . had toured', Osborne,
LB 219f.

'literally captive audience', ibid. 225

'I just went through it', ODID

'I've seen it before', Osborne, *LB*
229

'I had naturally', ibid. 235

'more weary than angry', ibid. 240

'dull and boring', ibid. 245

'something of a sinecure', ibid. 254

'the more tedious', ibid. 254

'Look at that', John Osborne and
Anthony Creighton, *Epitaph for
George Dillon* (Faber & Faber,
1958), 59

'Began writing', Osborne, *LB* 261

'I was working', ODID

'BARGAIN FROM STRENGTH',
illustration in Osborne, *LB*

'I feel like', Osborne, *LB* 270
'happy state', ibid. 263
'Something, I felt', ibid. 280
'I heard', ibid. 271
'We cannot have it', Roberts 3
'I want to have', Roberts 6
'Shakespeare, Sheridan', Hewison 8
'There is very little', ibid. 8
'The theatres remained', ibid. 9
'The postwar theatre', ibid. 9
' "phoney" drama', Roberts 37
'Most train journeys', Lord
    Harewood, *The Tongs and the
    Bones* (Weidenfeld & Nicolson,
    1981), 178f.
'a very promising find', Roberts 33
'If I didn't have', Osborne, *LB* 281
'homosexual plays', ibid. 286, 284,
    282, 289
'Perhaps Jimmy Porter', ibid. 280,
    278, 277
'Mr and Mrs Lane', ibid. 238, 277,
    279
'He is a disconcerting', Osborne,
    LBIA 1–4
'Anyone who doesn't', ibid. 47
'all that "in the movement"',
    Taylor, *Casebook* 38
'appeal to all Christians', Osborne,
    LBIA 7
[Footnote:] 'I've always thought',
    ODID
'God, how I hate', Osborne, *LBIA*
    8–11, 2, 14f.
'went to some', ibid. 44, 42, 27, 16,
    19, 49
'Why, why, why', ibid. 89, 31
'neither of [Jimmy's] relationships',
    Ronald Hayman, *John Osborne*
    (Heinemann, second ed., 1969),
    18f.

'Jimmy has a', Tynan, *Holiday*
[Footnote:] 'I love you', *Sunday
    Times*, 29.7.01
'If only something', Osborne, *LBIA*
    36, 33, 67, 70
'Mummy may look', ibid. 52f.
'So much malice', Osborne, *LB* 264
'For twelve months', Osbornc,
    LBIA 59, 96
'a great deal in common', Taylor,
    Casebook 154

CHAPTER 11

'carped', Osborne, *LB* 297
'plays by someone', Roberts 51
'an attack on do-gooding', Drabble
    211
'I suppose', Osborne, *LB* 299
[Footnote:] 'the story of ', Tynan,
    Holiday
'very drunk', Osborne, *LB* 299
'Look, Ma', Roberts 48
'This first play', Taylor, *Casebook*
    35, 39, 46, 51
'You didn't expect', Osborne, *LB*
    299
'an angry play', Taylor, *Casebook*
    46
'The write-ups', Osborne, *LB* 300f.
'Mr John Osborne', *Sunday Times*,
    13.5.56
'They are scum', *Observer*, 13.5.56

CHAPTER 12

'Osborne is a disconcerting', Tynan,
    Holiday
'People who like', *Times*, 26.5.56

'wearing false', Osborne, *LB* 307
'provocative, illuminating', Ritchie
    145
'is always a man', Amis, *WBJA* 89f.
'He greeted me', *Evening Standard*,
    4.5.56
'an Amis sort of play', Farson 204
'If I was in', *Daily Mail*, 13.7.56
'surprisingly gloomy', Farson 204
'Mary Ure', Colin Wilson to the
    author, 2.12.01
'Success has not', *Evening Standard*,
    7.7.56
'oh, this is an angry', Ritchie 27
'The postwar generation', *Daily
    Mail*, 12.7.56
'His name is', ibid. 13.7.56
'four new young', *Daily Express*,
    26.7.56
'For a few weeks', Wilson, *AR*
    27
'He lives in', Ritchie 147f.
'Francis was a Teddy boy', *News
    Chronicle*, 12.5.56
'Cecil Beaton photographed',
    Ritchie 147
'poets (who have all . . .)', *Evening
    Standard*, 9.2.56
'The current beau ideal',
    ibid. 11.3.57
'Rock'n'Roll', *Sunday Times*,
    30.12.56
'cared little what he wore', Dossor
    27
'If I hadn't', Wilson, *Outsider* 7
'I can't pretend', Osborne, *LB* 310
'The response', ibid. 302
'The houses', Irving Wardle, *The
    Theatres of George Devine*
    (Jonathan Cape, 1978), 185
'a play for adults', Denis Forman,

Persona Granada (André
    Deutsch, 1997), 80
[Footnote:] '*Look Back* waited',
    Osborne, *LB* 302

CHAPTER 13

'University students', Braddon 96f.
'a firm stand', Hugh Thomas, *The
    Suez Affair* (Weidenfeld &
    Nicolson, revised ed., 1986), 41,
    66, 56
'THIS IS FOLLY', *Daily Herald*,
    31.10.56
'deep anxiety', *Daily Telegraph*,
    2.11.56
'very great risks', *Times*, 31.10.56
'what I took to be', Braddon 96f.
'Suez . . . was a shock', *New
    Statesman*, 21.6.58
'I was interested', Braddon 124f.,
    225
'Actually I have', Leader 480
'to entertain', Jacobs 172
'the most valuable', Leader 489
'Adulterous husbands', Jacobs 177
'Russia's war', Amis, *WBJA* 201
're-hash', Leader 485
'an elderly young intellectual',
    Kingsley Amis, *Socialism and the
    Intellectuals* (Fabian Tract 304,
    Fabian Society, 1957)
'it may well have been', Braddon
    185
'A curious feature', Amis, *WBJA*
    201
'muddle of feeling', Osborne, *LB*
    317
[Footnote:] 'People . . . persuaded',
    ODID

[Footnote:] 'I'd heard it', ibid.
'the most CONTROVERSIAL',
  Evening Standard, 22.12.56
[Footnote:] 'amazing windfall',
  Osborne, *LB* 311
'I used to have', Osborne,
  Entertainer 37, 28, 33, 54
'theatrical effect', *Sunday Times*,
  14.4.57
'one of the great', *Observer*, 14.4.57
'plus thinking that', Roberts 60
'Miss Leigh', *Evening Standard*,
  11.9.57

CHAPTER 14

'Mr Braine', *Yorkshire Post*, 14.4.57
'as if I were riding', Braine, *WTTT*
'a callous, ambitious', *Observer*,
  17.3.57
'Joe Lampton looks back', *Punch*,
  17.4.57
'If I were given', *News Chronicle*,
  14.3.57
'three youngish men', *Daily
  Express*, 13.4.57
'wasn't bothered', Salwak,
  Interviews 51
'Looking at British', Allsop 84
'smoky valley', Braine, *WTTT*
'I'm the son', *Daily Express*, 23.5.57
'in a mental fog', Allsop 82
'There may have been', Braine,
  WTTT
'Here . . . in the Lounge', *New
  Statesman*, 8.9.51
'I had a talk', Salwak, *Interviews*
  43f.
'I had £150', Allsop 83

'In [that] land', Braine, *WTTT*
'a wonderful and bewitching',
  Allsop 83
'obtained for me', Braine, *WTTT*
'I had lost', Salwak, *Interviews* 44
'In January 1952', Braine, *WTTT*
'I heard you'd phoned', to Paul
  Stephenson, 1.5.52, WAC
'I was ill', Salwak, *Interviews* 44
'it wouldn't really matter', *DLB* 15
'By the time', Braine, *WTTT*
'Oh no', *Desert Island Discs*, BBC
  Radio 4, recorded 27 April 1971
'I returned to librarianship', Braine,
  WTTT
'pale, bespectacled', Amis, *Memoirs*
  155
'I half expected', *Books and
  Bookmen*, September 1957
'Braine [was] a nicer', *DLB
  Yearbook 1986*
'How like Joe Lampton', Amis,
  Memoirs 155
'What I want', *DLB* 15
'Joe Lampton isn't', Allsop 83
'It's already difficult', Braine,
  RATT 129
'Let's be frank', Alistair Horne,
  Macmillan 1957–1986, volume 2
  of the official biography
  (Macmillan, 1989), 64
'The bathroom was', Braine, *RATT*
  13f.
'Mr Braine's . . . eye', *Times Literary
  Supplement*, 5.4.57
[Footnote:] 'He's smashing', Braine,
  RATT 25
'Bags of money', Braine, *RATT* 39,
  134f., 29, 16, 157, 116
'has to make [Joe's]', *Spectator*,
  15.3.57

'One feels that', *Times Literary Supplement*, 5.4.57
'It is hard', *DLB Yearbook 1986*
'He has already made', *Books and Bookmen*, September 1957
'Mr Braine['s] first', *Daily Express*, 23.5.57

CHAPTER 15

'The fact is', Salwak, *Interviews* 51
'He was put', Amis, *Memoirs* 156
'. . . looking over', Leader 540
'ole John Whine', ibid. 513
'Thank you', Thwaite 272
'My own feeling', Wain papers
'An angry young man', *Daily Herald*, 21.2.57
'Mr Amis and Mr Wain', *Reynolds News*, 3.2.57
'became aware of', Wilson, *AR* 27f.
'strangers who claimed', Wilson, *RATR* 10
'oppressed by the *angst*', *Punch*, 11.7.56
'an excerpt . . . from', *New Statesman*, 18.8.56
'giving dinner', *Rain Taxi*
'Angry Young Man', *Daily Mail*, 20, 21 and 23.2.57
'COLIN AND JOY', *Daily Express*, 22.2.57
'felt like horsewhipping', *Daily Mail*, 21.2.57
'You've been mistreating', ibid., 29.3.57
'Egghead, scrambled', *Time*, 18.11.57
Before the year', *Books and Art*, October 1957, November 1957

'a remarkable book', *Times Literary Supplement*, 20.12.57
'I'm the greatest', Bill Hopkins, *The Divine and the Decay* (MacGibbon & Kee, 1957), 76, 187, 106
'the dullest rape', Allsop 184
'deep disturbance', *Texas Quarterly*, Winter 1960
'Of course the book', Hopkins interview
'better written and', *Observer*, 26.5.57
'*Emergence from Chaos*', Tynan, *Holiday*
'All Tynan thought', Hopkins interview
'I would hardly', *London Magazine*, May 1957
'I am not necessarily', Wilson, *RATR* 41
'rashness', *Manchester Guardian*, 25.10.57
'Wilson's second book', *Evening Standard*, 22.10.57
'Now that we have', *New Statesman*, 26.10.56
'Anyone who attacks', *Sunday Times*, 20.10.56
'mixture of banality', *Books and Art*, November 1957
'*The Outsider* was', *Observer*, 20.10.57
'I can hardly wait', *Daily Mail*, 13.7.56
'I am a busy', ibid., 28.9.57
'Surprise Success', *Books and Bookmen*, January 1958
'STOP PRESS', *News Chronicle*, 23.10.57

CHAPTER 16

'it didn't interest', Maschler

'I hate all this', *Declaration* 8

'It takes a lot', *News Chronicle*,
16.8.57

'He's not an angry', Leader 513

'demeaning to the', Maschler

[Footnote:] 'A formidable', Tynan,
Holiday

'very young', Lessing 208

'the writers who have set',
Declaration 7f., 91, 70, 22f., 25,
23, 15, 65f., 56f., 17

'two altar boys', Osborne, *LB* 375

'the Spotty Nietzscheans', *Time and
Tide*, 2.11.57

'the end of pure rationalism',
Declaration 138, 140, 185

'the mystique', *Observer*, 13.10.57

'young *Führers*', *Declaration* 116

'real left-wing', Lessing 211

'I want drama', *Declaration* 112,
166

'written hastily', Osborne, *LB* 376

'I want to make', *Declaration* 65,
68, 76f., 74f., 80, 83, 67

'criticism of royalty', Osborne, *LB*
376

[Footnote:] 'had got wind', Irving
Wardle, *The Theatres of George
Devine* (Jonathan Cape, 1978),
190

'a crumbling', Osborne, *LB* 376

'Everybody was waiting', *Books and
Bookmen*, December 1957

'why should a Socialist', *Tribune*,
25.10.57

'the Press is', *Observer*, 13.10.57

'about 20,000', Maschler

'I got so sick', *Rain Taxi*

'for a marathon', *News Chronicle*,
10.9.58

'Mr Wilson will be on', ibid., 26.9.58

'merely a social', Holroyd,
Contraries 145

'rather a decent chap', Allsop 161

'How anyone', Osborne, *LB* 377

'The play concerned', Logue 234

'custard-pie anarchy', Osborne, *LB*
377f.

'Colin, Bill', Holroyd, *Contraries*
168

CHAPTER 17

'Is the Angry Young Man label',
Allsop 8f., 181, 23, 178, 199

'In the United States', *Beat
Generation* 10

'incoherently', Amis, *Memoirs* 201

'kept diaries', *Punch*, 31.12.58

'*Woman's Hour*', *Encounter*,
November 1959

'Mr John Braine', *Evening Standard*,
21.6.58

'all smiles', Leader 498

'a skimming', Allsop 43

'politely', Osborne, *LB* 427

'Not many marchers', Lessing 266f.

'not a single', Allsop 205

'I believe [it] to be', Wesker,
AMAID 460

'a great deal', quoted in *DLB* 13,
543

'achieves something', ibid. 544

'John knocked down', Osborne, *LB*
xix–xx

'oblivious', Wesker, *AMAID* 399,
465

'Look, the mirror', ibid. 507

'their predominantly', John Russell Taylor, *Anger and After: a guide to the new British drama* (Methuen, 1969 ed.), 12

'There never was', quoted in programme for Bristol Old Vic production of *Look Back in Anger*, March 2001

CHAPTER 18

'I haven't given', Philip Larkin, *Further Requirements* (Faber & Faber, 2001), 112, 114

'He remained', Will Wain interview

'Several times', Amis, *Memoirs* 44

'feeling it wouldn't', Leader 756

'result of meths-drinking', ibid. 1008

'very hurt', Will Wain interview

'The novel which', *Reynolds News*, 3.2.57

'no prose stylist', *Times Literary Supplement*, 4.3.60

'an immature arrogance', *Encounter*, June 1960

'fairly successful', *Rain Taxi*

'I usually returned', Wilson, *Outsider* 8

'I accepted it', *Rain Taxi*

'It's Dante, Shakespeare', Leader 1028

'I suspect', *DLB* 194

'Obviously I'm pretty talented', Wilson interview

'which he intends', Allsop 192

'There is something pathetic', *Times Literary Supplement*, 15.5.59

'sincere', Ritchie 171

'He was an enormously', Hopkins interview

'left London', dust-jacket of Holroyd, *Contraries*

'Bob Guccione', Hopkins interview

'changing moral climate', *Penthouse*, March 1965

'scorpion', Hopkins interview

'. . . the . . . subject [is] Failure', *Times Literary Supplement*, 20.11.59

'the essential unfairness', Allsop 85

'an easy way out', *Desert Island Discs*, BBC Radio 4, recorded 27 April 1971

'a full-dress', Amis, *Memoirs* 155

'He has no politics', A. Watkin Jones to Michael Bowen, n.d. (1956), WAC

'In 1964', Amis, *WBJA* 200f., 207

'clubman, curmudgeon', Jacobs 170

'Seeing his moon face', Amis, *Memoirs* 156

'The only thing', Salwak, *Interviews* 52

'Even [their] reactionary tendency', Amis, *Memoirs* 158, 160

'fighting every day', Alan Sillitoe, *Saturday Night and Sunday Morning* (Flamingo, 1994), 219

'solid and accurate', Ritchie 198

'they chased me', ODID

'Most of my work', Osborne, *LB* 135f.; ODID

'sexually obsessed', *The Oldie*, April 2001

'the coarse posturing', Osborne, *LB* 551, 555

'I see him now', *The Oldie*, April 2001

'DAMN YOU OSBORNE', Osborne, LB 522

'Maybe the big', Humphrey Carpenter, *Dennis Potter: a biography* (Faber & Faber, 1998), 77, 102f.

'. . . the funniest review', *Observer*, 14 May 1961

'John Osbore', Humphrey Carpenter, *That Was Satire That Was* (Gollancz, 2000), 199, 243

'not only the label', Ritchie 207

'I think the Beatles', Braddon 184

'It seems funny', Wain papers

'The Sixties may', Alvarez, *Where* 123

Acknowledgements

I suppose I should begin by thanking whoever it was – and I have long since forgotten – who invited me to join him or her (I think it was a her) for something called Authors' Night at the Press Club. It was an unremarkable 'do' somewhere in or near the Daily Mirror building, which was then still in Fleet Street, but I do remember one event during it. I was talking to John Wain, whom I knew a little from parties in Oxford, where I live, when a heavily-built middle-aged man wearing glasses with thick lenses came up to us and began chatting in a cheery way. Wain responded easily enough, so I was a little surprised when the man moved on and Wain turned to me and said: 'Who was that?'

I knew, because I had recently interviewed him for the BBC World Service. 'John Braine,' I said. So much for the Angry Young Men being friends with each other – though to be fair on Wain, his eyesight was probably deteriorating already.

Over the years I had a few encounters with Kingsley Amis – always pleasant, though on the final occasion, my attempt to interview him on the night he won the Booker Prize, he had definitely had too much to drink. I never saw John Osborne in the flesh, and I had no acquaintance with Colin Wilson until my visit to him which is described at the beginning of the book.

I could not have written it within the allotted time without Harry Ritchie's *Success Stories* (1988), an incredibly well-researched account of most of the AYM. I am (as always) grateful to my agent Felicity Bryan for finding me a publisher, and to Andrew Rosenheim, then head of Penguin Press, an old friend who turned out to be that publisher. Alas, by the time the book was finished he had moved on; but I have been lucky in that the project was taken over and enthusiastically cared for at Penguin Press by Simon Winder.

Besides enjoying Colin Wilson's lavish hospitality in Cornwall, I have had the pleasure of making the acquaintance of another surviving AYM, Bill Hopkins. Two other participants in the AYM story, Hilary Rubinstein and Tom Maschler, patiently answered my questions. William Wain kindly lent me papers relating to his father. Bobbie Mitchell did the picture research.

ACKNOWLEDGEMENTS

The Kingsley Amis Estate (represented by Jonathan Clowes Ltd) kindly gave me permission to quote from a number of letters from Amis to Philip Larkin (now in the Bodleian Library, Oxford) which were not included by Zachary Leader in his admirable edition of Amis's *Selected Letters*. Professor Leader himself has been generous with his advice and encouragement.

I am grateful to Mrs Helen Osborne and John Osborne Productions Ltd for permission to quote from his memoirs.

Even with the assistance of Colin Wilson and Bill Hopkins, I was unable to trace Stuart Holroyd. If he reads this, I hope he will come forward, in time for an interview with him to be included in the paperback edition of the book.

Index